CHAOS:

A MEMOIR

CHAOS

Faking a Normal Life

A memoir told as a story – a story so twisted
that it took seven books to tell it all.

Book Three in the *Powerless* Series

LELA FOX

Cover designed by Queen_Graphics, Fiverr, Photography by Shutterstock

Chaos: A Memoir is a 90-percent-true story of eleven years of the author's life. Some
scenes and incidents are used factiously or may be products of the author's
imagination. Names of people and places have been changed. Any resemblance to
actual events, locales, businesses, organizations, or persons, living or dead, is entirely
coincidental.

Lela Fox
Visit my website at www.LelaFox.com

ISBN 9781090342195
Printed in the United States of America by A-FEX Publishing

DEDICATION

I dedicate this book to Dude and my friend Teri.

Chaos would have remained an unorganized series of vague memories without the inspiration and encouragement of my savvy friend and cheerleader.

Always the badass, she's as close to an AA sponsor as I've had outside of recovery, though she doesn't know it.

And Dude... each vowel and consonant, and the thought behind it, I owe to you. Thanks for giving me a challenging life and letting me write about it.

☼ ☼ ☼ ☼ ☼ ☼ ☼ ☼ ☼

TABLE OF CONTENTS

☀ ☀ ☀ ☀ ☀ ☀ ☀ ☀ ☀

FAKING A NORMAL LIFE

"An alcoholic is someone who can violate his standards faster than he can lower them."

–ROBIN WILLIAMS

HOW I GOT HERE
And Where I've Been

Somehow, I'm still alive in this part of the story and at a crossroads. A new Lifetime has begun. *Chaos* is the third book in the *Powerless* series, a tale of ever-growing mayhem in the life of a stubborn alcoholic.

It's the story of an unmedicated Bi-Polar alcoholic, making bizarre decisions while believing she's perfectly rational. Or maybe you'd call it a story about a resourceful alcoholic who goes through the motions of having a normal life, somewhat successfully, but feels terminal Guilt for living a lie.

One thing is for sure: it's the story of chaos... the saga of a formative eleven years in my life, ages 26 to 37, and the beginning of a long, slow simmer on the relentless flame of alcoholism.

It begins when my future was bright and blooming. Despite a rocky history, I had a career on the fast track and employers lining up to recruit me. No shit.

Chaos ends with a series of burned bridges, broken hearts, and an even-crazier Lela Fox.

A lot happened between my first drink and this apparently fortunate career situation. At age thirteen, an almost-instant addiction to alcohol made a tornado of my teen years.

An instant-fix to my alcoholism, in my brilliant 20-year-old-mind, was to demand immediate maturity – marriage, motherhood, all the trappings. That would fix me right up. And I truly believed that shit.

But it didn't turn out quite the way I'd planned. In fact, it blew up in my face like Mount Vesuvius.

I had chosen Husband #1 because he was an easy target and, more importantly, he could roll a perfect joint while balancing a beer on his knee. I saw none of the oversized red flags, so I interrupted my college career to fake my way through growing up. And I insisted that hubby follow my lead. Of course, he didn't, and I became a clueless single mother with ridiculous expectations.

In my early twenties, life was a series of weird things that revolved like a carousel in a horror movie. You'd assume I was destined for quick and complete ruin, with the inevitable bottom just around the corner.

But that's not how it happened.

Despite the odds, I endured.

You'll read how I did it here, as Lifetime Number Four begins.

ANOTHER CHANCE TO GET IT RIGHT
Lifetime Number Four

The way I see it, I've had nine Lifetimes.

Each book in the series covers a part of my life markedly different from the one before it. These "life parts" are what I call Lifetimes, and I've had nine. Nine Lifetimes of tumultuous changes, curious choices, a slew of trials and tribulations, dozens of great successes, and hundreds of poignant failures. By some miracle, I landed on my feet, like a cat dropped from a third-story window.

My childhood, Lifetime Number One, ended the moment I tasted my first cup of spiked punch. There's no reason to write about a happy, normal childhood, so that book remains in my head and heart.

Lifetime Number Two began in a gravel alley with two albino sisters and a six-pack. Four beers brought ease and comfort alcohol to my tattered ego and shameful self-image.

The addiction was instant. I wanted more of that, and now. So I screwed up my teen years, adding more and more notches of shame to my belt loop. Those experiences became *Powerless*, first in the series.

Lifetime Number Three saw me struggle through college, marriage, motherhood, and divorce from Husband #1. That's book two: *Denial.*

This book details Lifetime Number Four, ages 26 through 36, where I faked a normal life married to Husband #2, scrambling to be an attentive part-time mom with part-time freedom to play the party girl.

You thought things were crazy before? This is when the crazy chaos begins, in *Chaos*.

movin' on up

Chapter 1

My résumé was up to date but a pure lie. On paper, I looked like a kickass advertising writer with a promising future. While everything else in my life went to hell, I oozed pride in climbing my twisted version of a career ladder, fighting, biting, and scrambling for new clients willing to pay big bucks for the outrageous ideas offered by the remarkable Lela Fox.

In the advertising world of Rockville, Tennessee, I was 1985's rising star. And humility was not my strong point.

After discovering my first husband Andy's affair, our separation was immediate, but the official divorce took many more months. Not that it stopped me from moving forward with a series of drunken one-night stands... and hanging out with my lifelong BFFs: Guilt, Shame, and Remorse.

From my perspective, the real problem was the red-headed bitch Ella Perkins, my ex-husband's girlfriend and now the part-time mother of *my* son, living with *my* man in *my* house. She made me sick with her impeccable organization, nutritious menus, and always-perfect life management.

On the flip side, I was single and struggling to be stable and sane. The struggle was rocky because my focus was off-kilter, my Bi-Polar was showing, and because vodka was my best friend.

On the outside, I looked like a million bucks, arriving at the monthly Marketing Association networking meeting in a new, bright-magenta suit. I wore a double-squirt of confidence like expensive perfume, sure that my legs looked fabulous in black spike-heeled pumps and that my big-hair curls framed my face perfectly. I was kicking ass as a copywriter but always on the lookout for better opportunities.

Lo and behold.

Over cocktails, I got a lead on a job at a young and growing company called 14-24.

"Why do they call it 14-24?" I asked, trying to act cordial but cool and professionally uninterested.

The ad agency exec flashed a smile. "It's their target audience. Ages fourteen through twenty-four. You know... the influencers."

"Ah! Of course!" I chuckled as if I had known the answer all along.

"They're doing the marketing and advertising in-house, or I'd be knocking on their door myself. Thankfully, my position is pretty solid."

"You're James, right? At Sturbridge?" I reached out to shake his hand. "I'm Lela Fox. You'll be hearing my name quite a bit, for a long time, and you can say you knew me when."

James' handshake was firm, and his chuckle came with a toothy grin. "It's nice to meet a creative who has stayed humble." His deep, brown eyes charmed me. And it looked like my own brand of charm had found a sucker.

So far so good on tonight's alcohol consumption... or so I thought. I always seemed to overshoot the runway with cocktails at those networking meetings, so I had a standing babysitter, my buddy and ex-boss, Marla Brown. Marla was the writer/creative director at the agency where I had interned a few years before. As I stumbled toward the bar for the fourth time, she elbowed me in the ribs. "Slow it down, Lela."

I knew I could trust Marla and that I couldn't trust myself. At my first networking meeting months ago, the open bar screamed my name repeatedly, and I downed a half-dozen vodka-tonics in less than two hours. I stumbled to the fancy ladies' room and threw up in the handicapped stall. *Not cool, Lela.* I washed my face, then, literally, showed my ass in the banquet line.

Marla had led me downstairs and called a cab. That night, we set up the babysitting arrangement, and it seemed to be working. Each month, she elbowed me at just the right time, and I'd left before the shit hit the fan. But her elbow was stronger that night, and ten minutes after the servers whisked the plates away, she strongly suggested I get the hell out of Dodge. I guess I had gone two steps too far, maybe three, based on Marla's frown and glaring eyes.

I left in a hurry, saying brief farewells to the ones with the power to help my career. That's why they call it networking, right?

It was my son's weekend with his dad, so I stopped at Applebee's for another drink at the bar. To fit into the Friday-party crowd, I removed my business jacket, unbuttoned another button on my blouse, then paid for two drinks at once. It wasn't a two-for-one happy hour; I ordered that way to save time. Bartenders are slow on Friday nights.

I signaled the bartender for a third drink. Soon after, a good-looking man plopped onto the stool next to mine. "Can I buy you another?" he asked.

"Naw, I'll just take the money."

They say men study long and hard to perfect their pickup lines, but that was mine, and I used it repeatedly. Worked like a charm unless the man was a fuddy-duddy and disapproved... in which case he could kiss my ass.

I only took the money twice, but I put it in the tip jar. I do have *some* class.

The next day, after easing my hangover with a few glugs of Bailey's in my coffee, I wrote a killer cover letter and scheduled a courier to deliver my résumé to 14-24 at 8:01 AM.

Their half-page ad in the Sunday classifieds described the company and the job opening in detail. They sought a writer of direct mail brochures to sell the company's free, advertiser-sponsored educational magazines. For instance, the U.S. Army-sponsored *Careers*, a slick publication for high schoolers. I would promote the magazines to guidance counselors, convincing them to provide them at their school. If the educators didn't object to the advertising influence, the publication was an easy sale. According to the example in the ad, readership was in the hundreds of thousands, and Army recruitment was waaay up among subscribers. Everybody won.

And *Careers* was just one of the dozens of magazines.

As a local to Rockville, my sister Jennifer knew of 14-24 and the nationwide reputation they had built. *TIME* had featured them in the "Fastest Growing Companies" issue, she said, and the CEO made a "Top Influencer" list, blah, blah, blah.

But Jennifer seemed over-the-top excited. She upped the volume. "Lela, that company is hot shit right now. You need that job!"

Though I was dressed to the nines, the job interview was casual, with a tall and scrawny older woman named Marilyn. Butt-ugly, maybe, but she held her own in a match of wits in the interview, so I considered the job worthy of my station.

A pompous ass like me should've been shot. Back then, my ego was front and center, and fuck you if you didn't like it. *Fuck all of you.*

The 14-24 office was downtown on Marshall Square, a venue that overflowed with people day and night... all varieties of young, old, professionals, students, and families. Festivals began there, with a collection of bands on the outdoor stage, and the renowned weekend Farmer's Markets bustled under the concrete canopy on the far end. Yep, Marshall Square was the hip place to be.

With a unique product and an aggressive sales team, 14-24 had grown like a virus, first occupying one floor in the Walnut Building and now six floors. This quarter's growth had expanded staff to an adjacent building, keeping the six floors in the Walnut tower for support departments like Marketing.

"You'll find 14-24 to be a 'melting pot for creativity,' I've heard it called," Marilyn said, "Most employees are creatives like you... writers, designers, or illustrators. Plus, the casual dress code and lack of corporate nit-picking here make it a pretty chill job. You have to be self-motivated."

"I'm super motivated. Direct mail campaigns have been my specialty; I've built a reputation on them." I leveled a look at her and continued, "I have the ideal experience, Marilyn, and I'm easy to work with. Just tell me when to start, and I'll dive right in."

Maybe it was my confidence, or my lying résumé, or the new funky shoes, but she hired me on the spot, and at a salary that beat my current pay by fifteen percent.

I would start two weeks from Monday.

I stopped around the corner to use the phone. A cat and her litter of kittens curled into a corner of the phone booth, and Momma Cat screamed at me, daring me to mess with her family. "Just making a call, Momma. I won't give you any shit."

Coins for a long-distance call in hand, I dialed Mom and Dad with the news. They had just moved back to my hometown of Burgess, Tennessee, after a few years in the Armpit of West Virginia, and they cheered me generously, saying all the right things. Daddy erupted with another one of his meaningless lines, ones that still brought a smile. "Hooray for our side!" he said, and

"Never fear, Lela's here!"

Daddy gushed about my success, saying he was "crazy-proud," and that's exactly what I needed to hear. I had an unending hunger for my do-gooder parents' approval, and when it was due, they slathered me with praise.

But when it came to the "other issues," as they called them, they remained silent except to repeat their mantra: "You know how we feel about your drinking, Lela."

I hung up happy. Today I had earned kudos for being a "responsible adult." Then I wondered how many responsible days it would take to compensate for the past few weeks when I had been a useless drunk.

It doesn't snow much in East Tennessee, but it did on the day I started at 14-24. Instant memories of another big day in my life when it snowed at an inopportune time, my wedding day. It sucked.

Hopefully, it's not an omen like it was with Andy.

Though Rockville was a southern town that shut down in bad weather, I felt obligated to show up to my new job and show up on time. The problem was the long, slow hill leading to my apartment – it would be ice-packed in the morning. The city's resources could only scrape major roads; getting there was a crapshoot.

Thinking ahead, I took three-year-old Bo to his dad's for the night and parked at the bottom before the storm hit.

Early in the morning, I woke to a serene snowfall, perfect for sledding. It would all melt by noon, as always, but it was beautiful. As expected, I slipped and slid down the hill on my butt, sliding toward my Chevy Monza at an alarming speed.

Fingernails grasping the back tire stopped my slide. I struggled to get the snow off the windshield and windows, working up a sweat. "I guess I wore too many layers," I said to the silence. Inside, the car started, and I shivered as it warmed up.

My thoughts were in great conflict: happy for the job, determined to be there, and scared to go. I had never driven in the snow. Debating, I thought about walking back home, but bravery won, and I put the car in gear. *Here we go.* Though not Catholic and not religious, I crossed myself. *You probably did it backward, dumbass. But you're bigger than this silly fear, so just go! Go!*

It was iffy getting there, but once I got to the I-40 East ramp through town, the roads were clear. With only one terrifying moment turning left, I arrived to park in the garage as instructed.

But the garage echoed noisily; it was 100 percent empty on the ground floor. Now even more terrified, I took the first available space.

Walking to the Walnut Building proved eerie. Empty streets. A blustery wind blowing snow against the base of Marshall Square's vintage brick buildings. The sound of my breath through two layers of scarf, the magic of billowing white clouds that disappeared in an instant. And the odd, clunky squeak of snow crunching under my boots.

Rounding the corner, I gulped. *The building will be locked, you dumbass!* I pushed; the revolving door circled easily and opened to a three-story lobby where a smattering of people milled about, and a small group sat on the navy leather sofas.

Nobody looked my way as I stepped into the open elevator. In the familiar hum going up, I braced myself for making a noble first impression, whispering my parent's encouragement speech from high school: "You are invincible. You are beautiful. You are capable." I repeated it three times on the way to the fifth floor.

The elevator door opened. Silence and an empty set of office cubicles welcomed me. Only one rack of fluorescent lights glowed; the rest were a cold dull-gray, darker than silence.

Where do I go? Marilyn's office? I took a few steps toward her corner, then stopped. Perplexed for a pause, I decided the logical choice was to call out. "Hello? Is anybody here?"

A voice from the far end answered. "Hark! Who goes there?"

I smiled at the corny joke. "I'm new and don't know where to go."

"Where are you?"

"Back corner."

"Which back corner?"

"Marco."

"Polo."

"Marco."

"Polo."

A few more echoes of Marco-Polo and a man in a TSU sweatshirt and jeans rounded the corner. Wow. He looked at me with intense green eyes. An instant smile spread on his face, and there was a note of flirt to his greeting. "Hey there."

"This is my first day of work. I'm Lela Fox."

"Bless your heart! What a terrible day to start a new job!" He introduced himself. "Phillip Johnson, nice to meet'cha." Phillip led me to the coffee pot.

"I'm not even sure where to put my stuff yet."

"Why not sit here in the atrium for a while... grab a few of our publications and read. I mean, to see what we're about. Congrats on the new job. What is your position?"

Don't do it, Lela, don't do it! But I couldn't stop myself. "My position? Usually missionary."

Phillip made a noise that combined a laugh and a snort. Then his eyes bore into mine as he laughed outright.

There you go again... being nervous and saying the stupidest, most inappropriate things possible. "Sorry, Phillip. It didn't sound so bad in my head." I looked down and felt my face getting hot. The nervous buzz between my ears roared. "So much for a good first impression, huh?"

"Oh, it's a first impression all right!" he answered, still laughing. "Lela Fox, the new smartass employee. You'll fit in perfectly around here." Another peal of laughter made him wipe a tear from the corner of his eye. I could have laughed along with him, but decided silence was the best way to save face.

My silence seemed to make Phillip uncomfortable. Either that or he was just ready to end the conversation and get back to work. "Well... I'll let you get to reading, Lela, and it might be a day-long wait. See, you might be the only one who shows up. A snow day is like a day off around here."

Through a smile, I said, "I hated to take a day off on my first day, if you know what I mean." My smile turned into a laugh, and the tension evaporated.

"Yeah, I know what you mean."

"But will Marilyn be here?"

"Yeah, maybe Marilyn. She may think *you'll* come... well, you did! So she may show up. Either way, just chill. If you need me, just yell 'Marco.'"

I sat in the atrium of the refurbished Art Deco building and read the fantastic variety of 14-24 magazines. I scanned a dozen, impressed by the quality of the editorial content. Even an untrained eye would recognize well-written articles, outstanding page design, and top-notch printing.

I began to understand what my role would be. The magazine *Table*

Manners, sponsored by Seagram brands, featured articles helping restaurant servers increase their tip. To "sell" that magazine, I would address ads and letters to restaurant owners. It all began to fall into place.

Around two o'clock, the marketing people began a parade, stumbling in one-by-one. Lauren was the first to arrive. Until Marilyn hired me, Lauren was the only other copywriter in the department. My heart fell when I saw she was a redhead. *Another one!* I fought the comparison to my ex-husband's damn girlfriend.

As Lauren grabbed papers from a stack in the corner of her office, she said, "Here are brochures and stuff we've done in the past. Did you see *Table Manners* out there?"

"I did."

"This is the brochure for the smalls. We did another version for the large franchises." Again, the quality and creative approach of the advertising impressed me big-time.

More staffers arrived. I met an art director, Porgie, also a redhead. *What's up with the redheads?*

Porgie was a sassy, petite woman with purple frames on oversized glasses. She looked like the consummate creative person, complete with spiral-permed hair and no makeup. Her chime of a laugh seemed friendly, but I stopped short when hearing her hateful self-introduction. "I'll try to get along with you, Lela, but be forewarned: I'm difficult." *Wow. What a brazen remark. Better keep your eye on her.*

Lauren introduced me to the other two art directors fifteen minutes later as they arrived in the same elevator. "This is Brenda and Jay. Direct eye contact was obviously hard for the shy and tall Jay; he offered only a weak wave and a heartbeat of eye contact.

In complete contrast, Brenda wore a beaming smile atop an ample body and gushed about the info she had gathered for me to review. An instantly likable woman, a few years older but with a young and cheerful demeanor. Brenda would be a good friend; I knew it immediately, and I looked forward to becoming a cohort with the bouncy blonde.

Marilyn was last to arrive, around three o'clock. In her fluster, she seemed surprised I was there. Stumbling to cover her error, I supposed, she announced, "Meeting in the conference room to welcome our new writer!"

Unwrapping from layers of coat, scarf, mittens, and boots, Marilyn exposed her frosty face. A smile was underneath.

The ultra-casual meeting included plenty of laughter, furthering my feelings that this was the right job at the right time for me. At the request of my new coworkers, I "presented" my professional experience and strengths. Then they asked the more-personal stuff, interested to know the age of my son, my hometown, and hobbies.

I felt surrounded by an aura of respect, professionally and personally. For a minute, I thought I deserved it.

Fitting in wasn't a typical feeling for me, though I faked it well. I'd been a slave to alcohol for most of my life, but this was the time for a new start, I decided. A chance to fit in with normal sober people and be a sober, stable citizen.

After the meeting, Marilyn set me up in an office with a view of the square. *Wow! A window!* Brenda's office was across the hall from mine; our desks faced each other. At least once an hour, I caught her eye and made a funny face or stuck my tongue out at her, just being silly. She replied with the same.

☼ ☼ ☼ ☼ ☼

On the third day of work, a large project landed on my desk with Brenda as my assigned partner. The two of us sat down for a brainstorming session, promising an open mind on both ends. She breezed through the meeting, kind and happy; my anxiety evaporated quickly.

The two of us joked about our role in creating junk mail, the hated mailbox clutter, and laughed at the way mailing lists twisted names and addresses. Her last name was Bebing. Right: Brenda Bebing, definitely an odd name and always misspelled, she said.

Her face reacted in a sudden flash of memory. "In fact, I have a file... it's all the junk mail where my name is wrong." She flipped through a folder in her bottom drawer, handing me random pieces. "Oh! Here it is! The best one ever... Babbas Bean." I cracked up; we both did.

"That's perfect! Babbas fits you better than plain ol' Brenda! So, like it or not, that will be my new name for you, girl!" She blushed crimson but didn't tell me no, so I called her Babbas Bean from that point forward.

I also believed she was the best art director of the bunch. Babbas Bean never let a creative opportunity pass her by; low budgets seemed to bring even more determination. I had the same "creativity above all" attitude, and our mutual respect created a loud, unspoken affection.

Babbas Bean's ingenuity came in handy in many situations, some beyond the scope of marketing. Like when she came through with my first date, a lunch date just a few days later.

LUNCH ONE & LUNCH TWO
Chapter 2

I hadn't dated since the divorce, not quite ready to dive back into the shark-infested waters. Despite how my ex had duped me, I wasn't bitter about men, just skittish because I knew Lela Fox was a sucker for a good line.

The problem was I hung out at bars, dressed up and drunk, playing the tease and encouraging men to put the move on me. But I only *slept* with the barflies, didn't take them home to Momma. A relationship wasn't really in the cards for me, I thought.

Phillip Johnson, the guy who greeted me on the first day of work, had been flirting with me in glaringly obvious ways, raised eyebrows, sly grins, knowing laughs... the whole bit. He scared me, yet nothing was threatening in his manner. Nothing at all. The problem was in his appearance, and I felt like a bitch for feeling the way I did.

Babbas Bean knew him well, and the potential coupledom thrilled her; she urged me to flirt back. "He's a nice guy, Lela, and you're a catch. Name one reason you wouldn't go out with him."

"Well, he's definitely *not* good-looking, Babbas. Downright ugly if you ask me."

Babbas gasped. "*So what?* Aren't you mature enough to know personality matters *ten* times more than looks? Besides, he's not that bad." She rolled her eyes at me. Disgusted, she mumbled, "Worried most about looks! Come on, girl. Grow up."

Shame reared its ugly head for a flash, but somehow Babbas Bean could say shit like that to me without ruining my life. Instead of spending a week in bed, her advice to "grow up" opened my eyes. And other than the non-Adonis objection, I had no other reason to turn down his invitations. I vowed to accept his next offer, which came just a few hours later.

Maybe focusing on Phillip's negatives was a way for me to add distance to diminish the possibility of me liking him. *That's bullshit, Lela. Like Babbas says, "grow up," right? There's no reason you should be afraid to start dating... it might keep you out of trouble if nothing else.*

With a deep breath, I ran the bad-Phillip objections through my thought shredder and began anew.

There was a positive: he was muscular and fit, but... with a twist. The addition of a colossal beer belly under his sculpted shoulders was so out of place that it looked pasted on, like a man's fake pregnant belly. Worse, he didn't know how to dress to make the belly less noticeable. He wore tight crewneck sweaters with button-down shirts underneath – so *last year*. The tight sweaters were the worst. *Why can't he learn how a normal man dresses to impress?*

Despite my attempts to find positives, I continued to focus on the negatives. Beyond the hook nose, I saw sharp incisors that pointed to a pale and cracked bottom lip.

He'd take off the sweater late in the afternoon to reveal sopping rings of armpit stains as if he'd just come from a workout. The deep marks were more curious than gross; Phillip didn't stink, but my mind concocted a rain forest surrounding him... with recycled moisture dripping from his armpits and the trees overhead, and mucky peat moss at his feet.

If he's so horrible, why does he scare me so much? As if on cue, Phillip's confident grin popped around the door to my office and threatened to erase my fear. He said, "Lunch?"

"Sure! I'd love to."

The grin broadened, emphasizing the pointed incisors, but I noticed his bottom lip was flushed and supple... like perhaps he'd just lubed up with Chapstick. "So I'll knock around noon, okay?"

"That'd be great."

He exaggerated a wink, and I laughed. Then he spun out of my office entrance and down the hall toward the atrium. *Oh, shit! I did it! I said yes!* On the move, I dashed to Babbas Bean's office, finding three other team members there.

With a shaky voice, I announced my date. Then... remembering the morning's mirror-check. I said, "Oh, no! I forgot earrings today! There's no way I'll go on a date without earrings!"

Jay turned red and slipped out of the office without a word.

Porgie, pissy as always, said, "How childish that you would get nervous about a simple lunch date," then flipped a red curl over her shoulder with a smirk. I stared her down, thinking so loud I feared it was audible. *Rot in hell, bitch.*

Satisfied I'd put Porgie in her place, I turned to Babbas, wringing my hands. "Can I borrow your earrings, chicka?"

"No way, you need *anything* but gold. Your skin is too yellow to wear gold – ever. Remember that." Babbas Bean stared at me, waiting for an answer, I supposed.

After a few beats of silence, I took the hint. "Understood, my friend. But what about *today?*"

"Today, you need silver, maybe white." Her next look was comical, an "aha moment" played by a bad soap-opera actress. Then Babbas Bean performed her miracle with ease.

"These are perfect!" She placed double-stick tape on two Tic-Tacs and pressed them against my lobes. *Ta-da!* In her hand mirror, they looked like real earrings, and the matte finish matched the muted weave of my top. I couldn't have bought a more perfect pair.

"Wowzers, Lela. Knock 'em dead, you beautiful woman!" Babbas Bean encouraged, sounding like my father.

At ten 'til noon, I dashed to the bathroom to touch up my face, looking in the mirror and smiling at myself for the first time in months. *Maybe I'm okay, maybe this is what I'm supposed to do.* The final dot of lip gloss created the exact look I hoped for. *Go, go, Lela-girl. You're doing all right, kid.*

To be pleased with my reflection was a surprise. It had been over a year since I had seen myself as anything close to attractive. As for sex, Andy and I never resumed a suitable sex life after the baby was born, or nothing worthy of a mention. I guess that was another red flag I should have noticed.

But sex had always been a pucker-worthy topic, considering I'd been raped, not once, but twice. First at age sixteen by my brother-in-law, and again at eighteen by an ex-con who slipped me a roofie. I rarely thought about it, squashing the shame down with enough alcohol to keep me moving forward.

Checking the mirror one more time and thinking about sex for the first time in a while, I realized something shocking and said it aloud. "Hell, I don't even masturbate anymore!"

Someone in the handicapped stall said, "What d'you say, Lela?"

Oh shit. It's Marilyn. Without a word, I ducked out the door.

"Is Bailey's okay?" Phillip said, referring to the always-busy diner on Marshall Square.

"Sure, I love it! Especially the veggie plate, home-cooked like my Momma's."

"Bailey's it is, then." A broad smile brightened his face as we entered the elevator. We were alone for two floors before a loud and rowdy group joined in the ride to the lobby. The folks seemed like such good friends that it warmed my heart. *These 14-24 people are fun! I'm lucky to be surrounded by happy, creative people.*

But Phillip wasn't a creative; he was in Accounts Receivable. I never imagined we could have something in common, but, surprisingly, we found many topics to discuss. His upbringing was almost identical to mine, but with two brothers instead of two sisters. His parents were upstanding citizens in his small home town, and he also used my favorite term for his mom: Goody-Two-Shoes. Phillip had recently divorced, too, and had dated only a handful of women, he said, each for a short amount of time.

Embarrassed, I tried not to talk about my divorce or say that Andy had cheated on me, but Phillip said his wife had done the cheating, and he frowned. After that, I opened up a little, telling him about Andy and the Ella-bitch in a red-headed hell.

"So this Andy guy must be an idiot to walk out on such a fantastic woman!" he said. I felt the heat rise on my cheeks, and he threw his head back to laugh. "And you're cute when you blush like that." My reply was silence. *Dammit, Phillip! Quit!*

We walked back to the Walnut Building after an extra-long lunch hour. "This has been great, Lela. I'm just going to be honest. I like you. Maybe a *lot*. Let's have dinner tonight."

I froze. *Oh, shit. Way too much, way too soon, dude. I like you, I guess, but mostly, you were just an experiment in having a date after so many married years.*

So I lied.

"I have my son tonight, Phillip, and I promised a Happy Meal. Joy, joy!" I could feel my face burning with embarrassment... or excitement... or something uncomfortable.

Our walk resumed, but a few paces later, Phillip asked, "When can we have lunch again? Tomorrow?"

I refused to screech to a stop as I had done with the surprise dinner invitation, but my mind shot into overdrive. *Oh, shit! Phillip likes me. Do men really like me? I mean, like, NORMAL men? No vodka today, no flirting or teasing him, but he still likes me?* Finally, words came, filling the silence that had lasted too long. "Uh... do you mean lunch? Tomorrow?"

He ignored my stupid question. "I'd like to get to know you better, Lela Fox. Because I find you fascinating."

"But... I'm not. It's just... maybe... uh." I couldn't find a way to say: *I'm bad news, Phillip. Damaged goods. I have bad luck with men, and I'm a whore, spreading my legs wide at the drop of a hat. I can't say no, so please don't ask. I have nothing to offer, so go away!*

Phillip stopped walking abruptly and turned to take both my hands in his. I sighed and closed my eyes. Five seconds later, I opened them to find Phillip staring deep into my eyes. Another sigh. I said, "You're not going to let me get out of it, are you?"

"You don't need to be afraid of me."

"I'm not! I just... haven't dated yet and..."

When he saw I couldn't finish my statement, he jumped in with fervor. "It's not a formal date, Lela! Just *lunch!* A nicer lunch tomorrow, I'll see to that, but it's just *lunch*, okay? Surely you and your fear can handle that innocent kind of date."

Thinking in the silence, I knew he was right. There was nothing to be afraid of with Phillip. *He's a nice guy, Lela, and he likes you! If nothing else, take advantage of that! Maybe practice your don't-sleep-with-him-yet relationship trick.*

Phillip interrupted my thoughts. "Around noon, like today? I'll knock on your door."

I didn't know I'd been holding my breath until I let it out. "Okay, okay, I'll go." The rest of the fear came out as I babbled. "Honestly, I'm looking forward to it. A nice lunch, you say? You don't have to do that. Bailey's is always awesome."

"No, we need to go a little more special. Somewhere nice and quiet."

Nervous butterflies filled my gut as we parted at the building entrance; he smiled broadly and held the gaze too long. Finally, I looked away and mumbled a goodbye.

In the fifth-floor hall, I stopped by the bathroom to check my teeth for broccoli. "Oh, no!" I said to the mirror. No broccoli, thank goodness, but I had lost the left Tic-Tac earring.

"Probably fell in my green beans," I said aloud. Someone in the handicapped stall said, "What d'ya say, Lela?"

Dammit! Marilyn again! Ignoring the comment, I added lip gloss, kissed the mirror, and ran to tell Babbas Bean about my date.

☼ ☼ ☼ ☼ ☼

"Look at you! All dressed up today, Lela." I had taken special care with my makeup and wardrobe for the day. My bright royal dress looked funky and vintage, with a wide, angled black collar and oversized black buttons. The color brightened my skin tone and brought out the blue in my eyes. He repeated, "Wow! You look fabulous!"

"Thanks, Phillip. I see you dug deep in *your* closet, too. Very nice sweater." He looked atypically handsome; his clothes actually fit, and he'd tamed his fuzzy hair with a dollop of mousse.

"We have reservations and have to hurry. Are you ready?"

"Yes, but it's a great-big deadline day, so we can't stay forever."

"Well, let's do it. We're going to Reagan's."

"Reagan's! What the hell, Phillip? That's the most expensive place around! Why in the world would you take me there?"

"I told you... I want to get to know you better."

"We could do that at McDonald's!"

"We're going to do it in style, and don't try to talk me out of it. The Reagans know we're coming."

I still hadn't moved, stunned that he would take me to such an expensive place... so expensive it made me uncomfortable... so expensive that I questioned his motives. Phillip helped me with my coat; I moved as if in a trance.

I said nothing until we exited the building, taking a right this time. Phillip grabbed my hand, lacing his fingers into mine, and squeezed. I looked at him reluctantly. The full inch of those pointed fangs showed in his broad smile.

Thankfully, he didn't talk about me, or "us," or the lunch to come; he began small talk about the weather, gossip about fifth-floor coworkers, and the upcoming construction downtown that would require a detour to enter our parking garage.

When we entered Reagan's, the tuxedoed maître de rushed to take our coats. Phillip said, "I'm Johnson... reservations for the Elite Table."

With bulging eyes, I snapped a look at his grinning face. "*The Elite Table*? What the heck is that? What's going on here?" Panic – I didn't want any special treatment beyond this incredibly expensive place. Hell, I wasn't even sure I liked him enough to go to lunch two days in a row!

"Just the most private table. Don't freak out."

The maître de led us through a labyrinth to the back room, where a trio of musicians played for a couple at a table on the far side. Our host pulled a brocade curtain back to reveal a table from a movie set. Black-lace over a stark-white tablecloth, speckled with candles and fresh lilies. Private, indeed! The tuxedoed man asked, "To your liking, sir? Ma'am?"

"Perfect," Phillip answered as the maître de deposited leather-encased menus on the table. Like a gentleman, my date pulled out the chair and motioned for me to have a seat. The scene shimmered with beauty and class, and I shook with fear of the expectations involved as repayment for such extravagance.

"Phillip! This is too much! I'm not sure I want to be here!"

"Relax a minute before you decide. Lela, dear, you deserve to be spoiled, right? How can you possibly complain?"

"I'm not complaining. It's just..."

"Come on! Why not let me treat you like a queen? How could it be a bad thing? And you might as well get used to it, Lela, because I want you to feel special every day. I don't even care if you like me as much as I like you, which is what I suspect. But I just want to blow it all out. Please don't complain and hurt my sensitive little man-feelings."

I could see his sincerity with a slight begging in his voice. *So he's... uh... crazy about me. That's not cool, but what can I do, exactly?*

"Phillip, I just don't know if we should do this after only one simple lunch date at Bailey's, ya know? It's too much, too soon." I fidgeted, fingering the edge of the cloth napkin. When the silence became too much, I looked up to find him staring at me with intensity. I felt my personal space evaporating, and tension set my jaw on a line. "Just... back off a little, okay, Phillip? Please."

A disappointed look crept across his face, then a slow, genuine smile. "Okay, I'll back off. I promise not to indulge you or give you compliments. And I won't tell you how much I like you. Would all that help you be more comfortable?"

What could I say? Phillip wasn't really doing anything wrong, just liking me too much. Some would call that *my* problem and not his. I did what I knew to do, telling him it was too soon. "Too much, too soon." A three-year-old would understand what *that* meant, right?

As the server tiptoed into the picture to pour ice water, I waited for a full glass and gulped a tummy full. *Lela, there's nothing you can do but reinforce your stance on not liking him enough for all this. You'll never go out with him again, that's for sure. And you should probably tell him that.*

"Phillip, it's hard for me to be comfortable when somebody likes me, especially when it's, like, in-my-face obvious. But as long as you're not..." I searched for a word, "*obsessed* with me or something. And not a serial murderer, or a rapist, or some kind of weirdo-pervert..."

A funny noise came from Phillip's side of the table. I looked up to see him on the verge of tears with laughter. "Oh, Lela! You are precious when you're nervous."

"*Don't!* I just *told* you I'm–"

"Okay, okay... you're right. I take it back. You are in *no way* precious, neither cute nor beautiful, nothing even *close* to that. In fact, I don't even know why I asked you to lunch... because you're such a loser."

I couldn't help but laugh. And Phillip was right. Why couldn't I accept a simple and innocent compliment? "Okay. Now I say *you're* right. But..."

"Let's just drop it, agreed?"

We toasted with our water glasses, each hitting a little too hard. The sound was perfect in pitch, a vibrant tone that made me afraid the fine-crystal glasses had broken. We both looked at the points of contact, then back at each other, followed by peals of laughter. The laughter took several minutes to fade. Finally, I wiped my eyes and was able to catch my breath to speak. "Should we try that again?"

"Sure." He raised his glass. "A toast! To the appropriate amount of clink and the appropriate amount of liking each other."

Suddenly the waiter, tuxedo and all, appeared. I wondered how long he'd been standing there. It seemed he was waiting for a formal invitation to approach the table. When Phillip followed my gaze and locked eyes with the waiter, my lunch date nodded. "Yes, please," he said. My brow wrinkled, having no idea what was going on between them.

"Your champagne, sir..."

I raised my voice. "*Champagne? Phillip!* First, it's a workday, and second, it's the same 'too much, too soon' I just talked about!"

His genuine smile returned, spreading across that freshly scrubbed face. "Don't be upset, hon. I ordered it ahead of time... before I knew you didn't want me to like you." The sideways grin broadened.

With a smile like that, how can you be mad? Phillip burst with natural charm and friendliness, pleasant enough to compensate for his not-so-handsome exterior. His confidence was quite attractive, too, I realized. My "rejection" of him didn't change his demeanor.

I said nothing while the waiter performed the formalities of uncorking and serving the bubbly. With Phillip assuring the waiter we needed nothing further, he left, gently closing the curtains around the Elite Table. Now entombed in privacy, Phillip, again, raised his glass, "Here's to not liking each other at all."

"I'll drink to that!" There was a hint of snort in my laugh.

"Lela, I guess you realize how stupid that sounds, right? A toast to not liking each other."

"Yep," I laughed through the words, "But let's just keep up the joke."

WOW! The champagne tastes great! What are you going to do when you get tipsy on your third glass? How much will Phillip drink? Maybe he'll leave most of it for me – NO, NO! Quit thinking that way! You have a deadline today, so you've got to keep a clear head. Okay, then why does taking one little sip instantly take my clear head away? Why am I already on the road to getting drunk? In the middle of the day, at a restaurant too fancy for my tastes, with a guy I don't really like? What have you done now, Lela? How are you going to get out of THIS? You are so screwed.

Just as I suspected, Phillip stopped drinking after two glasses. I urged him to have another, which he refused. "So what are you going to do? Just leave it to be thrown away? To be wasted?"

"I got what I wanted out of it, so it's not a waste."

"Hey! There are starving children in Ethiopia, man!"

Phillip threw his head back to laugh. "Your dad said the same as mine, huh?" I nodded. Still laughing, he said, "But I think that's about meatloaf, not champagne."

"Maybe I should say 'there are thirsty children in France' then? Does that make more sense?"

"Just don't worry about it and have a third glass. I won't judge."

"Well, the boss-lady might."

"Nah... it's not like you're going to stumble down the hall and miss your deadline or anything."

That damn buzz in my ears began again. "Of course."

☼ ☼ ☼ ☼ ☼

"Dammit! No wonder you didn't want me to like you! You're a fucking drunk! Jeez, I can't stand it!" I saw the sweat on his upper lip as he made the final decision. "I'm leaving. The tab is paid. Just try not to fall down on your way out. It's not a place for drunks. And you should really call a cab, Lela. Your drunk ass doesn't need to be driving."

"Okay, Phillip. I unnerstand."

He stood and looked at me, a disgusted look on his face. My head wobbled as my vision of Phillip faded in and out. I had grand ideas of ways to defend myself, but I fought the temptation to speak; I knew slurring my words wouldn't be cool. I raised my hand and waved goodbye using only my fingers. "B-bye, Phillip. Tank you fer lunchhhh."

"You make me sick!" He glared at me wordlessly for a few seconds, then slipped into the overlap of the curtain. I heard whispering outside and realized he was talking to our over-attentive waiter. Minutes later, a cup of coffee appeared in front of me, along with a mini-pitcher of cream.

"Oh, what a cute little pitcher! Can I have it?"

"Uh, no, ma'am. It belongs to Reagan's."

"Okey-dokey then." I laughed. "Jus' dun't look, mister-sir, okay?"

I caught the last few drops of champagne on my tongue, then poured the cream pitcher contents into the flute. Again warning the waiter, I slurred, "No look! *POP*, it disappears! In my pocket. Bye-bye." I cracked up laughing, but the waiter turned on a dime.

dI drank the coffee and the second cup he brought without my request for it. I stood and turned at the same time and almost fell. *Maybe you should take a cab, Lela. Or... no, just another coffee.*

Thinking I'd page the waiter, I stuck my head out of the Elite Room curtain, gathering the fancy fabric under my chin so that only my face showed. Six eyes stared back at me from a table just outside the curtain. I felt sure it was a corporate group entertaining a client because everybody was all puckered up and nervous-looking. "Hi!" I said, focusing on the only woman in the group. A man at the far end signaled for the waiter, then pointed to me. I looked at the waiter, locking eyes with him as he took three long lunges toward the Elite Table.

"Ma'am, please, let me call a taxi for you. You can take a coffee to go, as well."

"Hey... shrimp cocktail to go?"

The waiter's eyes widened. "Yes, ma'am. Coffee coming soon, and I'll come to get you when the taxi arrives."

"Okey-dokey!" I caught myself, "Uh... I already said that, didn't I?"

"Thank you, ma'am," he said, disappearing behind the curtain.

Nobody heard me say, "Thank you, ma'am? Thank you for what? For being a stupid drunk in the middle of the day?"

I was drunk enough to laugh about it and drunk enough to cry about it. As expected, a half-dozen tears dripped off my jaw, landing on the tablecloth where they beaded up without rolling or spreading. "Too much starch," I spoke to the empty cubicle.

Ten minutes later, the waiter opened the curtain all the way and reached to pull me off the chair. "Let's walk slowly, okay. Hold on tight." I opened my mouth to speak, and he jumped to interrupt me. "Don't talk. Say nothing at all."

Suddenly, though it was surely hours later, I was home and eating steamed shrimp with spicy cocktail sauce, wondering what the hell happened.

SPYING, CRYING, DYING
Chapter 3

The custody agreement was working out just fine. Bo spent a week with his dad, followed by a week with me, and all pickup/drop-offs were at daycare. Going with the flow, Bo seemed to handle the changes well. Most importantly, Andy and I managed to keep our hateful feelings about each other out of the picture for Bo's sake.

But I still struggled with major resentments about the perky redhead Ella Perkins, the wholesome-looking harlot who stole my husband.

Work was incredible; my concepts received rave reviews from all concerned, including the Publication Managers. I had lunch dates with random suitors about once a week but never agreed to see them in the evening, never daring to show my alcoholic self as I'd done with Phillip.

The every-other-week custody schedule became routine. When Bo was with me, I cooked like a fiend and played four-year-old games, sipping wine until I could guzzle it after he went to bed. When Bo was with his dad, I was sober only at work. On no-Bo weekends, I hung out in West Rockville's bars playing come-hither games with a string of men.

On the way home from daycare on Fridays, Bo would tell me stories about his week with his dad. "Ella cooked s'ketti."

"Was it good?" I spoke cheerily but seethed inside. Just hearing Ella Perkin's name filled me with rage.

"S'ketti and brown-juice meatballs!" He threw his arms up in joy. Then furrowing his brow, "Ralph doesn't like popcorn."

"Ralph the big, fat cat?"

"And the sun... almost... got in my eyes."

I laughed. "Almost, huh?"

"And we played baseball. Wham! Mine went over the fence."

I imagined sweet blonde-haired Bo standing three feet from the fence with a bat, his Dad shouting cheers. My thoughts verified, Bo whispered loudly, "And the crowd goes wild!"

Though I boiled with jealousy for their Norman Rockwell family life, I encouraged Bo to share the details of his life. It was like spying on Andy and Ella.

Andy called that Friday night around ten, making small talk. Finally, I broke through the bullshit. "What do you want, Andy? I'm sure you didn't call to chit-chat when you have spaghetti and meatballs waiting." He didn't understand the slam.

"Okay, I'll say it directly. Bo is telling us disturbing things about what goes on over there."

My instant reaction was fear, but I laughed sarcastically. "What's he saying, Andy? That I'm a red-headed child abuser?"

"Lela, he talks about how much you like wine and said you talk on the phone all the time." *Ouch. Busted.* Yep, I was being "watched" by a four-year-old, and Andy was exactly right. Yep, too much wine and too many phone calls. Andy spied on me through Bo's eyes in the same way I spied on him and Ella.

With a new commitment, I put my sole focus on Bo. I quit drinking in front of him, and when my friends called, I begged off the phone. One-on-one, we created a happy family to rival the one he had with Andy and Ella, and for the first time in my 26 years, I had an extended period of no drama, no trauma, and outright happiness.

After a while, I even quit wondering when the other shoe would drop.

Bo and I went on a series of fun adventures, but always on the cheap. I made a good salary but found it hard to keep up without the benefit of child support. That was my fault; I wrote most of the divorce agreement. Maybe I was naïve about it, but I assumed Andy would always share Bo's expenses and time per the "rules" we'd carefully written.

But it was odd how things fell into place. Andy, or maybe it was Ella, bought my son an excess of clothes, toys, and miscellany. It was so excessive that I feared Bo would be spoiled rotten, thinking he could get anything he wanted on a whim. The solution for me was to buy him *nothing at all*, thus balancing everything out.

Little did I know Andy considered that an advantage for himself and Ella. At the time, I didn't even know he was working for an advantage.

There was more juicy gossip in response to the "Did you have fun with your dad?" question the next day. I discovered such tidbits as Ella wore red shoes to work, the cat threw up marshmallows, his Dad got the truck windows "blacked," they painted the living room, and his dad wore an ugly tie to church.

"Church?" I freaked.

The second we got home, I poured out Legos for Bo, and I hid in the closet to call his fucking father. I was growling mad. "How *dare* you take *my* child to a *church? I don't want that.* If you take him again, I'll take you to court."

The silence lasted a full fifteen seconds as I fumed. Turns out, they had gone to Ella's church, the Church of God, where parishioners speak in tongues and thump Bibles. I didn't want Bo to go to *any* type of church, and certainly not a crazy Pentecostal one chosen by a red-headed stranger.

Reluctantly, Andy agreed. Not because he understood or respected my point of view, I surmised. No, he agreed because he didn't want the courts involved. Andy knew I'd win.

I kept up with the questions on transfer days, learning dozens of juicy tidbits – he got a new *Mutant Ninja Turtles* comforter, they played games with shaving cream and his dad ate some, and Andy's brother Mott came to visit. I didn't hear another word about church, and my butthole had relaxed its pucker on the topic.

Nine months came and went with no issue. Then Bo dropped the juiciest gossip of all. He made a speech on the way home, a speech about cake. White cake. Stating rules about what kind it had to be… how tall, how round, what color, and used the word "frosting." *Kids don't say frosting. Kids don't care what fucking kind of cake it is. What's going on?*

"Why are there rules for cake, Bo?"

"B'cause you cut it. And a million people eat it."

"Where will they eat the cake?"

"Duh!"

Where did he get THAT word? What are those two teaching him? "Bo, don't say 'Duh.' It's not nice. So where will they eat cake?"

"They eat cake in *church*, Mommy. That's where they *always* eat!"

I coughed, half-choking, then pulled over. My hands were shaking too hard to keep the car on the road. With an audible swallow, I asked the question I didn't want to be answered. "Is it a wedding, Bo?"

"Yeah-yeah-yeah! That's the name! And I get to wear a bow tie."

"A wedding in the church?"

"Yeah, I walk to Daddy with a wing on a piddow."

"A ring on a pillow?"

"Duh!"

I closed my eyes and shook with a slew of emotions. Bo asked why we were "not moving" and accepted my silence as an answer. Like a four-year-old should, he made zooming sounds while pulling on his upper lip and other such other mouth sounds. Suddenly he said, "But Ralph can't go. He's too fat."

We idled on the side of busy Valley Pike for ten minutes or so as I hid my tears from Bo, squeaking short answers to his many questions. I ebbed and flowed with emotions. Anger, sadness, defeat, dread, fear, then more anger and more sadness. Finally, I put the car in gear and drove home to plan my speech to Andy.

Sadness enveloped me; jealousy oozed from every pore. *Oh, shit... Andy's getting married. He's happy, and I'm not! Because I'm a single-mother loser... a drunk, worthless has-been.* I wondered how Ella-fucking-Perkins could make him happy when I couldn't.

The worst part: they were getting married in Ella's Bible-thumping, tongue-speaking church. It felt like Andy was defying me, cheating on me again and again and again. My anger spiked, yet I cried with uncontrollable sadness.

Bo wanted to play leapfrog, but I couldn't bring myself to laugh with him. I poured a vodka-tonic, actually vodka with a splash of tonic, and could only sit and stare. I didn't cook my planned dinner, barely managed scrambled eggs and toast. Then I stared at Bo with crossed eyes as he ate.

"What's wrong, Mommy? Why are you crying?"

"Because you're so cute, baby. So cute you make me cry."

"That's silly."

"Yeah… I guess it is." So I forced a smile and tried to act happy for Bo's sake, managing a few corny kid jokes. A flash of memory of what Ella had done the night I called an "interrogation" had roused me. I moved the dining room chairs to the living room so Bo could play train.

I wrote out notes for my call to Andy, but my concentration waned. In the end, I vegged out to an episode of *The Smurfs* as Bo jumped around the apartment. Two more vodka-tonics and I fell asleep when putting him to bed at eight o'clock.

Their wedding date: February 8, 1986, a Saturday. When I realized nothing could stop it, I dove into a deep depression. So far down, physically and emotionally, I was lucky to do just the minimum of keeping my job and taking care of Bo. Otherwise, I slept. And drank.

When the wine ran out, I stocked up at Middlebrook Liquors. The vodka bottles were too big to fit in the cabinet, and they sat prominently on the kitchen counter to serve as a constant reminder of my weakness. My pitiful, disgusting weakness.

What a useless piece of shit you are, Lela Fox.

Thankfully, the depression was reasonably short-lived, a blip on my lifeline of Bi-Polar spikes. But all shrinks warned me of "rapid cycler syndrome," and I soon zoomed the other way. But mania and sadness are no better combination than depression and sadness.

Actually, mania doesn't mix with much at all.

On the night of their wedding, I stumbled into Applebee's bar. Alone, despondent, and wallowing in self-pity. The drunker I got, the more I wailed about my hopeless situation. Speaking with a rat-a-tat pace, I told my sorrowful tale to the bartender and every suitor who wandered toward me. "What a smack in the face," I said, "They're probably saying 'I Do' as we speak." A parade of men bought me sympathy drinks.

At last call, I looked to the right to find a faceless man on the stool next to mine. I don't remember our conversation, but I do remember asking if he wanted to go home with me, and I remember his response: "It would be my greatest wish," he said.

☼ ☼ ☼ ☼ ☼

Around five AM, I heard a zipper. His fly, I reasoned. The metal pieces of his belt buckle clanged against each other. I thought about pretending to be asleep but found myself curious and sat up. "Hey, dude, what's your name?"

"Russell. What's yours?"

"Ella," I said.

"Well, see ya around."

"Maybe."

"By the way..." He hesitated, sounding almost apologetic. "I probably just gave you herpes." The man turned and walked out of my bedroom slowly, and like always, the vacuum effect in the breezeway made the front door slam. *Bam!* It seemed even louder so early in the morning.

"Well, that sucks," I said to the dark room. With a sigh, I got out of bed and made a pot of strong coffee, splashing a shot of vodka in my first cup. I toasted myself. "Hair of the Dog, to the stupid-drunk single woman with herpes."

I sat at the breakfast table, deep in thought, sitting long enough to realize I probably didn't know the whole of my mistake.

I checked my purse and, as I feared, the Visa was missing along with about fifty bucks in cash.

Too drunk to cry, too drunk to freak out. With a calm demeanor and staccato voice, I called the toll-free number to report my credit card stolen, then splashed another cup of coffee with vodka from one of... *shit! Only TWO bottles now!* I screamed to the empty apartment, "The sonofabitch stole my bottle of Grey Goose! My *best* vodka!" I sat at the table and fumed. "What a sonofabitch... stealing my liquor... that's a low blow!"

I sobered up an inch at a time on that Sunday, using my weaning-off, fool-the-hangover trick. I thought I was smart to do it, sipping vodka in smaller and smaller quantities until sober enough to do without, usually around six PM.

How could I possibly drink *less?* How could an alcoholic purposely get un-drunk? It amazes me now. I guess I wasn't a hopeless drunk yet. But as my drinking continued for years into the future, I dove deeper into the bottle to drown my feelings, to make me fit in and feel worthy.

As the roller coaster of my life built speed, the need to self-medicate exploded into chaos, sending the roller coaster out of control.

But maybe the ugliness was just lousy luck, I thought. I dug deep for creative ideas to justify my behavior, blaming the men for tempting *me*, creating grand scenarios to prove I *should* get special treatment despite what the motherfuckers said.

I even thought maybe I'd been gay all along, and all the problems were caused by leading a false life.

I blamed everything but myself and the vodka.

BAD NEWS, GOOD NEWS
Chapter 4

Marilyn's boss Christopher called the meeting. "A change is coming," he said, "A big change." The entire Marketing staff traipsed to the upstairs conference room, all ears open to hear the head honcho and the "momentous change" he had promised. We'd been discussing possibilities all morning.

"All in-house marketing will cease at the end of this month. We have contracted the work to a local advertising agency." He kept talking, but I immediately zoned out... watching my life flash before my eyes.

I didn't hear the second sentence, either, knocked flat by the first. *I've lost my job. Unemployed. Single mother. You're fucked, Lela.* In an instant, I turned numb and didn't notice my tears until one plopped on the walnut conference table. *Plop...* loud enough to hear on the other side of town. Marilyn reached under the table to squeeze my knee. Her look was caring and full of empathy, her bottom lip pouting with exaggeration like a sad clown. Then she morphed the pout into a smile... maybe to encourage me? I didn't know.

It didn't work.

Throughout my life, tears had been my first and instant reaction; that's why Dad called me "Tear-Bucket Jim." My tears continued to fall, but my heart skipped a beat with the second announcement. Before the gasps and moans caused by sentence one drowned him out, Christopher purred sentence two. "But there's good news, too."

I doubted any news could compensate for the end of my career, but he kept talking, and the news was good. The local agency that won the 14-24 contract would interview each of us and planned to hire us one by one if we wanted to make the move.

"In fact," our CEO said, "Interviews with each of you was a contract requirement. We want *you* to train *them* about what we need and why. And with your knowledge and talent, you'll continue to work for us. Just... not here."

I breathed a sigh of relief, but a disgusted Porgie threw her notepad across the room and yelled at Christopher for allowing this "outrageous act." Marilyn reached across the table to grab Porgie's wrist, I assumed to calm her, but Porgie jerked her arm back and shot Marilyn a fierce "fuck-you" look.

Porgie stood, all four-foot-ten of her, and spat words like bullets, aimed at the spot between Christopher's eyebrows. She screamed, "You're selling us out, dammit! This will *never* work, and it's just not *fair!* Don't you know my work is far superior to what you'd find in this damn town!" And, for God's sake, I've been here for almost five years! I helped *build* this department!"

Marilyn was a true diplomat and approached everything with a calm and positive approach. In the silence that followed Porgie's outburst, her voice seemed loud. "Maybe you could think of it as an opportunity, Porgie. Weren't you talking about moving to Chicago with your brother? There'd be a ton of jobs for a good art director in the Windy City. And I'll write excellent letters of recommendation... for all of you, actually."

Porgie didn't reply but sat down in a huff. She clicked her ink pen in and out of the barrel, repeatedly.

Babbas Bean looked defeated. My friend opened her mouth to ask a question, or so it seemed, but closed it just as carelessly. Shy Jay's blazing-red face held eyes that darted around the surface of the table, avoiding eye contact with anyone. Lauren stared at a spot near the ceiling and spoke as if in a dream. "This is a sign. I'm supposed to head west. California," she said softly, "Just like my dream. It's time to go where the creatives create, where the gay women are gay."

Whoa! I never knew Lauren was gay and found it strange that she'd announce it here, in that way. The rest were surprised, too, it seemed, based on their shocked looks. In the poignant silence, all I could hear was Porgie's ink pen, clicking in and out.

And in and out.

Our secretary, crying quietly, would be out of a job, too. Christopher spoke directly to her. "Debra, we have a place for you. Assistant to Sarah Laughlin, if you're interested." He looked at Marilyn and grimaced.

With her head down, Marilyn mumbled, "It's early retirement for me. My husband will be happy." Her lack of emotion spoke of an emotional overflow; tears fell from her eyes, and I reached under the table to squeeze her knee as she'd done to me.

There were a few more questions from the others, more explaining from Christopher, but the sound of Porgie's pen overpowered the room.

Click. Click-click-click.

I screamed it, sending an echo, "Porgie! Stop your goddamn clicking!"

Her eyes flew wide open. Then they squinted, glaring at me. The bitch leaned across the table and sneered. "You're not the only one who's upset, Lela Fox. Although *you*, little missy, have the most reason to worry. People with your level of talent seldom go far."

Marilyn spoke up in a voice as sharp as her nose. "*Porgie!* We're *all* upset, and you have no right to be that rude to Lela! Or anybody!"

"I don't need permission, Marilyn," she snapped back. Silence, even from CEO Christopher.

After my rage at Porgie eased a bit, I asked Christopher, "What's the agency's name? The one who won the contract?"

"Sturbridge Advertising. Biggest shop in Rockville. It will be the son in charge now, Barry Sturbridge. He'll be the one to interview you and... hopefully, everybody."

Porgie huffed. "Not me! No way I'd work for that idiot!"

Christopher spoke like silk to Porgie, showing his charm. "Maybe he's not an idiot, Porgie. I found him professional. The entire board of directors found him and his agency deserving of our business, you know."

"And that's supposed to impress me?"

Christopher stared Porgie down. I waited for more silky words, more of the CEO's charm to calm her. But no... he squinted his eyes and took a deep breath as if changing personalities in front of our eyes. Thudding his index finger on the table with each word, he glared at Porgie, "This meeting is over." Then he stomped to the door, leaving us dumbfounded in our chairs.

Silence.

Porgie had managed to upset the stoic CEO of 14-24, something even Marilyn hadn't seen, she said. Babbas Bean stood and paced the room, ignoring Porgie's continued whining. Marilyn cooed assurances to all of us, and Jay's face transformed from baby-butt-red to flaming crimson.

I felt... crowded... as if the world was squeezing me closed. A pounding headache beat in my temples, leaving me sick with pain and anxiety.

I spoke, sharing perhaps the best news of the day. "I know Barry Sturbridge, y'all. He was the sponsor of the Campaigns class my senior year at TSU." Maybe only Lauren understood the enormity of that relationship via Campaigns Class; she was a TSU grad, too.

Lauren said, "Maybe he'll hire you, then. But you notice Christopher said only an interview was guaranteed, not a job. Big whoop. I don't call that 'good news' like he said. I'm already so glad I'm moving. I wish you guys luck."

Though I tried, I couldn't view the change as a "smart business decision," as the CEO had said; the news felt far too personal, like a direct slap in the face.

You're screwed, Lela. You only thought you were sailing on smooth waters. You relaxed too soon, assuming your future was secure. The bitch of it is you'll struggle to find work, just like Porgie said. Yep, you're in a world of hurt. And now destined for failure.

Though it was only two o'clock when we left the conference room, I gathered my things and left for the day, not asking permission. I tried to think positive and be grateful for an afternoon with Bo.

Outdoors and walking to the parking garage, my lungs begged for air in the summer humidity. *This morning's big problems seem so small now. Don't you wish the weather was the only thing to bitch about?*

I was flat-out terrified. On the way to daycare, I allowed myself to cry in traffic, then used a napkin and some spit to clear the mascara under my eyes. I vowed that neither Bo nor his teachers would see me upset.

"Did you have a good day, buddy? What did you have for lunch?"

"Hot dogs! Green jeans, too. Yuck!"

"You mean green *beans*, but they're not 'yuck' because even one green bean makes you strong!" I made The Hulk sound he liked. "And four green beans will make you strong enough to jump over buildings."

"No, Mommy. *Bread crust* makes you jump over buildings!"

I didn't think he'd ever listened to my teasing lies about food. "Oh, yeah...

I get them mixed up."

"My daddy eats *a lot* of bread crust, 'cause he's *crazy-strong*. He can even lift a truck." I laughed for Bo's benefit but dropped the subject immediately. I wasn't in the mood to hear about his damn dad and the perfect life he led on the Norman Rockwell cul-de-sac.

I parked next to the playground at Lyons Park. The slide was "ouchy," Bo said, and I assumed it meant "too hot" though the day was cloudy. His goal was to arm-walk the monkey bars; he'd been trying for weeks, losing steam before the final bar.

With a boost from me, he did it and squealed with laughter as I helped him jump to the ground. "Again, Mommy!" Then, "Again! Again!" Twenty back-breaking boosts later, I worked to change his focus.

"Good job, Bo-Bo! This calls for a celebration! How about... Putt-Putt?" His squealing continued, and he jumped up and down in answer to my question. Seeing a happy Bo put things in perspective. *I have everything I want right now, and I will rally with all the gratitude I can muster.*

That evening, after Bo hit the sack, I drank three quick glasses of wine. Notepad in hand, I planned my course of action and scribbled a few paragraphs about how to remind Barry Sturbridge of our previous relationship.

Then I made a phone call that sent my Adam's apple into spasms... to ask a question that would break a legal precedent. I called Andy to tell him I would need child support. He laughed. "Lela, you'll be waiting for hell to freeze over on that one."

I knew he was right; our divorce agreement was to split costs and not pass money hand-to-hand. Still, I thought I would ask; maybe he would take pity on me. I asked just before he hung up laughing.

"One more glass, and I'll call my parents." I emptied the bottle, finally making the call around ten. Only slurring a few words, I spilled my bad-but-could-be-good news.

Dad knew the pain of being without a job; he'd been laid off twice in his day. In the past, when I told them I would be immune to such tragedy, both had harped on me to put money aside. Did I listen? Hell no. I put a pittance into a savings account here and there, never imagining I'd need it.

From the beginning, I thought I was a "special case" and that my career was a lifelong sure thing.

After all, I was Lela Fox, Queen of Everything.

Without telling me what a dumbass I had been, my father pointed out that no one is immune to the whims of a corporation. "You're right, Daddy, as always." After a long silence and a big sigh, I said, "We're coming to Burgess this weekend – I need a big dose of Daddy."

My loving father assured me there was plenty to go around. Then, thinking of the secondary benefit of visiting the parents, I said, "And I need a double serving of Mom's chicken and dumplings!"

The prospect of losing my job changed how I managed my money for the rest of my life. With the next paycheck, I opened an IRA and a fancy high-interest savings account.

My "simple savings," I'd called it, had been spent on useless luxuries up until then. I vowed to return it to a balance far beyond that of my peers.

Unlike most alcoholics, I was curiously responsible and "paid myself first," as my parents, especially Mom, had taught me. I did it monthly until the shit hit the fan.

When I reached my bottom, drunk and sloppy in jail, I still had untouched money in the bank. That little bit of savings saved my ass.

But my best investment was sold in Lifetime Number Nine; I traded stock certificates for the will to live.

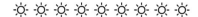

SHOW THOSE PEARLY WHITES
Chapter 5

The following week, Barry Sturbridge set up a presentation board in an empty cubicle on the fifth floor. He had come to interview those who wanted to "transfer" to Sturbridge Advertising when the 14-24 jobs disappeared. "Not a guarantee of a job," Marilyn reminded us again. She'd said it so many times that I wondered if she knew something we didn't.

Lauren wouldn't see Barry; the idealist soul was serious about moving to San Francisco, having signed a moving company contract within two days of the meeting. Porgie, still pissed, refused to interview with a "phony" like Barry Sturbridge, as she called him. She had her sights set elsewhere.

Bitch. I hoped she would be unemployed much longer than her money lasted.

Babbas Bean, Jay, me, and two designers who sat on the far side of the department signed up for time slots for an interview.

I went first. To my surprise, it wasn't so much an interview as a welcome to a new job. Barry Sturbridge didn't double-team me, ask the questions meant to trip up an interviewee, nor ask to see my portfolio. My false résumé was ready, listing a college graduation date that still hadn't happened, but he merely glanced at it.

Though he seemed perfectly normal, it was hard to look at him for long. Barry flashed the whitest teeth I'd ever seen – neon white and the center of a grin so wide that he looked like a cartoon. I seconded Porgie's "phony" comment... his charm was forced and very disconcerting.

Maybe he's as nervous as I am... maybe the musky cologne is a cover for lack of confidence?

I half-listened to the rest of his pitch, realizing that his anxiety, his not-quite-square jaw, even his teeth-bleach obsession – none of it mattered. And it didn't matter if I trusted him or not. I needed a future at Sturbridge.

Barry detailed such a future... the how, who, why, and wherefore of it all. Thankfully, his weirdness disappeared as he talked; I could feel the tension ebb word by word.

So maybe he's just nervous... a nice guy being a human being with normal feelings. He covers his insecurity with false bravado, just like you, right? But after the first impression, he's approachable and even kinda funny. So relax, Lela. You got this.

Boldness: I dared to bring up our history.

"Barry, do you remember when Sturbridge sponsored the TSU Advertising Campaigns Class? 1982? The convenience-store chain client?"

"Is that how I know you?"

"Yep, but I wasn't just any ol' student in that class."

Barry chuckled. "My guess is you're not 'just any old' *anything,* Lela. You're a stand-out."

"I wasn't fishing for a compliment, but thanks." I knew he didn't know if I was a stand-out or not... just romancing the new employee, but I kept talking. "If you remember, I was out-to-here pregnant at the time." My hands demonstrated where my belly had been in the ninth month of pregnancy.

Barry smiled that pearly-white smile again. "Oh yes, and the TV commercial your team produced," he paused for a genuine cackle, "A pregnant woman frantically looking for pickles!" He slapped his knee and laughed loudly, much louder than necessary.

It *had* been a funny commercial and a miracle that we pulled it off with the zero- budget of a team of five college students. "Remember, Barry? We won the competition that year. You chose my team as the winner."

"Oh, I remember you well now! All the more reason that I think you're a great catch for Sturbridge. That project... and this interview... you've proven yourself a brave, inventive, and creative copywriter. A star before your time, actually."

Still wondering why he'd be so complimentary so early, I asked, "Will we do projects for other clients? I mean, in addition to 14-24 mailings and presentations?"

"Absolutely. The agency is expanding like a balloon right now. My father retired two months ago, and I turned the sales staff loose with a plan that has worked. Worked wonders, in fact, and we're not finished yet." I nodded; his pride and excitement rubbed off on me.

He continued to babble about their new clients, along with the established ones. He mentioned banks, pet products, and a half-dozen other companies and industries I found exciting. "You and your coworkers here are part of the plan. We need good creatives, as many as are worthy."

Barry Sturbridge stood and reached for a too-firm handshake. "I accept the job, Mr. Sturbridge."

"No 'Mister" allowed at Sturbridge. Call me Barry. We're about to make beautiful advertising together!"

Cringing, I smiled and nodded, but I hated the phrase. Too flirty, and he did a lousy job at it. But I forgave Barry instantly when he stated my starting salary... double what I was earning now, and I was doing okay already!

Double the salary! I knew agency writers were the highest-paid, but I never imagined it'd be *double*. I looked away before my jaw unhinged; it took a minute to swallow the shock and re-assemble my professionalism. *Negotiate, Lela. That's what you're expected to do. But don't screw it up!* I mumbled a higher number and agreed to his counteroffer, adding an additional $3,000 annually. *Holy shit, Batman! I'm rich!*

Out the door as a nervous wreck, simultaneously excited and fearful for what was to come, my legs began to waver. *Don't faint! It's just... I have a job! A great-big job!* Bo and I could live well on that much money, and I could save tons more for the rainy days to come. Maybe I could even get a new car!

A few deep breaths later, I skipped back to my office; yes, I skipped like a little girl. A voice from behind sang, "Skip to my Lou!" and I froze in my tracks. Slowly, I turned to see Barry Sturbridge and his pearly whites gleaming. Though he seemed genuinely amused, I felt the familiar crimson rise from jaw to hairline. "Don't be embarrassed, Lela. I've never seen a new employee skip. I assume that means you're happy, and I love that! I try to make all Sturbridge employees happy. It's important to me." His grin widened, and I realized he was sincere. Amazingly sincere. Finally, he threw his head back to laugh out loud. "Yes, it's nice to see happy employees. I hope to find more happy employees down this hall."

No words came from my mouth; none seemed appropriate. I nodded and slipped into my office while holding my breath. Barry watched until I sat at my desk. As if on cue, Babbas Bean looked up and caught Barry's eye. "Are you ready for an interview, Brenda?"

"Yes. But please call me Babbas Bean."

"Babbas Bean?"

"Lela named me that, and I've decided it's the best name ever for an art director. It fits me."

"Okay then... Babbas Bean... are you ready for an exciting new job?" She nodded, stood, and picked up her resume file and oversized portfolio. As she turned to follow Barry down the hall, she winked and gave me a thumbs-up.

After the interviews, the department went to lunch as a group. Both Jay and Babbas Bean had accepted Barry's offer, as did the other two designers on the back hall. Although none of us quoted dollars and cents, the subject of salary came up. All seemed to feel the way I did – amazed and thrilled. I ached to rub Porgie's nose in my new-found success, but I had purposely sat on the opposite end of the table.

Two more weeks, and I'd never see her again. Or at least I hoped so.

SOMETHING ASTIR
Chapter 6

As promised, in the spring of 1996, the idealistic 14–24 creative team arrived at Sturbridge Advertising. The building had seen better days. Two floors of discolored yellow brick, a hundred yards from the Tennessee River, in the farthest, lowest corner of downtown. I parked in a large lot on the side street with a walkway to a private employee entrance. Sweet.

A group of twelve new employees stood in the triangle-shaped lobby of the building. Barry stood at the head of the group, ready to make a speech of welcome, I assumed. Suddenly, as in a cartoon opening, a rotund man with tufts of white hair bursting from the sides of his bald head toddled from stage-left to plant himself in front of Barry. Squinted brows above faded green eyes, he raised his right index finger and opened his mouth to speak.

"No, Dad!" Barry shouted, and stepped in front of him, not-so-gently pushing his father to the rear. He didn't want him to speak; that much was obvious, but he didn't make it in time. The Old Man didn't say words of welcome. Instead, he grumbled loudly, "Now get to work! You damn people are expensive!" Then he hobbled off stage. The shine of his bald head left a halo as he walked away.

Smiling through a nervous laugh, Barry looked at our group, locking eyes with each of us one by one. Apologetic and shrugging his shoulders with exaggeration, he said, "He's 81 years old, okay? What more can I say?"

Laughter rippled through the lobby. "Dad means well. Someday soon, you'll find him fascinating." Barry's pearly-white, cartoon-like smile now seemed appropriate and my admiration of him rose a notch. *Maybe he's not so bad. After all, he's your boss and taking the reins from a gruff old man – that has to be hard.*

There were newbies in the group, not just my 14–24 coworkers. Though Barry bragged on the success of their sales push, I knew it was risky to hire so many people at once. That risk worried me; my future depended on Barry Sturbridge's triumphs. But his promises of new clients signed and a list of those ready to sign eased my worries for the time being. But I didn't know how I'd feel in a month or a year.

One of the additional recruits, not from our 14–24 group, was an art director named Miller McKeown. I didn't know him personally but definitely knew *of* him. He was a freelancer with a stellar reputation... a company called Studio M. And who wouldn't notice such a hot and successful guy? His body came straight from a GQ magazine cover, tight abs and wide shoulders; he even had an ass... a very squeezable one.

From self-employment to a salaried job? Hmm. What's up with that? A few years ago at the Addy Awards, he won Best of Show for a kick-ass annual report. Yet here he stood; Miller McKeown dressed in khakis and a tie featuring flying pigs. I found that hysterical and, daring to speak to him, I commented on it.

"Here, you can have it," he said and loosened the knot.

"Really?"

"Yeah, when pigs fly." He chuckled through moist, kissable lips and he re-knotted the tie under his chin. Miller stared at me and cocked his head as if perplexed. "Don't you get it?" he asked, "Har, har."

I paused; it did take a minute to catch the silly joke. Then I laughed out loud, staring through Miller's round, wire-rim glasses and into golden-brown smiling eyes. Barry stopped in mid-sentence with my loud burst of laughter and looked my way; then *everybody* looked at me.

I felt the familiar buzzing against my eardrums, always my reaction on the rare occasions I felt embarrassed. "Uh... sorry. I didn't mean to interrupt."

Barry's mile-wide smile snapped back into place. "Thank you, Lela. And that brings up another point. Here at Sturbridge, we have fun. My father – we all call him The Old Man, meaning no disrespect – he's the gruff and overly serious one. But I know creatives work best in a relaxed and creative environment. In other words, don't be The Old Man."

During the rustle of the group laughing and talking to each other, Miller whispered in my ear. "The Old Man is a piece of work. I've known him for years." Then through a neatly trimmed spicy-red beard, he imitated The Old Man's facial expression: wrinkled brow, protruding bottom lip, and squinty eyes. I laughed out loud again, and once again, everybody turned to stare.

Shut up, Lela. Don't start off being a smartass. I looked at the group, then at Barry, clearing my throat, and returning to a professional stance.

A few minutes later, Barry introduced his assistant, Gail, dressed in a flowery blouse with a neck bow. Straight out of the seventies. As she spoke, Miller McKeown maneuvered to stand close beside me, and he playfully poked me in the side. I turned and smiled. His eyebrows jerked comically up and down and I sank into the depths of his brown eyes, spiked with golden spokes. *Tiger Eyes. Nice!* With those eyes piercing mine, never leaving my face, he said, "Hi, I'm Miller, officially."

I couldn't maintain the stare without blushing, and I didn't want to do that. As usual, social anxiety brought out the smartass in me. "I know who you are, Miller Officially. Me? Officially, I'm the Queen of Fucking Sheba. Unofficially, I'm Lela Fox."

Miller's grin was larger than it needed to be, sneaky and cute. Then he tipped an imaginary hat.

A squeaky voice turned my attention back to the front. Gail's voice dismissed all remnants of authority. "Let's go!" she said, and ushered the new creatives upstairs, leading each of us to our appointed offices and passing a stuffed-full garbage bag to each of us. The bag was heavy with rectangle protrusions; must be office supplies, I surmised.

At the last office on the left, Gail squeaked, "Lela Fox... complete with a nameplate on your door." Setting the lumpy garbage bag on the floor, she gestured wide and squeaked, "Welcome to Sturbridge, hon, let me know if you need anything." Then Gail slipped quietly out the door.

My office. Mine. Ta-da! Four walls; no partitions here. Four complete plaster walls! And a door! It closes and might even lock! Though I had a four-wall office at 14–24, this one was bigger, with a deep-cranberry accent wall and a desk of solid wood.

I felt like I had "arrived" and slid into a Moonwalk dance move, envisioning a multitude of pats on the back.

Sitting at the exquisite desk, I said aloud, "Wow! Even the chair is a luxury model!" The damn thing rocked and swiveled, too. Pushing hard on the edge of my desk, I spun around and enjoyed a moment of career ecstasy. *Yay! Here*

I am, ready to shine. At Sturbridge, I'd be busy, with a massive variety of products to promote and the creative freedom to do my best work. *Good for me! Hooray for our side!*

A few minutes later, as I pawed through my garbage bag of Post-It-Notes and paper clips, Barry summoned us with a shout. "All creatives! To the bump in the hall!" I knew what he must have meant; the hall included a section of wider walls and a bump-out toward the bathroom doors. He introduced us to each other and to the existing creative staff, promising better furniture for the conference room at the end of the hall.

During this nickel tour, I caught Miller McKeown looking at me eight times. Yes, I counted. The ninth time, he smiled like a light bulb and wiggled his eyebrows. *Could you be a little more obvious in your flirting, Miller? Jeez! I mean, you're hot, but not now... please.*

There was laughter up and down the creative hall, not forced, but genuine. The exception was a snub from the long-term Sturbridge copywriter Dorisey. Maybe she was simply having a bad day, but Dorisey was the very definition of a sour-puss. A matronly fifty-something and almost six feet tall, she looked at me under the rim of her glasses, studying me part-by-part. "Any Addy Awards at that 14–24 place?" she asked.

"Big time! Every year, we swept the direct mail categories," I spoke the truth.

Dorisey laughed. "Oh, you'll have to branch out from direct mail in about two seconds around here!" The woman cackled and threw her head back; the hall filled with a loud, high-pitched screech that put the hair on the back of my neck at full attention.

"Uh... Dorisey?"

"Yes?" She scrunched up her nose... as if she could smell it but not quite locate it.

"Do you... have a problem with me?"

"Of course I do! Who would welcome someone walking in to take their job?"

"But that's not what's happening! We are extras, newbies. Or at least that's what I've been told."

"If you win awards, you're sending me out to pasture. I'm an old lady, but not too old to make sure you don't succeed. Watch your back. And yes, that's a warning."

My eyes turned to saucers. *I'm being threatened by a matron copywriter?*

What the hell?

I scrambled to again assure of my innocence. "You have nothing to worry about, Dorisey. You have a long time before... going out to pasture, as you say. And aren't we all here to work as partners? Again, that's what I've been told.

I'd never heard such a loud and perfectly enunciated "*Hmmph.*"

THE SINGLE LIFE
Chapter 7

Every other weekend, I partied hard, running the bars. For a guaranteed partner in crime, my oldest sister Jennifer and I were both single at the same time... which made me estatic. It's like she had gained respect for me, liked hanging out with me. We had built a strong bond, becoming friends and equals through joint vacations, kid get-togethers, and now, singles happy hours.

Jennifer hung out with the "Glug Club," a hilarious name, I thought. The club's so-called "meetings" were Friday-night happy hours at various local bars. Laughing ladies dressed to the nines, men dressed in suits, and a few folks in work-casual outfits swarmed around a bar with drinks in-hand.

Of the three dozen interesting people, I found the men in suits the most captivating. Maybe because the men in suits found *me* the most captivating. The "new lady."

They gathered around me and took turns buying me drinks. Embarrassed a little, but I enjoyed the attention big-time. "Where do you guys work that would make you wear a full suit?" I asked with true intrigue. They answered simultaneously. One said "TVA." Another, "Self-employed," and another, "Tennessee State Bank." A far shot from my creative career.

These guys should be the most boring of the group based on occupation, but they weren't. Quite the opposite; they were funny and charming. Wisecracks and jokes ricocheted between them and all five had a quick and wicked wit. They found ways to include me in their group easily. I felt an instant friendship.

By the end of the night, I had more than enough to be tipsy; I was flat-out drunk... yet I hadn't spent a dime. Before I left, I gave lavish kisses to all the men *and* a half-dozen of the women.

That's when Jennifer pulled me out of the bar.

Outside, she shouted at me. "Enough, Lela! You are *bad,* disgustingly drunk! Go straight home – do you hear me? And drive slow, you idiot!" Then she spun and walked away. "Call me tomorrow!" she yelled over her shoulder.

Confused, I asked myself... *What did I do?* I couldn't remember any mischief or inappropriate things. But I sighed, buckled my seat belt, and drove home with one eye closed.

☼ ☼ ☼ ☼ ☼

The next morning, at 8:01 AM, my phone rang. One of the suits. I said, "I recognize your voice but can't put a face or a name with it. There were so many of you."

"Oh, trust me, Lela – Vick Belford isn't just 'one of the many.' I stand out from that crowd of ruffians for a dozen reasons. And I think you kissed me the deepest and longest in your final farewell."

Embarrassed, I said nothing. His confident tone struck me, intrigued me. With barely a pause, he asked, "May I take you to dinner tonight?" Again, I said nothing, realizing I hadn't had an official date since... hmm. *Does the disastrous lunch date with Phillip and the champagne count as a date?*

I opened my mouth to answer, but Vick stopped me after the first syllable.

"Before you decide, let me say we're going to the Sky Box." *Oo-la-la. Impressive! But also ridiculous. Why would a person waste so much money on food when it just becomes poop the next day? If the point is to throw money around to impress me, what does this say about Vick Belford's character?*

Deep breath. I reminded myself of the goal: date a variety of men but make sure they're not psycho. He wasn't a psycho, evidently, so why would I turn him down?

I vowed I wouldn't do what I had done with Phillip. *No getting drunk, no sloppiness, Lela.*

With just a touch of hesitation, I agreed to go. Vick replied with the shout of a cheerleader, which sparked a memory from the night before. I had teased

Vick about drinking more than I did and he objected, saying, "It's beer, Lela. I'm a tall, dark, handsome tall-dark-ale man. Besides, there's no such thing as 'too much.'"

"We'll have to meet later, Vick. I have to scoot home and change." He agreed and said "ta-ta" before hanging up. *Ta-ta? Who says that?* Then, in a snap, my feelings about Vick Belford took a back seat to the intricacies of the date itself. I'd need time to transform myself into a confidently single, affluent woman... a woman classy enough to eat at the Sky Box.

After hanging up, I realized my heart was beating double-time. The solution was to call Jennifer for reassurance and to bark a list of questions: "What should I do? What do you know about him? What do I wear? Help! I'm scared!"

She advised me calmly, as my sweet sister always had, and gave me the run-down on Vick Belford and the Sky Box. Jennifer even suggested an outfit she liked. Slowly, my nerves abated.

"Okay, I think I know what to do. Still, I feel like a child, meeting an adult for the first time."

"But I have a warning about that so-called adult, Lela. Listen carefully: he's not as nice as he looks. Vick is a cowboy."

"Cowboy? What do you mean?"

She struggled to find the words. "There's evidence that... he... well, let's just say he's not into protecting the honor of a woman."

"Good, neither am I."

"And he drinks too much."

"Good, so do I." Then I hung up the phone. I gave no more thought to her warning, assuming she was once again simply being overprotective of her little sister.

Excited, I had a hard time focusing on work for the rest of the day. It also didn't help that the sexy Miller McKeown kept bopping in and out of my office, uttering his cute-shy comments. He was a definite flirt, and I had to admit his interest in me turned my crank.

Mid-afternoon, he stopped by my office with a pencil behind his ear and day planner in hand. We had a project to discuss, our first as a team. "Tomorrow at one?" he asked, and a buzz between my ears began.

Another buzz started elsewhere, somewhere much more personal.

The thought of being with him in a small room sent my heart aflutter. Alarmed by the strength of my feelings, I warned myself: *This is your job! Quit thinking those thoughts! Don't shit where you eat.*

The Sky Box was the sphere atop a structure left from an International Faire hosted by Rockville in the early 70s. Striking artwork adorned every wall; dozens of polished metal and glass sculptures hung from the ceiling. A round structure, it boasted a monstrous round fish tank in the center.

While remodeling the sphere to create the restaurant, they had divided the cavernous space into intimate areas using six-foot-high brick walls; the room was open but intimate. Details matter and they had created a masterpiece. Warm and inviting, but funky.

We started in the bar. Vick remembered my drink of choice and ordered a vodka-tonic for me. My dad had always ordered for my mom, as a sign of respect, he said, and Vick's chivalry stunned me. But it wasn't just a regular vodka-tonic; he upped it to a call brand. "Tanqueray-and-tonic for the pretty lady," he said. That made me smile.

I asked, "So chivalry is not dead?" He wrinkled his brow, seemingly confused, so I explained. "Ordering for me? That's nice."

"It's just what a gentleman does. I was raised by a lady and treat each one with respect."

"That's not what my sister said."

"What? Why would she say that?"

"She says you're a cowboy. But I don't know what that means, exactly."

"Neither do I. And if she can't explain it, then you can't believe it." He took my drink from the bar and handed it to me. "Cheers." No clinking, just a raise of his glass.

Cozy sofas and plump side chairs in the bar area created a relaxed scene, much like a reading room in a nice house. I took a wingback chair and Vick sat on the corner of the sofa next to me. As soon as his butt hit the seat, he leaned forward to look at me with those magnetic brown eyes. "So! Lela Fox... tell me your life story."

It was such an abrupt and broad question that I laughed. First-date jitters made me drink the Tanqueray-and-tonic quickly and Vick signaled the bartender from the sofa. Suddenly, another drink appeared in my hand. *Don't do the champagne thing, Lela. Slow it down. Be a good girl.*

But I didn't listen to my own warnings and by the time the hostess escorted us to the table, I had a heady buzz. Happily, Vick had reserved a table in the casual section and not the hoity-toity section on the other side of the sphere. It was plenty formal for a small-town girl like me. Even in this more-casual atmosphere, I had seldom been around such extravagance and it made me uncomfortable.

Maybe it was the Methodist in me... the belief that extravagance is sinful.

On the flip side, after the fourth vodka-tonic, being surrounded by such extravagance felt thrilling, dangerous, and sneaky... and oh, how much I liked it! Here I was, living the high life... perched on a richly upholstered chair, drunk, with a sexy, rich cowboy who poured on the charm, flattering me and gazing at me adoringly. I felt like a million bucks.

"How's the steak?" Vick asked.

"Delicious."

"As delicious as your lips?"

"How do you know my lips are delicious?"

"They look delicious."

"Well, you know... looks can be deceiving."

"Not in this case."

"Maybe there are other parts of me that are *more* delicious..."

Vick threw his head back and huffed a laugh. He took a sip of his dark beer and eyed me evenly. "Lela Fox, you are a tease."

I finished chewing, contemplating my answer. "Guilty as charged."

Vick's eyes had never left mine. "I like a tease, all night long."

I smiled and lifted my drink. "Cheers! I like a man who isn't afraid of a vixen." All this was nonsense, but I enjoyed the witty flirting.

We toasted as Vick's eyes stayed glued to mine. After a few seconds, one eyebrow raised and his look became quizzical. I stopped in mid-chew, then hurried to swallow. "What?"

"Just trying to figure you out, Lela. You're a puzzle."

"Crossword or jigsaw?"

"I think maybe a word-scramble."

"I'm an old pro at word-scrambles. Or any word puzzle, actually. A writer should be, wouldn't you say? So maybe I can *help* you figure me out." Vick cocked his head but said nothing. I saw the gesture as an invitation to keep babbling. "See, I'm pretty much an open book. I don't hold back. As they say... 'I yam what I yam.'"

"What you yam… is sexy."

I blushed, shut down by embarrassment.

The teasing, going both ways, continued as we finished dinner and stretched it with coffee and dessert. Vick kept his comments R-rated and witty, flirting with me in a romance-novel sort of way. Never crossing a boundary, his manners were impeccable, but he expressed his desire with front-and-center certainty.

Vick Belford used words I had been desperate to hear from a man. The ex-asshole husband Andy had said things that were quite the opposite.

It was midnight when we stepped out of the elevator and waltzed through the elaborate lower lobby. Vick and I said our goodbyes and shared a kiss that was way too deep for a first date. I knew it wasn't a good idea, but I had no experience in demure, halfway kisses. Call me clueless. Or a slut.

After the thirty-second kiss, he squeezed me tight and mumbled with hot breath in my ear. "Follow me home, baby. I want to make you feel good." The devil and the alcohol in me wanted exactly that, but I declined.

When Vick complained that I had teased him too much to turn him down now, I told him he'd have to wait, take me out again. "See, Vick, I like to dress up and go to nice places, get drunk and eat good food. Everything else is a bonus."

I have no idea where this comment came from. It just… flew from my mouth as if I had experience in saying "no."

Probably, just as before, I'd overshot the runway in play-acting what I thought was a drunken-but-innocent verbal sparring contest. But I knew I wasn't "asking for a raucous roll in the hay," as he said.

Dare I tell him the truth? That I didn't want to sleep with him only because it would be the first time in my life I'd not slept with a first date after dark. I wanted a notch in my belt in a reverse kind of way.

☀ ☀ ☀ ☀ ☀

The next morning, I went straight to Babbas Bean's office per her request. She was eager to hear about my date, she said and wanted details about the interior of the Sky Box.

I could be honest with Babbas and shared the most surprising news, too. "The best part, Babbas Bean… I resisted and didn't get shit-faced drunk! Ta-da! I didn't even sleep with him!"

Within a beat, Miller walked into Babbas Bean's office. I reddened and sank into the side chair, trying to become invisible.

CREATIVE TEAM
Chapter 8

A few minutes before one o'clock, Miller McKeown slipped into my office and closed the door. A shy, crooked smile covered his face as he helped me roll the wood file cabinet from the corner to use as a table for our meeting. Each of us had read the project brief, and I stood to write the title on my whiteboard: Shaffer Flea Tablet.

Shaffer Industries was the largest client at Sturbridge Advertising. Most of their products were for large animals: vaccines for cows and horses, treatments for sheep diarrhea, stuff like that, but this project was for the small-animal division. Specifically, Shaffer FT, an old product we would revive, re-brand, and re-package for consumers, no longer just for vets.

Brainstorming without holding back, we threw around a dozen ideas. It seemed Miller wanted *a lot* of duality in the creative process and it struck me as odd. Usually, the writer and artist have mutually exclusive roles, and though anyone would agree that two heads work better than one... it just wasn't done.

The problem, if you want to call it that, was the way he looked at me: like he could see straight into my soul and was pleased with the sight. I felt so exposed and so... well... sexy. *Watch yourself, Lela Fox! Stay away! Your career is not a playground.*

It seemed like he respected me, which was weird. Then again, he didn't know me... didn't know my history or my shitload of character faults.

Almost against my will, I loosened up quickly; Miller made it easy. We brainstormed for nearly an hour, no holds barred, and laughed a lot. The whiteboard was full of possible product names. Miller liked my ideas, and I liked his, but the perfect one evaded us.

The solution was to combine our words and thoughts and as I put stars on those I thought may work, we both said in accidental unison, "Hey, you're *good!*" A voyage to mutual creative respect had begun.

Quit Yer Itchin' would be the new name for their flea prevention product, along with the tagline "Make Fleas Flee." Miller winked at me as he left my office. I felt my heartbeat pounding against my chest and echoing in my head.

Wait... Am I dating Vick Belford and shouldn't be so, uh, "inspired" by Miller McKeown? Alone in my office, I shrugged, realizing I hadn't a clue about how to be single. But I knew playing the field didn't mean a commitment after three dates and, so far, no sex.

So Miller is sexy and makes me feel sexy, too. I like him, respect him. Is that a sin? Happy and feeling verified, I bounced through the rest of my day with a shit-eating grin, though I paused often to quake in my boots about what might become a "normal" relationship with a man.

Having multiple people desire me sexually drove me at this time in my life. The reason, I think: still-shameful, I believed sex and more sex was the only good thing I could offer. So the more people who wanted me sexually made me more important, more confident, more worthy of life's blessings.

But in one hour's time, Miller McKeown put me in a crazy-uncomfortable place. He treated me with respect, apparently admiring me professionally and creatively, too... not just sexually.

It was the kind of respect I'd never had from a man, or had never acknowledged. It made me uncomfortable.

The sensation of feeling appreciated was so foreign that I felt like a big, fat, ugly fake... a counterfeit fuck-up pulling shreds of bogus knowledge out of my ass.

I'd be caught soon, I knew; he'd find out how much of a worthless drunk I was. It would be best to avoid circumstances where I might earn respect, I decided, but how could I avoid Miller?

BEST OF BOTH WORLDS
Chapter 9

Miller wanted our first date to a trio with Bo. Our plans depended on what "the boy" would like to do, he said, and he hit me with a barrage of questions and suggestions. The final choice was a Tex-Mex restaurant and a kid's movie – *Teenage Mutant Ninja Turtles*.

As we took our seats in the cinema, I put Bo on the end of our threesome so I could sit next to Miller, my date. But Miller insisted we change seats, putting Bo in the center. "Share him with me! I want to see his reactions, too," he said. Thrilled and miffed at the same time, he acted like his date was with Bo, not me.

The second date: a Putt-Putt game that left us all dripping with sweat. Miller taught Bo how to stroke the ball smoothly and with the right amount of force. It almost worked, considering Bo's three-year-old attention span. The third date: Chuck E. Cheese. On the way home, as Miller teased Bo about the games they'd played, I began to wonder if he was flirting with Bo to connect with me, or if he was being a selfish wanna-be father and I was just along for the ride.

Bo's big blue eyes twinkled when he looked up from hugging Miller's leg. My boyfriend, if that's what he was, was crazy about my son and reached down to rough-up his thin blonde hair. Bo said, "Miller, you're fun-fun!"

"I am?" Miller's eyes also twinkled. "Maybe it's just because you and I have fun *together*. You-you, dude-dude, are the fun-fun guy."

The interchange brought a case of Bo-giggles and, a few minutes later, both were squirming on the floor, laughing, and "arguing" about who was the most fun. Bo was in love with Miller and had been since the first date. Miller made sure the love affair continued.

I watched the two of them with a dreamy smile. A smile broadened on my face; it felt good to be a family, to have somebody to share the love and wonder of Bo. Family time was absent with Andy for the last year of our marriage, the time it should have been our major activity and shared joy.

The first time Miller and I made love, in my bed after putting Bo to bed, he gave his all, being attentive and gentle. He reeled in total awe of what he called "my crazy sexy side." His comment, "so responsive!" was a compliment to both of us, I thought.

We hadn't talked about it yet, but I assumed he, too, wanted more children. I was impatient and started early with fantasies of an expanded family with Miller McKeown. He seemed to be the perfect father and a dependable family man.

Then I questioned myself. Is that what I truly wanted?

I partied with Vick on non-Bo days and had a great time... drunk and sloppy as my party friends expected me to be. By the time the parental custody changed, I was eager to be with Miller and jump head-first into his adoration for Bo and me.

Feathers flew. Miller and I had arguments about me dating Vick every-other-week, but his approach was to shame me about it... to call me selfish and accuse me of purposely hurting him. I didn't want to hear that shit; it made me pull away from him. My explanation of this didn't seem to crack the stubborn of his brain.

Maybe things would have been different if he'd asked me out for a one-on-one date, but he never asked. Not once. Instead, he would spend hours planning activities for the days Bo could make it a threesome. I never told him how much that hurt my feelings, but I also didn't ask what he did when I was partying with Vick.

The reality of "joint custody" with Bo's dad was exactly joint, down to the minute. As it was, I had the best of both worlds, being a part-time mom and part-time party girl. Andy wouldn't let me have extra time with Bo, even if I asked nicely, but if something came up on my end, like one of Vick's extravagant weekend adventures, Andy was eager to be my backup.

Yep, the best of both worlds.

On a scale of one to ten, sex with Miller was an eight at best. He sweat too

770-691-0372

much and didn't have much of an imagination. On the flip side, Vick offered crazy-good sex, peppered with the titillating sometimes-addition of Sara, a beautiful and uninhibited woman. With Vick Belford, there were no rules, no lines to cross, all was celebrated. And the vodka kept me from feeling guilty about such lewdness.

Vick made me laugh. Maybe because I was always drunk, but probably because he liked to act silly like my Daddy. He made up parody song lyrics and sang loud in inappropriate places. I drank top-shelf vodka at his insistence and we made fun of people at the bar, creating soap-opera life stories for each of them. Giggles galore.

With Miller, I was mostly sober... not drinking until after Bo's bedtime. Though he wasn't as sour as Vick thought he was, Miller wasn't much of a laughing guy. Serious, but also not a good partner for discussing serious topics, especially about himself or his past.

Another good thing, I knew Miller must make the big bucks at Sturbridge, but he rarely spent much. Definitely conservative, you could even call him a cheapskate and I respected that, assuming his savings account was large and organized. Another "family man" check mark in the pro column.

My sister Jennifer was one of the few who knew I was sleeping with two men at the same time. Maybe she didn't realize I already felt the overwhelming *wrong* in my bones because she asked me about it.

"Why would either of these men accept your infidelity to them?" Jennifer wasn't being prudish but asking a legitimate question. Sleeping with multiple men at the same time was even more of a "no-no" in the eighties than it is now.

"I know I'm playing with fire, sister, and pissing both guys off in the meantime. But they're so different! I can't just choose one. I like them both, for two completely different reasons."

"Tell me what you mean, dammit."

"Don't be mad about it! It's just... Miller has never asked me out without also inviting Bo. Flip side: Vick has never asked me out if Bo was around. I have two different lives, two different boyfriends."

"Which leads to what I *really* wanted to talk to you about. Lela, it's like... you also have two different personalities."

"Ha, ha. Like that movie?"

"Not like that, sis. You're so damn different when you drink. It's disgusting, to be honest. What you have, I'm afraid, is regular, old-fashioned alcoholism."

"What the hell? Bullshit!"

"You said it yourself. You have your party boyfriend... because Vick is *definitely* an alcoholic if you don't know... then you have your family boyfriend. How much do you drink when Bo's around?"

"Actually, one little drink after he goes to bed. Or if it's wine, maybe two glasses. But that's all. And alcoholics can't do that, right? They can't drink sometimes and not drink other times. But I can. So chill out, Jennifer. I'm not wallowing in a gutter! Stop with your fucking accusations."

"But isn't it the alcohol that lets you feel okay about sleeping with two guys at the same time? Tell me about your shame, Lela. We have the same mother, remember?"

I burst into tears, never offering a reply. Tears dripping from my jaw, I gathered my son and our belongings and left. Her accusations hurt and I refused to let hoity-toity Jennifer make me feel even worse than I did on my own.

Yes, I knew to date two men was wrong. I even knew *why* I was doing it. Shame, my old friend, filled my confused mind.

I would soon choose between the two, and go down kicking and screaming.

☼ ☼ ☼ ☼ ☼

The next day, Vick Belford called with another lunch invitation. I agreed and, to my surprise, he said he would pick me up at work. I told him I thought that was weird, but... what did I know about dating now?

Not ten minutes later, Miller squeezed his way into my office door. "Wanna go to lunch?"

"Uh... can't. I'm having lunch with a friend." His face fell comically; an instant sideways knot appeared on his brow but I dared not laugh. Finally, his brows relaxed but the glare stayed as he spread a half-dozen sketches for the *Quit Yer Itchin'* package on my cluttered desk.

"Which ones do you like best?" he asked. Shocked, I couldn't believe an art director would want a copywriter's opinion on a layout. It just wasn't done that way. But Miller asked, so I critiqued and narrowed the selection down a little.

Suddenly, Vick appeared at my office door. "Hi," he said. Same goofy grin, same stunning brown eyes, and as always, dressed in a three-piece suit. I had expected him to go through the lobby and have the receptionist call me, like with a normal visitor.

"How did you find me?" I asked, surprised and a little pissed.

"Uh... a map?" he said, "And the guy at the end of the hall told me which office."

"You came through the private entrance to the building?"

"Doesn't say private, so what the hell?"

Miller stood with his mouth agape. He looked angry, snatching up his sketches with a scowl and enunciated indignantly, "We'll get together when you have time." Then he shot Vick a look filled with poison darts. Vick smiled back at him with an eerie calm. I noticed neither reached for a handshake. Instant tension; static made the hair on my arms stand at attention.

Despite my pleas to stop, Vick would pop into my office at random times during the day... whenever he had a nearby client appointment. It never failed that Miller was there, or in the hall to see him coming or going. Both bitched at me about the other but neither made an argument to encourage a choice between them. I was dating two men who hated each other, and I was in the middle by choice. *Who does that, Lela? You must choose... or break up with both of them!*

I kicked myself day after day, never doing what I knew must be done. I believe something or someone would eventually decide for me. Someday, somehow... I'd get what I wanted. Problem: I didn't know what I wanted.

☼ ☼ ☼ ☼ ☼

At one of our many Monday lunches, Vick flared his nostrils and slammed the navy cloth napkin on the table. He had asked what I'd done the previous weekend and didn't like the answer. "So how am I supposed to feel, Lela, knowing you're dating somebody else?"

"How am *I* supposed to feel, Vick, knowing *you* don't want to see me on the weekends I have my son? What do you expect?"

His lips formed a straight line, pressed together in frustration. "But you know I'm not ready to be a father!"

"Again... what do you expect me to do?"

"But you're so much fun to party with, so goddamn sexy, and free. I want you all to myself." He gulped half of his beer, quivering with emotion. "And, baby, I love to watch you make love to Sara in my bed. I love her in our crazy sex nights. You can go all night long! I'm crazy about you, girl. Crazy!"

"No, you're just crazy about part of me. And Vick, I don't hear the 'L' word... just 'crazy.' Don't you dare question me about what I do when you're not around!" I had found my independent, badass side and let him have all of it. "See, Vick, we have fun. We eat and drink. We get drunk and have sex. Hell yeah, the sex is great, and I appreciate you introducing me to Sara. I'm crazy about *her*. But going out and getting laid... that's all you get from me because that's all I get from you."

"Why can't we just have a part-time but exclusive relationship? You like being a one-on-one mother anyway, right? So maybe you just need me in the non-mom half of your life."

"Damn, Vick, you've got a lot of nerve!" I slammed my napkin on the table, loud enough to rattle the dishes on top. "Get the check, please. This is bullshit and I'm outta here."

"Oh, don't be so dramatic, Lela!" Suddenly he whispered, acting embarrassed in the uppity restaurant.

A deep breath, in through my nose. Then I closed my eyes and tried to control my anger, but it sat in my gut, churning like a hurricane. "And you're out of your fucking mind if you think I'll accommodate *your* needs when you won't accommodate mine! You've never even *met* Bo!"

"So I suppose Bo's father-figure is that asshole Miller McKeown? 'Mr. Miserable?' Or 'Mr. Zero-Personality?'" Vick blew a sarcastic laugh. "What kind of example is *that?*"

"He has plenty of personality! In fact, he's *nice!* Miller just hates you and hates it when you magically pop into my *private* office. So, of course, he's not going to put his best foot forward to his rival. Get over it!"

"And you defend him..." Vick rolled his eyes with his lips pressed together in disapproval. "Damn! Lela, I wish you'd just–"

"Look, asshole... Lela Fox runs the show, not you." Anger had increased my heart rate and I willed myself to sit back and relax. "Get the goddamn check, please. I have work to do."

Vick leaned back in the chair as well, studying me. "But... you're free this weekend, right?" I nodded. "Good news! I made reservations for a nice bungalow in the mountains... you, me, a gram of coke, Sara, and maybe her friend Steve. Are you up for a crazy party?"

As mad as I was, I snapped stiff with attention. When I shook myself back to reality, I sighed. "I'm not in the deciding mood, Vick. Just... just shut up about it. In fact, shut up about everything."

Vick laughed his trademark charming chuckle; he knew he had me. Both of us knew what my answer to the invitation would be. And now faced with understanding the sheer power Vick had over me, my anger and shame exploded. *But it's not just me! It's HIS fault.*

I raised my voice, too loud, "Vick, you motherfucker, you planned all this. All this... all everything... it's *all* your fault!"

It's odd how my reactions to Vick compared to my reactions to Miller.

Vick filled a hole in my soul that let me continue to be a misfit, a no-good drunk. He gave me permission to continue hating myself and feeling heartbreak and shame. Those feelings were comfortable and familiar.

On the other hand, Miller scared me. He seemed to be a good guy who led me to good things... things I didn't understand or know how into incorporate in my life. He thought I was normal and the pressure of his expectations made me push him away, though I never pushed far. At least not yet.

Should I be a no-good misfit or a professional, loving wife and mother? The true me was somewhere in between.

If I chose to be a wife and mother, I could only see the extreme example of my mother, and that brought paralyzing fears of being a Goody-Two-Shoes like she was.

The fucked-up thing: a Goody-Two-Shoes was exactly what I yearned to be. I wanted it more than anything.

Either way, I found myself lacking. The answer, of course, was alcohol and more alcohol. Vodka became a working solution, and it worked until a different kind of shit hit the fan.

SMOKEY'S COUNSEL
Chapter 10

I could only see the right side of Vick's face as he drove. He'd been silent for a while, as I rattled on about the scenery and our unknown destination. "It kills me that men like to just jump in the sports car and drive... like hearing the purr of the engine soothes you or something. Me? I say it's too much worry. It's not like you can zone out while driving because you'd be over a cliff in a heartbeat, driving straight on these curvy roads. But the mountains are nice this time of year, I'll agree with that. And today is–"

Blatant interruption. "I want to take you somewhere. Somewhere very important." Vick's demeanor was curiously serious. His two eyebrows created one; there was no teasing in his tone and no hint of sarcasm.

I was feeling no pain and no inhibitions that day, a six-pack deep into a case. "Sure... I'll go, though destination unknown again." When his expression became even more somber, I added. "Or maybe not. What's important about it? Vick, you look like somebody died." I paused. "Or like somebody is getting *ready* to die."

Vick didn't answer immediately, feeling for his bottle in the console and taking a long drink of beer. "I went to church today." He spat the words in one quick push... as if afraid to say them.

"Church? Today is Monday! What the hell?" When Vick didn't reply, I continued talking, trying to drop the accusatory tone. "That's not like you, Vick. Did you even go as a kid? Which church? And why?" Still no reply and my concern grew. "Vick? *Did* somebody die?"

"I just... lately I've been feeling... like I need to talk to somebody. I think the guy who gave the sermon would be somebody I could talk to. His name is Smokey."

My eyes popped wide with surprise. Vick didn't talk about personal things at all; that's not the kind of closeness we shared. Even with his eyes focused on the road, I could see them glass over with tears.

What the hell is going on? Should I reach and hug him? Pat his leg? Or maybe I should freak out and ask him to take me home. A tear dripped from his eye and I found myself touched by his vulnerability. Tears rose to my eyes, too. *Don't do it, Lela. Don't let him make you cry!*

"Smokey is Puerto Rican, I think. Maybe Jamaican, or some island. Dark-skinned but bright-blue eyes. And such *kind* eyes. It was like he looked straight into my soul or something."

Treading softly, I paused before asking more about his sudden need for church. "What kind of church?"

I felt the hackles on my neck rise. I was an adamant non-Christian. *Maybe God Himself is a thing, but not the Jesus stuff and not the fictional book they call the Bible... that part is bullshit and I won't have a thing to do with it. Please, please, please don't say Baptist, Vick!*

"Episcopal."

I had no clue about Episcopals except Jennifer's ex-husband was one. "They have, like, priests instead of ministers, right?"

"Yeah, Smokey was wearing a robe."

"Wasn't that kinda weird?"

"Actually, it left me wondering if he was hanging loose or wearing boxers, tightie-whities, or what."

Despite my effort to be serious, a laugh burst through. "That doesn't sound very spiritual to me."

"Actually, it was spiritual as hell, Lela. I cried."

"You *cried?* Why? What's going on?" Again, I felt a lump growing in my throat. My badass attitude was waning, suddenly wanting to play nursemaid to a man in distress. So I sat on my hands, willing the urge to pass.

Vick took off his sunglasses and shot a look at me. "Let's just go together."

"To the Episcopal church?"

"You have a problem with it?"

"Not really. Just... I'm blown away by this 'revelation' of yours, and curious as hell. Something must have happened because you're just not one to... what would I call it? Uh... share your soul with somebody. Especially somebody who wears a robe."

"It all depends on his undergarments."

Not knowing if he was serious or silly, I looked up to find the flash of his charming smile. He huffed a chuckle before returning the sunglasses to his face. His smile continued to glow and I laughed. "Vick, you're a hoot! I never know if you're serious or being whacky on purpose."

"Gotta keep you on your toes, dear." I felt weird, a little uncomfortable; this conversation was way more personable than our typical. He continued. "So, Sunday? I want to see what a large service would be like. The sanctuary is huge. Lots of stained glass and stuff."

"Is it the one way up the hill off Naperville Road?"

"That's the one. All Saints."

Saints! More Jesus shit. "So what is an Episcopal? More like a Methodist, or more like a Catholic? Please say it's not like Baptist or Church of God..."

"I wouldn't know, really. Not Baptist, though, thankfully. I've had enough of that shit." A few minutes of silence as the sports car smoothed around a series of Great Smoky Mountain curves. "Long ago, I heard somebody said they were a 'Whiskey-palian.' I guess that means they're closer to Catholic." He laughed, one snort.

Silence enshrouded us, and I let it sink in as I thought deeply about the importance of this "church Vick" persona. I murmured, "To be honest... a mystery religion makes me nervous."

"Let's just go check it out. I think you'll like it."

"You know I haven't been to church since I was – wow – it was a long time ago. Maybe ninth grade. In fact, I quit going when I got caught drinking at Youth Camp."

I could have told him the whole, disturbing story about cutting the tents and the psychiatrists thinking I was a skitzo, but I let it slide. "I'll go. What the hell... maybe it will help me, too."

☼ ☼ ☼ ☼ ☼

"Peace be with you," the thirty-something lady said. Her blue dress was casual cotton and her smile beamed toward me, a stranger. She'd been sitting in the pew in front of me, her blunt-cut blonde hair sweeping her shoulder blades.

I didn't know why she had wished me peace but noticed all the parishioners were turning to their neighbors and grasping hands in a "Peace be with you" greeting. The expected response, I finally understood, was "And peace be with *you*."

The massive stained-glass windows at All Saints rose to pointed arches, and most were geometric designs, not pictures of Jesus on the cross and shit like that. Vick had said the church was huge, and he was right. I considered it "cathedral-size" and the word seemed right because of the wrap-around balcony filled with ladies wearing hats.

The procession of the altar boys and drama of the candle-lighting freaked me out at first. Yep, definitely more like Catholic, I thought. But it wasn't weird, wasn't "in-your-face," just ultra-traditional and ultra-reverent.

We had walked about halfway down the center aisle, choosing one of the forty or so pews on each side, all padded with extra-long blue-velvet cushions. A series of flip-down kneeling benches in a warm wood tone connected to the pew in front of us.

At first, I found the side area mysterious. It seemed only families sat in the section with fifteen-or-so pews. A baby cried, a mother stood, and I understood immediately; there was an easy-exit in the back of the side section. *How clever is that!* I'd never seen such a thing.

Up front, two priests sat in straight-back "throne chairs" as a sixty-strong choir belted hymns. One I recognized, but most could be called dirges. Solemn, serious, and all with a deep baritone solo mid-point.

There was a reading about Jesus, and a chant they called an oath, but I didn't feel they had shoved something down my throat. Nobody lectured about sins, spoke in tongues, or accused the congregation of being a bunch of reprobates.

Instead, it felt natural, spiritual, and I welcomed the experience. The scary part is that I could say I welcomed the *spirit*. There was a lot of kneeling during the service, which I found odd, but overall the formality of the Episcopal approach was more intriguing than upsetting.

I knew their communion wine would be with real wine, not grape juice like the Methodists use, but that's not the reason I didn't go to the altar. I stayed seated, half afraid and half disgruntled by the emphasis on symbolic Jesus blood. Vick tiptoed to the altar for communion, though, and I was glad he did. Whatever he was feeling about the whole church thing was making him kinder and somehow more respectful of me. Weird, but nice.

When the service ended, I expected the members to pounce on us, trying to convert us as some Christians do. I was ready to run, but the reality was far from a pouncing. Instead, people smiled sincerely. "Welcome," was all they said.

Several parishioners said, "Terrible day to be your first," and the explanation was eventually clear as more people commented. Turns out, that Sunday was the annual Youth Rally day and chaos reigned. Everyone seemed so happy and enthusiastic; I hoped it was always that way, so I found the Rally news disappointing, but any enthusiasm is better than none, I thought.

The sanctuary emptied in mere minutes, only a handful stopping at the exit to speak to the priests.

Vick stopped to shake hands with Smokey, booming his voice in greeting. "Hello, Father Smokey. Remember me? I met you earlier this week."

A gentle cocoa-toned face lit up in a broad smile. Smokey was small in stature, large in personality... an instantly likable man. "Just call me Smokey. No 'Father' needed. And of course, I remember you, Vick! A newbie, right?" Smokey's laugh began in his generous belly, honest and infectious.

"And this is my friend, Lela."

"So nice to meet you, dear," he said, covering my right hand with both of his. "You've picked a crazy Sunday for your visit. I both apologize for the commotion and welcome you to our... I guess you'd call it 'passion.' We're always celebrating something but the Rally is a super-fun day."

Vick ignored Smokey's speech. "I loved your sermon, Smokey. It filled me with some kind of spirit I've never felt before. I think I'm... uh..." Vick's voice dropped to a whisper. "Smokey, I want to make an appointment with you. I need to talk to somebody safe and smart... to make a confession."

Smokey's reaction was odd, I thought. He had been so happy and wholesome until that moment, and in a snap, his face showed fright – as if someone had threatened him. *What's that about? Don't Episcopal priests counsel members like other pastors do? What's going on?*

My radar detector screamed in a high pitch. The priest said, "Today... well, can I just ask you to call the front desk tomorrow? They have a list of people you can talk to. See, I'd normally be your man, right now, but the kids have me first in line for the dunking booth." He chuckled, though not in the same comfortable mode as before.

Smokey turned toward me, smiling so kindly I could see why Vick had said the priest looked deep into his soul. "Please come back, Lela. We'd love to have you. You can find peace and purpose here."

"I'd like to come back," I said, and I meant it.

"God bless you," Smokey said. And to Vick, "Hope to see you soon, son."

Smokey looked past us to the next church-goer in line. We stepped forward hearing his voice fade as he greeted someone named Paul with the same bubbly enthusiasm he'd shown to us.

Vick took my hand in the parking lot and we walked in silence for about thirty yards. "Well, what do you think?" he asked.

"I liked it. And I felt moved. God, or whatever you want to call him, or *it*, hasn't roused within me for years and years. And when Smokey said you could ask God to take away your burdens, I *did* ask. Call me crazy, but I swear I felt something, like, floating away."

"That's bizarre."

"I'm not saying I've been saved or any of that bullshit, but I felt *something*."

"I can't wait to talk to Smokey! It's like I'm bursting at the seams to talk to somebody."

"Yeah, you said 'a confession.' What the hell did *that* mean?"

Vick laughed, squeezing my hand. "Silly, if I could tell you about it, I wouldn't need a priest, right?"

I didn't reply but knotted my brow. *A confession? For a crime? Must be a big one because I've committed a bunch of them and don't need a fucking priest! What kind of sin does Vick need to confess?*

We continued our walk to the car, swinging entwined hands in time with our steps. *Or maybe he's feeling bad about our sexual stuff... like, deviance or something? But it's not a crime! And if he talks about our sex life... that's like telling the priest MY business!*

I had to say it: "Whatever you do, don't talk about me. Understood?"

"Of course not." Vick's comment was too casual to convince me he understood my viewpoint.

"Hey, I'm fucking serious, okay? We've done things you might need to confess about, you know. But leave me out of it. *Nothing* about me, not even an alias of me. I mean it."

"You think you're that important, huh?"

My stomach fell to my ankles. "You're an asshole."

< < < < < < < > > > > > > >

Vick and I attended church again two Sundays later, with my Bo-weekend between. In the meantime, Vick had met with Smokey and attended a half-dozen noon services. "We can take communion for sure, now, I found out. Smokey said they have an open communion policy here."

"*Policy*? You mean there are *rules* about it?" I was incredulous. "That's bullshit!"

"Of course there are rules!" Vick seemed confused by my skepticism. "But don't worry. You don't have to be a member of the church, just baptized somewhere."

"Still, that's bullshit! I've never heard of such a thing!" My brow wrinkled, wondering if only the Methodists had a "no rules" approach. Methodist was the only denomination I knew, and I also knew our family did something against the Methodist's rules and it suddenly mattered.

With my mother's insistence, they had not baptized us as infants. As if we were Southern Baptists, Mom decided her children would choose for themselves. When we felt "saved," or "moved by the Lord," she believed, we would ask for the symbolic sprinkles of water.

It would happen in our own time, according to my mother. But the fever never struck me... I never had a time. My throat closed as I admitted the fact to Vick, a fact that had plagued me for many years. "But I've never been baptized." He snapped a look at me, a look of horror, reinforcing my shame.

Beginning at age sixteen or so, on lonely and depressed days, I had wondered what would happen if I died without being baptized. I believed in Heaven... believed in Hell, too, but I doubted a made-up symbol like dipping people in water could determine a final destination. In my mind, the ritual was bullshit... yet suddenly I needed the insurance coverage.

"Maybe you should get baptized by Smokey."

After a pause, I spoke slowly. "I wouldn't flat-out reject that idea. But we'll see. Today's service may determine a lot.

It did determine a lot. Listening to the depths of my emotions, I found I craved communion, craved the feeling I'd discovered in the past two Sundays when connecting to the "God phenomenon," as I had come to call it.

During the week that followed, I attended church during my lunch hours. Vick continued to meet with Smokey, had seen him maybe six times before Smokey stopped me in the hall after the noon service ended.

"Lela." It was a statement, not a greeting.

"Smokey! Good to see you!" Not understanding he wanted my complete attention, I blabbed. "I have a request for you. I want you to baptize me, Smokey! How can I set that up?"

Smokey's face registered shock – so much shock that I thought of a cartoon character and the splashes of sweat the cartoonist might draw. "Uh... sure, Lela. I'd be honored to perform your baptism. We schedule them on the fourth Sunday. You'll certainly be the only one not wearing a diaper!"

"No, not in front of everybody... can you do it privately? After the service or something?"

"Yes! Just call the office to schedule it, but what I need to talk to you about... is... well–"

"That you don't want to baptize an old lady?"

The infectious Smokey-chuckle filled the hall. "Right 'Old lady,' my big toe!" Before our shared laughter would have naturally ebbed, Smokey shot words that sent me a step backward. "Lela, I have to talk to you about Vick."

"About Vick? What? About what he's told you? I didn't think you could–"

"Right. I can't say specifics. What he's told me is personal and protected."

"So then... what?"

As we passed by the church library, Smokey grabbed my hand and stuck his head inside the door. "Let's go in here," he said. We settled in the upholstered chairs and my heartbeat increased exponentially.

"What's this about, Smokey? You're scaring me."

"Oh, don't be scared, dear. It's just..." He pressed his lips together and closed his eyes behind an audible sigh. At that moment, I decided what the problem was. Vick had cancer and had only weeks to live. Either that or Vick was a fugitive from justice, a gangster, something horrible. With my imagination running wild, every part of my body squeezed tight anticipating Smokey's words.

"What is it?" I urged him to hurry.

He spoke cautiously. "I can't exactly say, but Lela... I urge you to, uh, stay far away from Vick, honey. I don't think you know what you're dealing with."

What the hell? Why would a priest say this? What kind of wrong impression did he get from Vick? Something must be seriously wrong. "But Smokey," I said, "I don't understand... why would you think there's something wrong with Vick?"

Smokey repeated his warning word-for-word. "And I ask that you not tell Vick I've spoken to you. It may spark some... resentment, something neither of us wants."

"Smokey, what in the heck are you talking about? Vick is harmless, a little loopy maybe, but harmless."

He took a deep breath through his nose and held it as his chest expanded. All the while, his eyes remained wide. "I can't say any more, dear. I beg you to heed my warning."

"But you must have mistaken something he said! There's nothing worthy of a warning, and he's just an every-other-weekend boyfriend, anyway. It's not like I'm going to marry him or anything.

Smokey's jaw clenched and he didn't speak for several seconds later. "It doesn't matter. My first comment stands."

"Sorry, but I forgot your first comment." I wasn't being a smartass or trying to be snarky; I was so shocked by this... whatever it was... that I couldn't focus.

In a calm voice, Smokey repeated, "You don't know who you're dealing with, Lela. And as time goes on, it's becoming worse and worse. Please. I believe it all."

"Believe *what?* What is *'it,'* Smokey?" He didn't answer. Instead, he shook his head and looked deep into my eyes, purposely stripping my defenses, it seemed. Then his warning hit home and the buzz of fear spread throughout my body. Yep, I believed him. Something was wrong with Vick. I asked, "How bad is it? Should I talk to Vick?"

His head shook harder, back and forth. "Please don't, Lela. Don't tell him we talked." Smokey's eyes were pleading, so sad and full of pity, yet radiating genuine care. As was common in that "filled with God" phase of my life, my heart swelled with love... for Smokey, for my family, for God, for the beautiful spring day, for everything.

But I wasn't 100 percent convinced and asked for more evidence. "I just don't see any... danger, or whatever you're trying to say is wrong. Surely you've misunderstood something he said."

"It was a confession, Lela."

"Oh... yeah. That's what he said."

Smokey reached for me, wrapping his arms around my shoulders in a loving embrace. "God bless you, Lela. God bless you every day."

In the time between Smokey's warning and my baptism, I went to church several times a week, always on Sunday, once taking Bo, and usually two of the noon services through the week. My day-to-day worries dissolved inside that building.

I prayed my ass off, begging for relief from the addiction I thought I had kept a secret. Tears flowed as I cried to a God that eluded me, searching for a peace that eluded me, feeling only frustration about being left behind.

Why can't I be normal, God? Why can't I do what I'm supposed to do... at the time I'm supposed to do it? When did I become a fuck-up?

I paused my prayer, waiting for feedback, hoping for a sign that some*one* or some*thing* was listening. Nothing changed. Nobody answered. *I get it. Why would you mess with a screwed-up person like me, anyway? But please... if you're listening... help me NOT be a fuck-up. Please help me NOT drink, at least not during the day. Help me stop at... maybe just two or three drinks at night. That's all I ask. Please, God.*

I never received assurances or answers to my questions, only the echo of my ping-pong thoughts that brought more questions. God wasn't listening, I concluded; I felt no connection. He'd turned his back on me for good reason, though. Lousy drunks don't get pointers from God.

However, I did believe he'd listen after my baptism. Then he'd be able to hear me and I'd be able to hear his answers, I thought. *And then the great God will help me be a better person... a productive citizen instead of a lousy, lazy, drunken fuck-up.*

During one of our casual chats about God, I asked Smokey if it was okay to just skip the Jesus part and go straight to the Man with the Plan. He chuckled, thinking I was kidding, maybe, but I was definitely not kidding. "Lela, Lela, Lela... that's not the Christian way. Each time you come to church, you take the apostolic oath, chanting with the congregation that you believe in Jesus. That's what Christianity is! You can't just take a shortcut!"

I knew Christianity was the point, or at least that's what Mom would say, but I also knew I'd never fully accept the Jesus thing. In the meantime, I could just fake that part, I decided.

The third time I mentioned the God-only approach, Smokey huffed at me. "What makes you think you have the right to custom-design your own religion, Lela?" Though I remained silent, my mind replied. *Why can't I do EXACTLY that? Why do I have to believe the way others do? Why are there so many rules? Wouldn't God be happy with anything he got? Any belief at all? Why is it all or nothing?*

The appointed Sunday came; I wore my favorite ivory-and-pink dress and new ivory shoes. Karen had come from Jackson City to support me, along with her not-so-happy-about-it husband, and Vick stood beside me as my third "witness," per church rules.

I felt the aura of kindness and love radiating from my body. *This is the time, Lela. In five minutes, your life will change.* I prayed aloud in the bathroom: "God, whoever you are, please help me. Please let this be what changes me for the better." I pushed the knot of doubt in the back of my mind as far away as possible.

Smokey's voice boomed in the empty sanctuary. "I baptize thee in the Name of the Father, and of the Son, and of the Holy Ghost." He sprinkled me with cold water and paused to smile at me and the small audience. "Amen."

It happened in an instant. As soon as the dribbles of water ruined my hairstyle for the day, I felt ridiculous. Like a fraud. Not only did nothing change... there was no lightning bolt or voice from above... I had just made a fool out of myself.

You, Lela? Deserving of change? Ha, ha, ha. Who do you think you ARE, Lela Fox? Some SPECIAL kind of drunk? Hell no ! You're forever a piece of shit. There is no magic God for you.

I looked at my audience, sure they had heard my thoughts, but no. Karen was smiling ear-to-ear; Vick snorted a laugh but I saw nothing but a blur. Nothing had changed.

A regular human has sprinkled you with a symbol of something you don't believe in, something representing a Jesus you don't know or WANT to know. And the Holy Ghost part... think about that and it's flat-out creepy. What the hell?

Smokey turned into a cheerleader and I felt like an asshole for faking the emotions this ritual was supposed to bring. I felt just as much of a misfit, just as alone and stupid as I'd felt before. *Still one of God's orphans, Lela... on the outside looking in.*

To appease Karen and Vick, and certainly Smokey, I thought it best to squash my feelings and doubts, keeping my tears at bay until I was alone. A long afternoon began.

I attended church only a handful of times after the baptism. I'd been duped, I thought, robbed of the chance to have a close relationship with God. *It doesn't matter... God wouldn't like you, anyway. What have you ever done for HIM?*

I hoped for an instant cure, assuming a cocoa-skinned man in a beautiful building could miraculously ease my mind and abate my addiction. When the miracle didn't come, I hid from God and Smokey both, diving into a bottle of vodka without coming up for air.

And despite my promise of secrecy, I told Vick about Smokey's warning, repeatedly asking what could have upset the priest so terribly. Each time, Vick's reply was nothing more than a pair of thin lips, pale and in a straight line on his face. Vick would never discuss it with me; I felt I had no choice but to ignore Smokey's warning and go on as it was, sailing in the same free-and-easy relationship with Vick.

Later, I found out the truth and my jaw hit the floor. *Bang!*

Vick had thrice complained that his father's suicide had messed him up. I understood; that would surely screw up a twelve-year-old.

But as it turned out, his father's death wasn't a suicide. His only son shot him in the back as he sipped iced coffee at the kitchen table.

Had I known the truth, even the fearless Lela Fox would have run from Vick, full-speed ahead. But I chose to ignore Smokey's warning so I could continue the twisted relationship with the murderer.

I shiver to think of what I could have avoided if I'd listened to Smokey's counsel.

FIRST AID COTTAGE
Chapter II

Sometimes Vick and I seemed almost normal, like an all-American married couple doing normal married-couple things. Scary at first, I found myself liking to "play house" and pretend to be in an equal, respectful relationship with Vick. It felt like cheating, if that's the word, and I was thrilled to simply sit in Vick's den, reading the paper while lounging on his leather sectional sofa.

I nonchalantly slid into the kitchen to mix a drink and grab another dark ale for Vick. His social calendar hung prominently beside the fridge and I noticed two consecutive weekend trips. Our "extra" weekend, when Bo's dad had agreed to keep him, and now a third weekend would be added. Only minutes ago, he'd invited me to spend the weekend in Charlotte, including a day at the Carowinds theme park.

I'd have to call Andy again to beg for another weekend "off." So far, he'd never said no, and I still had no clue he was marking my extra requested days on a special calendar.

When I returned with the drinks, Vick looked up from the brochure he'd been reading. "There are nice hotels on the theme park property. Cabins, too, and tons of downtown high-rises. What's your preference?"

"Hey, whatever... I'm easy to please."

"Or maybe just easy..."

"Ha, ha, mister. But there *is* one thing I demand."

"Oooh! Lela *demands*..." Vick laughed through the words. "What do you demand, my queen?"

"That you win a teddy bear for me on the midway."

"Consider it done."

I remember riding a few rides, eating funnel cake, and being on fire. It was hot as hell though the thermometer read 72 on the asphalt, according to the digital sign. Sweat ran down the back of my neck and gathered in the small of my back, and as always, my upper lip sported a waterfall of perspiration. The next moment, the slight breeze chilled me to the bone, evaporating my sweat.

My legs seemed to weight thousands of pounds, maybe just from the miles we'd walked in the park, but I knew it was something more serious than that. All the while, my head pounded and exhaustion drained me like a wind-up toy on the way to zero. I was doing nothing more than faking a good time.

I did get a teddy bear; Vick won it by throwing darts to pop balloons. It only took sixteen tries at three bucks each, easily twice the cost of the best toy-store teddy bear. Maybe it's just a Southern thing, but the guy *must* win a carnival prize for the girl. It's absolutely mandatory in a romantic situation, and though ours was far from a storybook romance, I wanted that damn teddy bear.

As we walked further, the barkers along the midway put me past the limit; my headache was crashing in waves of pain, and I was freezing cold. Weak with wobbly legs and a heavy head, I tucked the teddy bear under my arm and finally admitted to Vick that I felt sick.

Keeping it light, I said, "I just need some Tylenol, I think. I saw a first-aid place not too far back. Let's turn around."

I overheated on the way and collapsed in what they called the "Feel Better Zone." The nurse took my temperature. 103.6, and I'm usually under the norm. A cold compress and two Tylenol.

Young and dressed in all-white, the nurse clucked like a mother hen and said I should stay out of the heat but the party girl in my head refused. There was more to do at the theme park, not to mention in the hotel. *Because hotel sex is the best ever, right?*

I awoke at three AM sweating like a fat man in July. My fever had broken, and I slept fitfully until dawn when my fever rose again. Full of regret, I told Vick I had to go home, had to get to a doctor, then went to the bathroom and filled the toilet with bright-red pee. *Yep, something's definitely wrong.*

Though the sun was blinding as we headed east, I slept all the way back to Rockville, hallucinating with a sky-high fever. Vick drove straight to the Emergency Room where they took a urine sample that glowed in the dark with a deep crimson tint.

In those days, if you entered through to the ER, they admitted you... no question. Also without question: a catheter if you had a kidney infection. They took me upstairs to settle into a room and I asked Vick to call Jennifer. Of course, my sweet sister came immediately, by my side within the hour.

I have no memory of the hour before she arrived; I was delusional with fever. But when Jennifer waltzed into the room, I heard Vick frantically ask her a barrage of questions. "Is it contagious? Am I going to get sick, too?"

He was in a panic, mumbling about how we had kissed, he'd drank after me, etcetera. Smartass Jennifer told him, "You'll get sick for sure if she peed in your mouth."

Vick didn't laugh. Instead, he left. And he didn't call or return for the three days I stayed in the hospital.

☀ ☀ ☀ ☀ ☀

"I'm glad you're feeling better, Lela. I kinda freaked when they said you were in the hospital." Miller laid the bouquet of daisies on my bed sheets. "Maybe the nurses will have a vase? I'll ask them."

"Thank you, Miller. They're beautiful and thank you so much for coming. And for having everybody sign a card. Makes me smile." Still smiling, I opened the card slightly and set it on the tray table. "Front-and-center display." I hoped my face showed the deep appreciation I felt, along with a bit of lovey-dovey stuff. This time he was being nice to *me*, not just Bo.

Miller's visit melted my heart and made me think there may be a Lela-and-Miller relationship after all. The fact that he came to see me, and his series of loving looks... those must be the result of loving feelings, I believed. I wanted to believe it, anyway.

Vick's abandonment hurt, especially coming just when I thought things were heading in the right direction for us. In a moment of clarity, I realized he was nothing but a fair-weather fan, only around when things were happy, healthy, drunk, and sexy.

That wouldn't stop me from using Vick for fun, though, because in the second moment of clarity, I realized I would've done the same. I justified it easily... neither of us were looking for a long-term relationship, right?

Vick was a party. Miller was a patriarch.

LEAKAGE

Chapter 12

After spending three nights in the hospital, I returned to work on Wednesday. The doctors had determined my infection was an unusual one; it didn't start in the urinary tract but went straight to the kidneys. Dangerous, they said, with the nurse's warning, "Take good care of your urinary system, Lela." Every time I thought about the fat, gray-haired caretaker saying that phrase with such a straight face, I cracked up laughing.

I remember the dress I wore my first day back to work: a blue and gray jumper with accents of blue plaid. Before I left home, I sucked down my usual three cups of coffee, plus a glass of water for taking the monstrous antibiotic they had prescribed. Even after all that liquid, I couldn't pee. It just wouldn't come - and I tried several times.

Later, after arriving at the office, my bladder hurt from being so full, but I still couldn't pee. Pain, then more pain. Concerned, I swung into Babbas Bean's office to tell her I wasn't feeling well, and to tell her about the hospital stay.

Like me, she was furious at Vick for leaving me at the hospital alone and thrilled that Miller had brought the card. "And flowers! Those were *his* idea, honey. Lela-Lou... he's sweet on you!" she sang.

I felt sick and scared, my skin stretched to the max as if a balloon were inside me. After a dose of her sympathy, I left Babbas Bean's office and tiptoed back to mine, shutting the door.

Closing my eyes, I imagined a babbling brook, the waves of the ocean...

trying to work up a stream of pee. But all I could hear was the pounding of a headache, squarely on both eyebrows.

Urine retention. What does that MEAN? Maybe I should call Jennifer and let her look it up in her books. And the pain down there! It fucking hurts, dammit. Is that leftover from the catheter? Is ALL this the fault of the catheter?

At four o'clock, Babbas Bean opened my office door and found me on the floor, curled in a fetal position. My bladder and everything internal hurt. "Lela, we're going to the hospital. Can you get to the car, you think?" she said, flying into mother mode.

☼ ☼ ☼ ☼ ☼

I remember little about that ER visit except that pee spilled on my new dress when I overflowed the first catheter bag. When the second bag was almost full, they told Babbas Bean that retaining four liters of urine was a serious issue. But they told *Babbas*, not me. Finally drained, I felt fine, back to normal. So I asked for the release papers; I wanted to go home.

"No way," said the nurse. They admitted me, determined to diagnose the kidney issue. It took two days to run every test imaginable, but they all came back negative. My kidneys were fine, the infection was almost gone, and there was no evidence tying the urine retention to the weekend's infection.

Dr. Law wouldn't let it go at that. "Lela, I have a theory and I hope I'm wrong. I want to test a sample of your spinal fluid."

"Spinal fluid? You mean like a spinal tap?"

"That's not the medical term, but yes." Then he explained his theory.

My jaw hit the floor at the first mention of his suspicions. "These are common symptoms of Multiple Sclerosis," he said.

"*What? No!* Dr. Law, what does this mean to my future?" I freaked out, asking a jumble of questions without pausing to hear his answers.

"Read this," he said, quoting the title of the brochure, "A Thorough and Practical Guide for Patients with MS."

Fear, shock, sadness. And more fear.

Dr. Law continued, "Urine retention is rare and points to MS when neither the kidneys nor urethra are involved," he explained. When I told him I'd been calling the urethra "Aretha Franklin," he chuckled briefly. Dr. Law was all business.

For the spinal tap, I would come as an all-day outpatient on Monday; for now, I could go home... released from the hospital for the second time in a week.

Because I hadn't heard from Vick, I called Miller to ask if he would come to get me. The sweetheart dropped everything to be there ASAP. Although he seemed a little uncomfortable around me as a sick person, his kind and caring attitude shined through brightly. I thought his embarrassment was compassion in disguise, and cute as hell. It touched me.

On the way to my apartment, Miller listened as I blurted out what the doctor had said. He nodded and poured on the sympathy as I babbled about the fear of having MS and being disabled or dead. Of course, being "Tear Bucket Jim," as my Daddy called me, I cried. Like an assuring nurse, he patted my leg. After fifteen minutes or so, Miller changed his demeanor, perhaps uncomfortable with my emotions flying all over the place. I tried to stop sobbing, but I couldn't.

On the following Monday, I fought the traffic to TSU Hospital for the day-long admission and spinal tap procedure. Around five o'clock, when I thought I could leave, the nurse told me I'd have to lay completely flat and still for *another* eighteen hours. Otherwise, she said, "the spinal fluid will leak and all hell will break loose." I didn't ask for details.

I called Miller to ask for a ride. Again, he was A-1 nurse and supporter, gentle and kind, but still with an undercoat of embarrassment... or was it aggravation? I couldn't tell which but felt a touch of his "Mister Miserable" personality coming to light.

I didn't spend much time analyzing his feelings because I was on the verge of throwing up as he drove to my apartment. Dizzy from my ankles to my brain, weak and nauseated. The worst came as I walked up the gyrating steps and across the carpet to my bedroom.

As my knight in shining armor walked me through the hall to my bedroom, his hand gently cupped at the small of my back, he purred assurances. "I want you to feel better soon, Lela. Do you want me to stay? What do you need? Some water? Are you hungry? A glass of wine or something? What can I do? I'll do anything."

"Only some Tylenol. I've never had a headache this bad in my life, and I've had some killer hangovers, ya know?"

"Tylenol coming right up!" Miller said with a smile straight from Central Casting. He let go of me and turned left toward the bathroom medicine cabinet. Instantly faint, I grabbed the door trim for support and suddenly the world spun backward on its axis. Miller said I grunted when I collapsed.

I found out later that my hot-blooded, auburn-haired caretaker had scooped me from the floor and slid me under the covers while I was passed out cold. It was he who set the phone and a monster cup of water beside my bed, kissed my lips gently, he said, and slipped out, locking the knob.

I felt so loved that it scared me.

Dusk. Awake and depressed, I laid there and worried. *Multiple Sclerosis, wheelchair, paralysis, how could I take care of Bo? How could I ever have sex again?* I slept fitfully. Though I heard the phone, I let it ring. I awoke in what looked like early morning light, again at dusk, again in the dark, and again at dawn. With two full days of zero activity, I still felt sick, but I knew I had to get to work. *Barry Sturbridge is ready to bust my ass, I guess. Who knows how many projects are in my inbox?*

With a mountain of effort, I showered and tried to get ready, but I had to lay down between each task. *How can I possibly have a productive day? How can I push through this?* My thoughts reeled between sessions of gagging. *Does a spinal tap do this to everybody? Damn!*

Not stupid, just stubborn. I knew my reaction wasn't normal, and that it had leaked like the nurse warned. Still, I refused to admit defeat and wouldn't stop tottering around. Moving like a turtle, I walked to the car with the concrete steps buckling and twirling. By some miracle, I made it to the car without fainting. The second I sat in the driver's seat, I leaned over and threw up in the passenger floorboard, on top of a sweater set aside for a return to Target.

Maybe an hour passed; the driver's door was still open and the apartment maintenance man found me in the fetal position. "Are you okay, ma'am?" The man touched my ankle with his canvas-gloved hand, but my first thought wasn't that he could help me. No, I first thought: I'm flashing him, wearing a skirt and pantyhose.

"No, don't!" was my answer.

"What, ma'am? I'm here to help. Do you need a doctor?"

"Oh," I said, realizing he was on the up-and-up. "Can you help me get up?" The man pulled my arm so hard I thought it had popped from the socket, but suddenly I was sitting upright behind the wheel. The change in perspective helped somehow but every inch of my skin prickled with stinging heat despite the cool morning.

"I'll help you walk up the steps if you want," he said, and I nodded slowly. With a kind and easy bearing, he walked me step by step to the door, catching me when I stumbled. By then, the world was a blur and the worst-possible headache pounded throughout my body. I tasted nothing but bile and flashed through a series of hallucinations while turning the key.

"Do you need a doctor? You don't look so good."

I'm not sure if I spoke out loud or not; it hurt to talk. "No, thanks," then I fell into the foyer of my apartment, splayed like a bear rug. As it often did, the wind caught the door in the tunnel of the breezeway and the door slammed with a bang. Loud. I'm sure it scared the maintenance man but I was too loopy to react.

Maybe I slept, maybe not, but after a rest, I crawled into the kitchen and pulled myself up on the bottom cabinets. The wall-mounted brown telephone roared a dial tone until I found the hospital number on a fridge magnet. A chirpy voice sang, "Please hold, ma'am."

Two minutes and a hundred years later, a nurse came on the line. She said there was nothing to do but wait it out. "Lay still and completely flat for a few more days. No pillows," she instructed. *How can I miss more work? Barry will kill me!* I called nobody else but crawled to the bedroom and under the covers – skirt, pantyhose, makeup, and all.

☀ ☀ ☀ ☀ ☀

I awoke to the heat of someone's breath on my face. Slowly, achingly, I opened my eyes to see Miller's face inches from mine, a glint of light sparkling on the side of his eyeglasses. He shook me and repeated my name. My eyes closed, then opened again. "Hi!" he mocked, "You've come back to life! It's a miracle!" For the first time in days, I laughed.

Miller came in search of me because I hadn't called work. "Instead of worrying," he said, "I jumped on my white horse and galloped west to help a damsel in distress." He had gone to the apartment office, and they had let him in, he said.

Glad he'd come... thrilled he'd come, I explained what happened and quoted what the nurse had said. "All I can do it wait," I whispered, trying to protect my head from the still-pounding headache. Miller sighed, tucked me in, and brought a variety of random things to my bedside. I kept my eyes closed through most of it.

"Hey, I'm taking your keys if that's ok," he said. Without opening my eyes, I murmured agreement. "I'll be back after work, honey," and he kissed my cheek. I scooched further down into my new white duvet and smiled. *He called me honey.* If I hadn't been so sick, I would have jumped for joy.

As promised, Miller came back after work, bringing me a chicken dinner I couldn't eat. He came again close to midnight, and the next morning, and at lunch, and dinner time again. That sweet man came every four hours or so until I felt strong enough to walk beyond the bathroom.

"You've had half a sandwich and a full glass of water, Lela. That's good. Maybe you're getting better." Miller said.

The sofa – finally, I could make it to the living room. "It's about damn time I got better! How long have I been in that damn bed?"

"Too long without me in there with you."

"Miller McKeown in a sick bed? That doesn't sound so sexy..."

"But you are sexy even when you're sick, Lela Fox." His eyes glistened, filled with adoration. Too much adoration; I felt uncomfortable, but I continued the teasing.

"If you keep flattering me, Bo will get jealous."

"Let's just not tell him. We can keep secrets from our son, can't we?"

"*Our* son?"

"You heard me."

I didn't know what to say. Miller had said romantic things before, but nothing so blatantly based on the future of our relationship.

As I opened my mouth to speak, Miller interrupted. "I love you, Lela."

Seconds ticked by as my head spun. *He just told me he loved me... he loves me! Oh, shit! Do I tell him I sometimes feel ignored... that he pays more attention to Bo than he does to me? Should I just say "Okay," or "I'm flattered," or what? What do I say?*

"Well?" he asked.

Tell him you love him, too! It's the only way out! Tell him! Say it now. I stammered, "I'm... I'm... Wow, Miller. It's a little–"

"Don't worry. It's early. You'll come around. Either way, I'm going to stay and fix you something to eat. Do you have ground beef in the freezer? I'll make spaghetti."

Miller stood and swaggered to the kitchen. There was no more talk of love.

From the kitchen, Miller shouted, "A glass of wine, dear, or the hard stuff?"

"Guess. I haven't had a drink in almost a week."

"A double?"

"For sure. And use my new bottle of Tanqueray, please."

"I thought you drank Grey Goose."

"Uh..." *Dare I tell him the Herpes guy stole my last bottle? It's probably something he needs to know, Lela, because you're getting ready to screw his brains out, right? And you haven't told him YET. Just because you haven't had a second breakout doesn't mean you won't have another. Tell him! And tell him you love him! Don't let him get away!* I shucked my thoughts aside, answering his question. "Used to be Grey Goose, but Tanqueray is better and cheaper."

"As much as you drink, something cheaper is needed. You're a lush."

"Not a lush... try 'lush' with an 'usch.' Luscious – that's what I am."

Three days later, Dr. Law called with the results of my spinal tap. I pushed away from my desk and turned my back toward the open office door. "Dr. Law... you're calling in person? Oh, God, that's either good or very bad."

"*Good* news, Lela," he said, "but only 'somewhat good.'" The pause tasted like copper. "The results are inconclusive and, in these instances, there are many false positives on a diagnosis of MS."

I squeaked, "*False positives!* Then why did you put me through all this mess? I've never been so sick in my life, Dr. Law."

"Yes, I see notes from the nursing staff, but leakage happens if you don't lay still."

"But I *did* lay still! Something went wrong, maybe you used too big of a needle, something like that. Believe me – it's not *my* fault because I did exactly what they told me to do!" I felt my heart rate shoot to the sky. Despite attempts to calm myself, I thought the doc was incompetent, and I fumed with anger and indignation.

Dr. Law ignored my comment and continued his explanation. "Listen carefully, please. The only way to confirm the diagnosis is with a brand-new technology called Magnetic Resonance Imaging, or MRI." I asked for an explanation, and he spilled a five-minute speech of how it worked, ending with, "The technology is fantastic, but there's a problem."

"What problem?"

"It's brand new. There's not an MRI machine in Rockville, so I've contacted Vanderbilt University Hospital in Nashville. Theirs was installed just a few months ago. The process has begun and they'll call you in the next few days with an appointment time. But there's a problem."

"Don't tell me about more problems, Dr. Law."

"Because it's one of the few machines in the Southeast, radiology is backed up. It may be a few months before I get your results."

I sighed. "Great. More time to worry."

GRANNY KNOWS BEST
Chapter 13

Now living "on the road," my 88-year-old Granny Liz rotated in residence, spending four months at a time with each of her nine children. That spring, it was Mom and Dad's turn to have Granny and the whole family gathered to welcome her. Happy times.

I was flat-out crazy about my grandmother, united with her in a way I'd never connected with another human being. She was my dad's mother, but Mom loved as her own, too, as she'd told me all my life. Granny was spry and adored being the plaything for her grandchildren, all 22 of them.

As the second-youngest grandchild, I was treated special. Knowing winks passing between us. I felt sure she didn't see the problems in my drinking, thinking her lectures about my now-dead, worthless drunken grandfather would keep me off the sauce. She didn't know my nasty truths; I had no reason to be ashamed while around Granny Liz. That, alone, brought an incredible sense of freedom.

I hung on her every word. We all did.

The house radiated happiness when Granny Liz was in Burgess. She told my aunts and uncles more than once that she enjoyed being at Mom and Dad's most because of our family's "open love." Whatever that meant exactly, I'll never know, but it sounded good.

To celebrate her weekend arrival, the whole fam-damily would gather at Mom and Dad's house. Lucky weekend; the schedules worked just right and everybody was able to be there.

Miller didn't freak when I invited him. In fact, he said he was honored, and I'll quote him: "I want to meet the people who made you turn out the way you did." So Miller, five-year-old Bo, and I got up early to drive the two-plus hours to Burgess, Tennessee, my tiny, conservative hometown.

The moment we arrived, Miller's happy tune changed. Once again, his off-putting air came forward; the better-than-you, chest-puffed-out asshole persona that Vick called "Mr. Miserable."

Bo felt the tension rise, too, it seemed. He grabbed onto my leg as Miller shook my father's hand... but you couldn't really call it a handshake. Daddy was being his silly self, overly welcoming, and the sonofabitch Miller wouldn't even look him in the eye, offering no more than a perfunctory how-do-you-do. He acted as if Daddy was of no consequence at all.

Oh, I was pissed to the max! Nobody – *nobody* – disses my Daddy without ruffling every feather I have.

I couldn't shrink as small as I felt; I had brought Miller to show him off and he acted like an ass. *Stop that shit and do the right thing, Miller!* Evidently, he didn't recognize my discomfort, not looking at me in the face either. My nervous titter echoed in the foyer, drifting to the attached living area where all sat in anticipation of meeting Lela's new beau.

Thinking that pointing out the wrong of his behavior would make it worse, I pretended all was well. Yep, I pretended he was still the prize specimen I promised to bring.

Then, ignoring all of us, Miller said to Bo, "Hey big guy, you want to play catch?" Of course, my son agreed, and I nearly collapsed with embarrassment when they abruptly left through the back door without saying hello to the full crowd.

He's just nervous... but why? And why does his anxiety make him so rude? Miller, dammit! This isn't the time for your twisted fears to lead your actions.

Over the past months, in our after-sex talks in bed, Miller had shared about his family's dysfunction and said it had always been uncomfortable to visit them. But I couldn't figure out why he was acting like *my* family was the same kind of weird. I promised if we kept dating, I'd "loan" him my family so he could have a good one. "A much better alternative," I said. *So what makes him think they AREN'T better? Why did he not even give us a chance?*

Though the introduction was wrong on all levels... I felt hurt, confused, and embarrassed. I wanted everyone to think I had a boyfriend deliriously crazy about me. Sigh. *Play it, Lela. Cover for him - just to make your point.*

Don't let him change what you came here to say.

Mortified but acting casual and ignoring the tension, I tried to laugh it off, but everybody had noticed. And they all looked at me with pity, or at least that what it felt like. I countered the looks. "What, guys? It's all cool! Lela's fine. Miller's fine. And Bo is *most definitely* fine!"

Mom and Dad's backyard was a full acre, maybe more, but Miller and Bo stayed close to the deck as they played catch with their freshly oiled gloves; Daddy joined them a few minutes later. Mom, Granny Liz, and I watched from the living room window.

Karen had arrived just a few minutes before we did, driving from Jackson City and dragging boyfriend-du-jour. Jennifer and the kids had come early; my oldest sister was always the one to help in the kitchen. Her oldest, my sweet niece Bella, was now a lanky teenager, a little shy. Jen's youngest was named after Granny. Six-year-old Lizzie was capped with a bright-blonde curly mop that jumped along with her as she ran and ran... and ran and ran.

Lizzie ran circles around Bo and Miller, literally, and screamed shrill giggles every few seconds. I was struck by the difference in having a boy versus a girl, feeling sorry for Jennifer. But I imagined Jennifer felt sorry for me.

Eventually, Bo will pair off with Lizzie and my supposed-best-boyfriend Miller will have to come to play with the adults. Please be sociable, Miller! Please be humble! And don't you dare dismiss my father again.

Meanwhile, inside, we gathered to share our hopes and dreams with Granny, who truly wanted to know what we were about. I sat at her feet until she motioned for me to sit on the arm of her upholstered chair so she could kiss me.

Though Granny Liz always smelled musty, like a closed-up attic, I loved being close to her. As we spoke, she made a point to share her happiness that Bo would have a new father figure after my divorce from Andy. "Well, it's not for sure we'll get married, Granny! Miller's just a boyfriend and a good friend for Bo-Bo."

Glancing out the window, she said dreamily, "But it seems Miller loves Bo more than he loves you!" She laughed, and all who heard did the same. Maybe they thought it was a Granny-joke... or a good thing... or impossible... or whatever, because they laughed like banshees. But it was like a punch in the gut to me. *How could she know already?*

I felt busted. No doubt, my grandmother was an intuitive woman, wise and sensitive, yet she knew as much about modern-day issues as she did about being the mother of a dozen during the Great Depression.

I swallowed hard and excused myself, then tiptoed to the back bedroom for a private cry. Knowing me well, Karen sensed my upset and followed. As she'd done all my life, Karen dropped everything to help her Little Sis, offering hugs, a broad shoulder to cry on and an open ear to hear me bitch.

I started slow. "Karen, I've learned to call him 'Bo's boyfriend,' halfway a joke, but to make it sound like it's a good thing for me, too. Everybody thinks we're the world's cutest couple, Karen! How can I argue with that? They think we're a happy family of young professionals, destined to live the American Dream or some shit like that."

Karen interrupted. "Does he treat you like he treated Daddy? Because that was—"

"No. That's his 'Mr. Miserable' side. I think he has what my therapist calls social anxiety. You can imagine meeting all of us at one time would be intimidating as hell, right?"

"Yeah, but—"

"I know, I know. It's not cool." I almost told her just how pissed off I felt, but decided to hold back. I had to make her feel there was *some* worth to Miller, right? "But can't you see he's perfect for *Bo?* My son is over the moon and demands to see him every second he's with me. Even Andy called to see who the hell 'this Miller' was." I huffed a sarcastic laugh. "As if it's his business..."

"Hold on there... it *is* his business. Just like how Ella treats Bo is *your* business."

I rolled my eyes. "Okay. You're right. But everybody sees Miller with Bo and thinks the with-Lela part must be just as good."

"And it's not?"

"*Hell no.*" Tears carved a river on my cheeks. "But who am I to bitch, really? Shouldn't I be thrilled with a man who loves my son so much? Isn't that the most important? The top priority?" Karen had no answer to those questions; there was nothing to say, no answers to offer. I continued, "A happy son *is* my top priority, but it feels..." My words trailed off into thirty seconds of silence.

The questions I didn't *scream* in that silence churned in my gut: "Why am I being ignored? Why am I the baggage and not the package? What am I?

Chopped liver?" Guilt, my old friend, made me swallow all that unhappiness and continue to depend on Miller for a sense of family, to keep him for the appearance of propriety.

It could be said that Mom had raised me to be a doormat, but I was a modern woman with way too much pride to settle... or so I thought. I spoke again, with my chin on Karen's shoulder. "My other boyfriend is the opposite. It's all sex, drugs, and rock-and-roll. Without Bo, of course."

"Your *other* boyfriend? Lela! Shame on you!"

"But he doesn't like Bo! He's the every-other-weekend boyfriend."

"No, girl, no, no, no. You need somebody who loves you and Bo equally."

"And it does kinda suck dating two guys."

"You're sleeping with both of them?"

"Yep."

She mumbled through a series of Oh's, Wow's, and Hmm's. "Not good. Again, you need to find somebody who loves you enough to occupy your whole life and heart. Somebody who thinks you're as fucking awesome as I do."

"Yeah, I'm not so bad, right?"

"Not even on a bad day, girl." I cheered the break in tension. I just needed my sister to let me know I was okay... to celebrate me for who I was, and she was always good for that. "Enough of this shit!" We laughed together in the way we always had. Karen's love for me was palpable and her protection of me went to the extreme of a brother, I'd been told.

"But you know, Karen. One day... eventually... one of them will fight for me. Either Miller or Vick will demand to be the only one. And sooner or later, I'll get the love I need." More tears flowed as I lowered my head into my hands. "Oh, God. It's *love* I need, Karen. Plain and simple. Like a fucking romance novel. I feel like an idiot."

More hugging, more assurances, more laughing and, finally, a trip to the bathroom to fix our mascara. "Okay," I said, "Back to Granny Liz. I don't want to miss a minute of her."

"Me neither." Karen and I locked arms and fought for the lead in a walk down the hall. Karen, always silly. The woman never failed to make me laugh.

☼ ☼ ☼ ☼ ☼

Miller was silent during dinner, though he laughed along with the crowd as Bo ate "lots and lots and lots of 'hicken." No shit... the kid ate nine chicken legs.

It was a long farewell; Bo didn't want to go with Lizzie still there. He stomped his feet in what we called a "Benningham fit" in our house, and squealed, "*Unfair!* Mommy, you're *mean!*"

Before I could reply, smartass Miller murmured sympathetic "ohhh, poor child" comments to my son. "I understand how hard it was to leave, buddy. But Mommy said 'go'... and we have to do what Mommy says, right?"

"No!"

Without thinking, I snapped, "Don't you *dare* make me the bad guy, you sonofa..." I cringed to have to keep the language clean. I fumed silently until we hit the interstate, deciding what to say to Asswipe. It would be a relationship-defining discussion, I knew.

Not wanting Bo to know we were in a disagreement, I only hinted about what a worthless piece of shit he was, slamming his character in a teasing voice for the benefit of the backseat... wearing a hard, accusatory face to make my point in the front seat. Miller questioned me but barely, also sensitive to Bo's presence. I had the final word. "We'll talk later." A pause. "No, I'll talk you you'll listen."

A fake-gruff voice boomed from the backseat, "Yeah, *Miller*... we have to do what Mommy *says!*" Bo's tiny voice playing the demanding boss was a hilarious contrast but I refused to join Miller in the laughter. My anger simmered as we neared Rockville and I planned the conversation, bargaining with myself about which answers I'd accept from him and which answers would cause me to kick him to the curb.

I'd just had two beers in Burgess; it was all I thought Granny Liz would "allow" me without the evil eye. But the cooler in the floorboard held six ice-cold Miller Lite bottles, and I had three in quick succession.

Bo fell asleep in his car seat when darkness fell, and I ended up feeling overwhelmed with love for him... and wanting to give him the same family life he had with Andy and Ella.

As I drank more beer, my heart softened more and more, and by the time we parked, I was a tender-hearted, all-accepting, world-loving, peace-filled drunk mother. And as requested, the "father" carried my sleeping child to bed.

Miller poured a drink and we settled on the sofa. But the conversation wasn't the bitchfest I planned. I didn't scream or make demands but simply stated what I wished had happened.

I tried to explain how my family was "different," how their "odd ways" were really meant to be open and funny. I had never used those words before; my family was a loving picture that needed no other explanation. There was nothing odd or different about them, but I said so for his benefit, thinking it would help him eventually trust and accept my perfectly acceptable parents and sisters.

I talked for a long while before Miller replied, and when he did, he seemed confused. Point-blank, he asked if I was trying to tell him something without actually saying it. "Okay, you're right," I said. "My point is... you acted like an asshole and I didn't like it at all." *There, you said it, Lela... and he hasn't run out the door yet. See, you had nothing to worry about.*

Silence. Miller leaned forward, elbows on his knees, and ran his finger around the rim of his scotch glass. "Well..." he said.

Tension squeezed my throat closed, but I couldn't let the silence stand. "Well what?"

In a calm voice, he spoke words that stung like poison arrows. "You're just covering for them, Lela, instead of seeing the truth. You're fucking *scared* of them! You don't feel qualified to be in that nice family! Admit it. And where does that leave *me?*" My mouth was open but no sound came out.

Miller continued. "But the real problem is..." He stopped, shook his head, and tipped his glass of scotch back to drain it. Without a pause, he dashed to the kitchen to pour another.

I shouted at him as he walked. "The real problem is *what?* Finish your fucking statement!" I had to admit he hit the nail on the head about how I felt with the family... how inadequate I considered myself when around them. Yet, despite the deep hurt, I hadn't dared to cry in front of him. *I shouldn't need to cry! Instead, I should be mad as hell! What a fuckhead he is!*

"The real problem is they know your secret."

"What the hell? Even *you* don't know my secret."

"Ah ha! So you do have a secret!"

"Fuck you, Miller. We're talking about you, not me." Then I re-upped my complaints about his rude treatment of my family members, with specific examples. His comeback was to toss it back in my lap; he blamed me for expecting too much. "Do you think I'm a mind reader? Only a nagging wife would demand something so specific from a husband. Quit that shit!"

"Specific? No, it's generally expected to shake hands with my father... looking him in the eye like a *real* man would!"

"So now you're saying I'm not a 'real man?' Bullshit!" That comment flipped the switch; I cried. He had rubbed my face in it, twisting the conversation back on me so I couldn't defend myself.

Miller threw his hands in the air. "Jeezus! Don't start with the damn waterworks, please! Look, I love you, Lela, but I can't handle your tears and fucking rules about how I should act!" He growled in frustration, then continued his rant. "I'm not a child! I know how to treat people!"

I stood. Miller stood. We locked eyes, mine glassy with tears and his tiny slits. For a snap-second, I thought he might hit me; there was fire burning within those slits. Trying to be firm, I spoke, but my voice squeaked. "Look. Just... get out. Just *go!*"

"No, wait! I didn't... I'm sorry! Obviously, I said the wrong thing. Or maybe I hit too close to home. Either way, it's okay to have a weird relationship with your parents – God knows *I* do! It's just... they're conservative as hell, Lela, and they expect the same of you!"

A tear rolled down my cheek and I looked away from his knowing gaze, using the back of my hand to wipe the evidence of my shame. "They know I'm not conservative, Miller. They may not understand me exactly, but I'm not *scared* of them, for God's sake! Where did you ever get *that* idea?"

With a chuckle under his breath, Miller pulled me toward him and wrapped his arms around me tight. "It's okay, sweetie. I didn't mean to hurt your feelers. I know you think you've got them fooled, but I don't think that's true."

"But I don't need you to tell me how I feel about my parents, you ass. I keep the perfect appearance!"

"But... do I have to do the same? Is my presence and perfect behavior part of your perfect appearance? You can't count on me – or anybody – like that. I'm not a mind reader. I called it like I saw it and I'm sorry it wasn't up to your standards."

"I'm *NOT* afraid of my family!"

"I won't call you a liar, Lela, but you might want to think about that before you state it so fiercely."

I snapped my head up and pointed to the door. "Out. Like I said before. I want you out."

"Relax, sweetheart. Sit back down and I'll get you another beer. Sit down and rest." He put his hand under my ankles and lifted them to the coffee table. "Here, put your feet up... we can find something interesting to watch on TV. We'll chill out, cuddle on the sofa, revel on being in love. That's what we're about, baby. Please breathe now. Please breathe."

He rattled more bullshit on the way to and from the kitchen. His last words were "I'm just sorry I didn't perform to your standards. But I know them now, so it won't happen again."

I was looking into his eyes, testing his honesty when a much smaller voice spoke. "What won't happen again, Miller? Do you mean *me?* Is that what you are yelling about? Tears spilled from Bo's beautiful blue eyes. "I'm sorry if I was bad, Miller!" My inner mom cringed, embarrassed and determined to set him straight.

I rushed to my boy, kneeling to look him directly in the eye. "No, baby! You *weren't* and *aren't* bad in *any* way, *ever!* Bo, you're awesome! We weren't talking about you at all!" He whined and I hugged for a few more minutes before I asked, "Why can't you sleep, sweetheart?"

"Cause you're arg'ing in front of the chuuldren," he said. I couldn't help it; I laughed. Obviously, he'd been listening to his dad and Ella.

"Let's go, big guy. Back to bed. I'll lay with you for a while."

When I came back to the living room, Miller was naked, rubbing his penis. "Hey... you want some of this?" he asked.

Hmmm... hot damn! The man is hot! So, so sexy! And look at that smile... and he's getting hard already. I smiled at Miller when he wiggled his eyebrows at me like a horny Groucho Marx. I took a step toward him, then hesitated.

Think first, Lela! If he's wrong... if your expectations really are unrealistic... his behavior was just social anxiety, right? The poor guy... he can't help it! Rudeness, Mr. Miserable... that's his only defense against what's basically a mental disorder. A real girlfriend would understand. Same thing you hope would happen if he came face-to-face with your Bi-Polar shit... wouldn't you hope he'd understand?

"Well?" In the pause, Miller had never stopped smiling; by then he looked confident and relaxed.

I played along. "Do you think you can appease me that easily? Buy me with the promise of a roll in the hay?"

"Uh... yes. Yes, I do!" His silly grin charmed me and I teased back.

"Well, it's not going to work." I ran my tongue along my upper lip in a sneaky, provocative move.

An exaggerated, comic frown. "What if I throw in a beer?"

"You're getting warmer."

"Warmer? But baby, you're already *hot*. Keep standing there... just breathing. That's all it takes. The longer I look at you, the *hotter* it gets in here."

"Just tell me something."

"Anything..."

"No... that's the problem. I don't want to hear 'anything.' I want the truth."

A smile crossed his face. He continued to rub his penis, and something must have happened because he jerked. He closed his eyes and mumbled, "Ask away. I shall give you the unadulterated truth."

"Miller, do you really love me?"

His eyes popped open with an instant answer. "Absolutely I love you! That's the easiest question ever! I've loved you for a long, long time, Lela. All I want is for you to drop that sonofabitch Vick and come home to Miller-Baby. Home to a family that's in the dictionary under the word 'happy.'"

"Ha, ha."

"Admit it, Lela. You know I love you... and you love me, too."

I felt my face crawling with red. "I, but...actually..." I threw up my hands. "The only thing I know is you look hot. And in response to your first question, the answer is yes."

The comedy act continued as he exaggerated panic, fingernails between his gleaming teeth. "Oops. What was the first question?"

"Yes, I'll take some of that."

"And a beer?"

"Absolutely. As long as you never try to analyze my relationship with my parents again."

"Promise. Never again. But promise *me* one thing."

"What's that?"

"Talk to a therapist."

"Fuck you. No! Fuck *me*. Shut up and fuck me."

RESULTING DECISION
Chapter 14

The next Wednesday, mid-day, my phone rang and somehow I knew it was *the* call. I stared at my dull-beige telephone with a blank expression, counting the number of rings. One ring, two, three, four. My peripheral vision blacked out; I was laser-focused on the phone.

"Hello?"

"Is this Miss Lela Lynn Fox?"

"Yes... Dr. Law?"

"Yes, it–"

"Just tell me, Dr. Law. Hurry."

"Well, it's good news, Lela. *Very* good news. No lesions on your brain. No evidence of MS. I still don't know what's wrong with your kidneys, but the problem is not MS." *I don't give a rat's ass about my kidneys! Now I can live a normal life. And that's the best news ever.* Finally, I heard what I wanted to hear.

"Thank you, Dr. Law. Thank you, thank you, thank you!" He was still talking when I hung up the phone and ran into the bump of the hall, shouting so all could hear, "Everybody! It's not MS! IT'S NOT MS! I'm not going to die, not going to be in a wheelchair!"

All my coworkers came running, cheering and standing in line to hug me. I blushed when Miller bear-hugged me like a lover in front of everybody. His voice boomed, "I love you, Lela Fox!" and I stopped in my tracks, shocked and embarrassed. Miller's smile beamed enthusiasm and his eyes looked moist when he kissed me. Not once but three times. Everybody clapped.

Amid the hoots from my friends, Miller knelt. On one knee, he presented an ink pen with two open hands, like a gift. "Lela Fox, will you marry me? An ink pen is all I have right now but... would you be my wife?"

The world stopped. My mind's silence was soon followed by a whirlwind repeat of his words. The echo of *wife... wife... wife.* It pounded against my temples in the hollow of my head. *Miller McKeown just asked me to marry him. What the hell? Oh, that's good... no, that's bad! It's an ink pen! A fucking ink pen.*

Those words bounced together, twisting and garbling to become a mix of nonsense syllables. In a blurry halluiation, I stared at ink pen as it spun out of Miller's hands and whirled out of control, spiraling upward to the ceiling. My eyes followed its movement as the cacophony in my brain increased in volume and pitch.

Miller's gorgeous golden-brown eyes looked at me like a hopeful boy in a candy store. His broad smile showed every tooth... those perfect, white teeth... against a strong-but-tender handsome face... connected to a rock-hard body. It was as if I looked at him for the first time, instantly attracted and lustful. *Lustful... but marry him? What is happening?*

"But... Wha?... This... I... But... Can?" I began a series of incoherent sentence-starts, finally settling on a whispered, "What did you say?"

"You heard me, Lela. I want to spend the rest of my life with you and Bo."

Still addled, I stood with an open mouth, unable to answer. The stuttering sentences began anew. A voice rose from the group surrounding us. It was nasty Dorisey. "Say something, for God's sake!"

My eyes fell on Babbas Bean who looked like a deer in high-beam headlights. I felt my eyes drilling into hers, begging for an answer. She opened her eyes even wider and shrugged. *Lots of help you are, friend!*

I looked back at Miller. His smile was gone, replaced by a confused and concerned face that had turned pasty.

"No... I mean yes... I mean, well, I have to ask Bo."

"Ask Bo? Why?"

"Because... you know why!"

"Is that a yes or a no, then?"

"It's a yes that I will I'll ask Bo. But I'll need something more than an ink pen, shithead." My heart rate slowed, now seeing the humor in such a non-traditional proposal. "And another question when we're *alone*, please!"

"We'll go to the jewelry store together." He was still kneeling and the hopeful-boy look returned.

I sighed, preparing to ask the question that had plagued me from today's first kiss. "Stand up. Let me ask you something." Miller stood, taking both my hands. "So... you want to marry me only because I don't have Multiple Sclerosis?" My voice raised an octave on the last few words.

"Well, that's not really a fair question..."

"Sure it is. I sure as hell need to know that! Shit happens, you know... it's a lifelong possibility for health problems or family problems or any kind of problem."

"Honestly?"

"Of course."

"I'm not sure I could handle a wife in a wheelchair, knowing you're suffering and having to take care of everything. Who could handle a disabled wife who is sad all the time?" He said it with a loving look, but the selfishness of this comment wasn't lost on me.

He's just caught up in the moment of the good news. He's just seen me at my worst the last few months. That won't be the case in the future. He wants me happy and how can I argue with that?

No red flags went up in my mind. *He's really not selfish. He can't be! Think how beautifully he took care of you with the spinal tap leak. Actions speak louder than words. Besides, he just wants a happy-go-lucky life... and so do I, so what the hell? We can have that together!*

"I'll ask Bo. But we all know what he'll say. He doesn't understand this stuff."

"I know, but I realize you need to think it through *because* of that sweet boy. And that's because you're a good mother... a *great* mother. In the meantime, I'll be shopping for a ring you'll be proud of."

I couldn't think of anything to say, still overwhelmed by the concept. He presented the ink pen one more time. "And you can keep this special pen. Maybe we'll frame it sometime when this fiasco of a proposal is the beginning of our happy marriage."

Dorisey blew a *pffftt*. "You guys are going to make me puke."

Babbas Bean piped in with a high-pitched comment. "I think it's sweet!"

"I just want out of this hall. I have a deadline." Rusty, our token gay guy, turned and left.

"He's just jealous," said the long-time art director Jim, who also headed back to his office.

My knees began to waver, suddenly feeling the weight of the circumstances and the decision I was due to make. "Deadlines are the furthest thing from my mind."

Miller nodded. "Mine, too." He kissed me again, eyes open and smiling. Never moving his lips from mine, he spoke. "But I have a meeting in five minutes, baby. I gotta go." I laughed, still pressing my lips to his. *This is craziness! Who proposes like this, minutes before a client meeting? He's crazy-cute!* He said, "Sorry to propose and run." Again, I laughed.

We stepped apart slowly, keeping our hands touching until we could no longer reach. "Goodbye, my handsome hunk," I said.

"Goodbye, my luscious lady."

I stumbled back to my office, feeling weak in the knees and startled by the speed of rat-a-tat shaking in my hands. *Oh my God, he wants to marry me! He asked me out loud!* Thoughts of Miller's proposal melded into those of Dr. Law's good news. *Oh my God, it's not MS. I'm not going to be disabled! Everything is going to be okay!* "Holy shit," I repeated to myself, my thoughts churning.

Also repeating in my head was the echo of an alarm, the daunting truth that my three-month-long debacle had uncovered: I needed someone to take care of me. Like I'd told Karen, I need love. Desperately. *So why in the hell would you walk away when it was offered on a silver platter?*

I'm not the independent badass I think I am, and I don't want to be single and strong. I need someone to take care of me. It's not a built-in need like having MS, but at some point, I'll need someone to walk for me when I break an ankle or something, someone to speak for me when I can't, to be a parent to Bo when it's too much for me alone, or at least someone to take me home when I'm too drunk to drive.

Will Miller do that? He inferred he wanted a happy wife. Is he saying he won't help me? Is that what he meant? What if I get depressed like I did with Andy? Will he leave me like Andy did?

A vision came to my mind... Miller carrying me in his arms when he put me to bed the day I collapsed in my apartment. Another flashback when Miller taught Bo how to stir cookie dough. *Miller will do it. Miller loves me, and when you love somebody, you'll do anything!*

My mind clicked into overdrive and a new era began in that critical second;

Miller and I would marry... the Advertising King and Queen of Rockville, together with the world's cutest blonde-haired boy, would become a Cindrella story.

Now I just needed to break it off with Vick and say goodbye to my crazy lifestyle. No more sex, drugs, and rock-and-roll. *I can do this, right? I'm ready to settle down and be a healthy, happy, sober mom with a picture-perfect family, right?*

The "official proposal" was three weeks later... under an oak tree on a trail of blooming dogwoods in the Smoky Mountains. He said we were going hiking, but I knew something was up because the weather sucked that day.

With the traditional words and stance, he popped the question in the rain, and my first glance at the engagement ring made me laugh. Not why you think. And we both laughed.

The exact moment he opened the hinged box, a gargantuan raindrop fell on the ring with an audible *pop.*

It was the wrong size, easily fixed, but a pear-cut design... my least favorite. I said nothing, of course, thinking I would replace it someday when I got rich and famous.

We carved our initials on the tree with the knife Miller brought for that purpose.

He assumed we would move in together immediately and began talking of those details, but I disagreed. "Not yet," I said.

He freaked out, but the truth was I accepted the proposal in a knee-jerk decision, thinking it may be my last chance.

There was much left to learn about Miller McKeown, much left unsaid on dozens of topics.

But we held hands walking back to the trailhead and sang songs together in the drive back to Rockville.

I broke it off with Vick the next day and it took every cell of my body to say goodbye; I still ached for the wild and crazy party he represented.

A full-time boyfriend? A fiancée? I'd have to ease into that slowly.

WEST GROVE VILLAGE
Chapter 15

When my lease was up, I moved to a nicer apartment, closer to work. Two bedrooms and, again, a brick wall in the living room. Indoor brick must have been a thing in the 80s. West Grove Village was a smaller complex with fewer rednecks and, though there wasn't an official playground, I saw several kids playing together at the pool.

Inside, the layout was not typical of an apartment. A double-sized living room featured a large window connecting to a private patio. An oversized kitchen with a huge island led to a square dining room with a wall of sunny floor-to-ceiling windows. It was a shame I had no dining table to sit and gape at the view: high enough to see the famous multi-layers of the Great Smoky Mountains, even the pinnacle of Mount LeConte.

I will be happy here. It feels like home and it's been a long damn time since I felt like I had a real home. Time to chill out and grow up, Lela.

☼ ☼ ☼ ☼ ☼

Just a few weeks after I moved into West Grove Village, I met a woman who could out-drink and out-stupid me. She would be my running buddy for years, despite Miller's disdain for her.

Here's how the saga began:

Early in the spring of 1986, on a Sunday, I donned my new black-and-white-striped bikini and walked two buildings down to the pool. I found a lounge chair at the shallow end and leaned over to arrange my towel, sunglasses, tape player, and red-and-white Playmate cooler of beer. At the deep end and within the three-sided shelter, a big group of people partied hard. Hmm... several very nice looking men, my age, and a dozen laughing girls. All were drinking beer from red Solo cups, poured from a keg wedged in the back of the shelter.

As I settled down on my chair, three more partiers came running to the pool, carrying the largest inflatable I'd ever seen. Round, red and orange, and almost as wide as the pool. When they threw it in, I saw it said "Party Island."

The partiers cheered and jumped in the pool. Some landed on the raft, some splashed high rooster tails with cannonball jumps. Chaos ensued, and it had happened in a flash.

I locked eyes with the blonde who carried the raft and she dramatically waved, imitating the guy on the old TV show, *Fantasy Island*. Exaggerating her motions, she said, "Join us on Party Island, my friend." She looked about my age, wearing a tie-dye one-piece. Based on how often people were saying her name, she must be Jill or Jilly.

"Jilly" disappeared into the depths of the shelter, then reappeared carrying two cups of beer, speed-walking toward me. "Join the party, curly-girl! It's a 'Kill the Keg' bash! You should have been here last night! It was one helluva party!" I smiled and accepted the cup of beer. She jerked, "Oh! I'm Jilly." Her right pinky finger cocked out and curled toward me. "Pinky shake!" I reached to hook my pinky into hers, laughing. The movement was awkward, but it seemed to amuse her. Jilly laughed. Rather, she snorted as an imitation of a laugh.

"And I'm Lela," I said, in the throes of laughter. I liked this woman; there was an instant connection. She no longer had a hangover today, she said, because of this morning's "Kill the Keg" bash. Intrigued by that, I thought of how long it'd been since I'd had that bad of a hangover. It's like I'd outgrown them and, when they happened, I sipped my vodka-spiked coffee until my body returned to normal.

But lately, I'd been too busy being a mom and kick-ass advertising writer to do too much partying. *Wow, you've been doing well on the drinking thing, Lela. Maybe drunk just three or four times a week. Not bad.*

"Thanks for the beer, Jilly, but it's not a hangover-killer for me today. I worked last night. Working... always working.

"Well, Curly, it's time to change that shit. Cheers!" We clinked glasses. "Come on, I'll introduce you around," Jilly said, and I entered a mass of people who would become my late-twenties' peer group and my downfall.

They called themselves the Hooligans and Jilly seemed to be one of the leaders, certainly the funniest of the bunch. She was relentless with hilarity, doing impressions of the others, cracking jokes of all genres, and blowing it out with silly puns she thought of on the fly, it seemed.

Without a doubt, I knew I had found a friend. A best friend.

That summer, it was Jilly and me against the world. We drank together, laughed and cried together, wreaked havoc at the pool, and embarrassed ourselves at every opportunity. The two of us went to every possible party, sometimes with Miller and sometimes with one of Jilly's many boy toys.

She was the best-possible bad influence for me.

On non-Bo Sundays when Miller played golf, Jilly and I spent the day on Norton Lake in her brand-new ski boat. Sometimes just the two of us hit the lake, other times we joined a mass group, a subset of The Hooligans called, appropriately, "The Lake People."

Jilly and I understood each other at a deep level. It was unspoken that neither of us were emotionally stable and that we both drank too much. Also unspoken: neither of us cared about the repercussions of our actions. We were the life of every party and I stayed happy with a huge group of socially active, crazy-party friends.

On the few occasions Jilly and I talked seriously, I discovered that she, too, had been diagnosed Bi-Polar at age sixteen and had struggled lifelong to fight mood swings.

Like me, alcohol calmed the static that dictated her moods. Together, we were self-medicating sisters and partners in crime.

Early in that fateful summer, we spent many Sundays in our swimsuits at Bob Pullet's backyard parties. We drank along with the thirty-strong crowd and played volleyball too competitive for a bunch of drunks.

Bob's Golden Retriever Gracie pranced around the court, biting one edge of each beer cup and turning it up, letting the beer flow into her mouth. Who knows how much beer the poor dog drank... like us, she was drunk by mid-afternoon.

The crowd found it funny, but I did not. Definitely not. With the power tools my father had given me (his "old ones" he'd recycled in some crazy way), I built two free-standing "shelves" with drilled holes to hold our cups while playing. I did it all for Gracie.

Bob wanted to pay me for the shelves but I refused. A much better payment was being applauded by the crowd. *Lela the Great, the Famous, the Generous Comrade, the Handy-Dandy Curly Friend with her Head on Straight.* Somehow, I truly believed I held those flattering titles. Those that judged me otherwise... fuck 'em! I had the support of the majority and thought I fit in with a worthy group. It was one of the rare times in my life when I felt solid and comfortable in my own skin.

Somehow I was still an appropriately sober mother every other weekend – barely buzzed for a week, then shit-faced the next. Best of both worlds for Lela Fox.

Miller moved in about a month after I did. I'd finally asked who he loved more – me or Bo. The look on his face was pure shock. He answered with wide eyes that twitched looking at mine, and a comment sounding more like a barf, combining "You," "Kid," and "Fuck!"

In the end, Miller said everything I wanted to hear and promised a future of family harmony and a social presence in the community. "We're at the top of our game, Lela! You, me, Bo! We're meant to be! And we'll have another... hell, we'll have a *whole baseball team* of kids!" That made me smile broadly. I'd always wanted to have two more children... assuming there would be no divorce.

One concern: I tried to talk about money to compare our philosophies but Miller bucked hard, puffed up, and turned defensive. It was as if I'd accused him of some horrible failing, and his comeback was to accuse me of drinking too much. Uh oh.

If I hadn't stopped it, a fight would have escalated. We agreed to split the bills and left it at that. But I didn't consider his reaction completely whacky because Andy had also been uneasy talking about money.

The main problem, I knew, was me. After almost losing my job the year before, I became a penny-pincher from hell, managing every nickel and dime. *As long as he lets me handle the money for the family, things will be fine.* I did get that assurance and he seemed grateful. "I hate that shit and always end up paying late just because I hate to deal with it," he had said.

"I love to keep it organized, so I think we'll be cool on that."

"Done deal. Now don't talk about it anymore."

A week later, Miller put all his furniture in storage and moved in with nothing but suitcases. Overall, it wasn't much of a change. My running around with Jilly and the Lake People didn't change at all because Miller spent all Sundays on the golf course with his wannabe-community-leader friends.

Red flags sailed by on the road to building the relationship. So what if Miller wasn't perfect? No big deal; I would fix him; take away his flaws and replace them with Daddy's traits. The fact that I'd tried (and failed) to do this with husband number one didn't enter my mind as a comparison.

I was in love and stupid. The calendar said I was age 27 but my behavior and beliefs pegged me as a much younger woman. Young, dumb, and drunk.

There was so much I didn't know about Miller when he moved in, and dozens of issues we hadn't discussed. I knew it, knew the danger, but thought I was in too deep to back out. I continued to invest heart and soul in him.

My belief was that to start anew with a perhaps-more-suitable partner would be too much trouble, too much change for Bo. So I stuck with the one I knew was "good enough."

My approach to the relationship was like my mom's. Her view of marriage to my dad: when you fall in love, you get what you get. The good and the bad, the strengths and weaknesses are all part of the package you bought. No returns.

So I focused on the good stuff, basked in the happy family times, and searched for ways to connect with Miller otherwise.

I bought sexy lingerie and pampered him.

I learned to bake, cooked lavish dinners almost every night, receiving thankful comments in return.

I dropped sweet notes on his desk and worked like hell to be the best creative partner imaginable.

Come hell or high water, I'd have the idyllic marriage my parents had. That was the plan.

WHACKY ADDYS
Chapter 16

January was Addy month. All the Sturbridge creatives gathered the past years' reprints and ad slicks, and filled out forms for the submission log; it was a long and arduous process. Though only the first-level local Addys, the awards were a damn big deal at the agency and to the creative community in Rockville. Local winners went to the state level for judging... then to regional... and national. Not only that, the Addy banquet was a long-standing tradition in Rockville, not just a dinner, but a drunkfest, a party where anything goes.

In preparation, all the women tittered about what to wear. Of course, I had nothing fancy in my closet, nothing at all, even though the dress code was "funky" rather than "fancy." My solution was kick-ass, according to me. I bought a pair of offbeat black satin pants, poofy in the thighs and tight in the calves, ankle-length like a jester's pants. Worn with a custom-fit rented tuxedo tail-coat and black stiletto heels, I looked... even I knew it... I looked fabulous. Hot, hot, hot.

Thankfully, I stayed sober enough to walk through the banquet line in those heels before I ditched them. As I played the flirty vixen with the men and women in the crowd, comments ran the gamut of "You look marvelous" to "Damn, you hot momma!" I was floating on Cloud Nine and my own personal awards were adding up. My "Queen Copywriter" title was now a proven fact; the bulk of the Gold awards went to projects with my name on them.

Maybe one-third of the way through the hours-long presentation, our drunken art director Rusty slurred, "Damn, Lela, you're leading the pack with awards. The Copy Queen of Rockville!" He raised his beer bottle for a toast and smashed it into my plastic cup, way too hard.

The cup cracked; my vodka-tonic sloshed all over my hand and onto the tablecloth. "Dammit, Rusty! You can't hold your liquor worth a damn. No wonder you're single," I said.

"All I know," he continued slurring and leaned closer to my ear, "If I was into girls, I'd go for you in a minute." I found that hilarious, as did everybody at the table. Somehow, I was flattered.

Desperate for a replacement drink, I excused myself and dashed to the bar for a another. While returning to the table, maneuvering through the pattern of round tables in the ballroom, the emcee announced the winner of the direct-mail postcard campaign: the winner was Lela Fox. *Oh shit, I know what that means. Get ready, Lela.* The smartass lighting director, a friend of mine, must have seen me coming back from the bar and turned the spotlight on me just as I stumbled on the leg of a chair.

The emcee boomed, "Lela Fox, once again, folks... the winner of a Gold Addy Award!" Then as I righted myself, only to stumble again, he joked into the microphone. "Looks like she's already had that free cocktail!" Though by tradition, everybody got drunk at the Addys, the sting of embarrassment twisted my stomach in a knot, but I held my head high; so high that I didn't see another chair leg in my path. Another stumble, another laugh from the crowd. Then, thank God, the spotlight snapped off just as I stumbled for the fourth time in ten seconds.

Damn, Lela! You aren't even wearing your shoes and you're falling-down drunk? Get your shit together, woman! You can't be the star of the show and the drunk in the gutter, right? Straighten up!

There was a short intermission before the announcement of the Best in Show award. The tension was high and the buzz of conversation competed with the loud, frantic music. This intermission was also time for all to refresh their drinks. Hundreds of drunk people scrambled to be first at the temporary bars lining the outside walls of the ballroom.

I plopped down in my chair, returning from the bar with another vodka "just in case." Suddenly, I felt faint. The room was spinning, my eyes crossing, and the cacophony of voices vibrating in my ears. "Miller! Listen!"

"I'm right beside you, Lela. You don't have to yell."

Taking a breath between each word, I finally finished the sentence, "I think I'm too drunk to be in public." Then a thought struck me and I shared it with my also-drunk boyfriend. "Hey, baby... take away one letter from 'public' and it's 'pubic,' right?" I cracked up laughing, my head lolling onto my shoulder, mouth open.

"Oh hell, Lela. Not now! Please!" Miller used one hand to lift my head and put his arm around my shoulder. "Keep it in the road, kid. Be cool and don't show your ass."

Right, listen to him, Lela. Be cool, as cool as you look. You have a fucking reputation to protect! Then I chuckled to myself, knowing the reputation also included being the leader of the party crowd. *Sure, you can do both, woman! Just don't fall down.*

The emcee began the buildup to the Best of Show announcement, proceeded by the Lifetime Achievement Award. There were a dozen possible winners, and The Old Man was one of the nominees. He had me write an acceptance speech if he'd end up in need of one.

The Lifetime Achievement Award was a big deal, an honor few had earned. Lo-and-behold, The Old Man won. The grumpy curmudgeon was a legend, a creative trailblazer, but his speech was humble by design.

The Old Man could hardly lift the massive trophy. He was a small man, now bent forward with advanced age, and the trophy looked larger than he did. I wasn't the only one who found it funny; laughter speckled the ballroom.

He waddled to his table, adjacent to ours, and I raced to peck a kiss on top of his bald head as I had always done to my Daddy.

A brilliant idea crossed my mind In the middle of the kiss. I decided a French kiss would be even better, so I licked his bald spot and moaned with lust for several seconds, rubbing my boobs against the back of his shoulders. Seconds later, as if I'd sobered in that little flash of time, I saw my smeared lipstick on The Old Man's shiny crown and the glaring error of my ways.

A sober Lela wouldn't do that; a professional Lela wouldn't do that. This was my boss! No, the boss of my boss!

The Old Man's wife, with perfect circles of apricot blush on her cheeks, flashed a Southern Lady look of horror. She pursed her lips at me as her husband's body stiffened. Barry, the Sturbridge son, sat across the table with a face registering both shock and disdain.

The Old Man turned to look at me and as he turned, I hoped his face would show humor... the same innocent humor that had driven me to kiss his bald spot in the first place. But no.

He threw his napkin on the table and stood, all five-foot-eight of him, his crooked finger pointing at my nose. "*YOU!* You drunken dog! What sloppy, *crude* reprobate would lick my head? You are an embarrassment... unbecoming female scum!"

I didn't think he'd be that mad, but the steam coming out of his ears wasn't just a cartoon illusion. With a clenched jaw and his hands shaking with anger, The Old Man opened his mouth to spout another insult as the taste of bile threatened to sober me up, and I couldn't let *that* happen!

"But, sir, I didn't–"

He interrupted with a scream to stop me. "No apology can change it now! Didn't your momma teach–"

As if on cue, the band's drummer began a loud and amusingly dramatic rim shot. The emcee boomed his accompanying line. "And now... ladies and gentlepeople... the top three choices for Best of Show!"

"Gotta go, sir. Congratulations!" I said, already on the move back to my table.

Miller had seen the entire scene and looked at me dumbfounded. Speaking an octave above his normal tone, he croaked, "Why in the hell would you think it would be okay to lick The Old Man's fucking head, Lela? Like you were fucking him from behind!"

I ignored Miller's concern, though I felt as ashamed as I'd felt in a long time. Pretending to be in control, I said, "It's Addy night, Miller... anything goes."

"Maybe anything but *that.*"

"He already gave me hell... called me a drunken dog and a reprobate."

"Oh, God! What else?"

"Unbecoming female scum. I think that was the line."

Miller put his head in his hands, supported by elbows on the table. Then I noticed his button-down shirt and the tablecloth were sopping wet. "Your behavior affects *my* reputation, too, you know," he said.

"And your wet elbow needs a professional explanation, too, you drunk fuck." That was my way of turning the problem back on him, keeping him on the defense. But he didn't defend himself at all; Miller stared at me with a look of pity. Oh, how it pissed me off! I shouted, "Just... stop! Whatever! Be quiet... here's the announcement. And the top prize is anybody's guess."

It seemed the spotlight brightened us before the emcee said our names. Miller and I won Best of Show for the *Quit Yer Itchin'* campaign. Applause all around for Rockville's Advertising Queen and King.

As instructed, all seven-hundred-plus people in the banquet hall rose to toast us – well, all but The Old Man and his wife. The moment I noticed this, a drink appeared in my hand; Babbas Bean brought the perfect gift.

The band opened with "Shout!" and Miller and I ran to dance. I forgot about the faux pas I'd made earlier, even when witnessing the elder Mr. and Mrs. Sturbridge dancing cheek-to-cheek... even when The Old Man glared at me over his wife's shoulder.

Too drunk to know how drunk I was, and with Miller feeling no pain, either, we danced the night away in the most literal sense. Our reservation for the honeymoon suite, the top floor above the ballroom, was supposed to be for a romantic interlude but as we tried to sneak away, others followed. The party lasted until five in the morning when I removed my jester pants for some reason and danced on the sofa to music that wasn't playing; it only played in my head.

For the second time, Lela Fox showed her ass on Addy night. It certainly wouldn't be the last time.

The following Monday morning, I took a seat on the leather sofa in The Old Man's office, per his request. Barry sat in a leather side chair and his father sat on a manager's chair set at a comically low height. Not much more than his head and neck peeked above the desktop.

The Old Man began the lecture. I felt not one ounce of remorse for what I'd done but kept my head down and mumbled the expected apologies.

Barry's comment at the end of the meeting was the one that stung. "Though I'm thrilled with our showing, and yours in particular, what you do reflects on Sturbridge. No more drinking when you're representing this agency. Obviously, you can't handle it. Lela, it's probably best that you be the designated driver at next year's Addy banquet. Are we on the same page?"

"Uh... that's a pretty stern punishment, Barry. I thought–"

Barry's eyes widened as he rushed to interrupt me. *"Punishment?* That's not..." He stopped to huff a breath of irritation. "I can't believe you think it's punishment!" Then his brow wrinkled, and he leveled an accusatory look at me. "That sound like something somebody would say if they had a problem with alcohol... is that you, Lela?"

"Of course not, Barry!"

"Then you should know the 'punishment,' as you call it, is common sense and professionalism. Surely you understand that concept."

Again, I mumbled an apology, and a half-assed agreement to honor Barry's request. I wanted to end on a high note, complimenting them both to assure all was forgiven, so I beamed with a false smile, changing the subject. "I'm so blessed to have you two for inspiration. At Sturbridge, I'm able to do my best work, alongside the forward-thinking staff that lines the hall upstairs. I will not let you two down again. Trust me on that. On the contrary, I will make you proud."

Both men mumbled a response as I excused myself. My parting comment, said with a smiling broadcaster's voice, brought two blank stares. Maybe they weren't sure whether to nod or shoot me. "Okey-dokey, then... my nose back to the grindstone. I'm working on another award-winning campaign for Sturbridge Advertising!"

I hightailed it upstairs, scooting into Miller's office and closing the door behind me. Breathless, I told him what had happened and, of course, he said I was lucky to just get a lecture. "You're right. I'm lucky. But the punishment is a bummer. What the fuck? I may not even go to the Addys next year. Why bother?"

"You staying sober might help *me* have more fun, knowing you're not going to do something stupid. Girl, you're wild when you're drunk!"

"So now you tease me like it's funny? What the hell, asshole! You sure didn't say it like that yesterday!"

Miller had been on my ass all day Sunday, harping about the stupidity of my actions, the vulgarity of my drunkenness, and the general inadequacy of my personality. I'd cried, and he seemed to enjoy the result of his purposeful shaming.

At least that's how I remember it.

☼ ☼ ☼ ☼ ☼

With such a booming business, it was time to move the agency to allow for growth. The Old Man sold the downtown building and bought a new and bigger one just outside of downtown. Sturbridge made the news. We were growing fast.

When The Old Man first bought the building, I freaked; everybody did. It screamed "ugly" in twelve languages – dulled chrome and garish turquoise.

But by the time we moved in, the 100-percent-remodeled and professionally designed office had stone accents everywhere. The lobby featured a fake-rock waterfall. Trendy digs in those days.

I didn't envy the receptionist. She complained of the humidity every day, grumbling that it affected everything from her hair, now fuzzy, her fingertips, now prune-y, not to mention the now-thick sheets of paper she sorted through every day. After the third complaint, we called her "Steamy," and not just behind her back. The creatives didn't show mercy to anybody; eventually you would get a nickname and probably a derogatory one.

When the kinks were worked out, I called the media and wrote a series of press releases: "Something Astir at Sturbridge." The newspapers complained about the headline. "Too much cutesy-advertising," they said. When The Old Man called me in to complain, I told him he should hire a Public Relations person if he didn't want an advertising approach. "Advertising is all I know, sir!" I argued. We had a two-person Public Relations department within the week.

The Old Man had an office in the basement, and I wandered down sometimes just to talk to him. It took months, but he had forgiven me for the Addys banquet assault, and, surprisingly, we'd become fast friends. He respected my work, he said, and I'll admit I respected his business acumen.

He pronounced "business" as "bid'ness" and talked about the responsibility of creating a reputation. Living up to your reputation, he said, makes for a lifelong successful career. The word "reputation" made my stomach grumble. It meant a lot of things to me. One a creative reputation; I was cool with that. But the other side of my reputation was seriously tarnished. And to think of that made me know it was because I drank too much. I wanted to sweep that fact and those self-hatred feelings deep under the proverbial rug.

But when writer's block struck, or when I needed a kick in the ass or a pat on the back, I went to the basement to talk to The Old Man. We talked about anything except the project at hand. His brashness re-routed my brain, removed the ping-pong thoughts that screamed "You're no good," and sent me back upstairs with a new, can-do attitude.

☼ ☼ ☼ ☼ ☼

Employment as a copywriter had benefits, and serious pitfalls. It's creative and free, yes, but still a business. Billable hours ruled. Sometimes I wrote five words for a billboard or shelf sign and typed it in the correct format. Two minutes of my time, but the minimum billable copywriting time was one hour. *Ca-ching* for the Barry Sturbridge cash register.

On the flip side were writer/producer projects. Barry never understood why they took so long and I never understood why he never understood. The copywriter was responsible for the script – both audio and video, *and* responsible for props, casting, schedules, shooting, recording, editing, finding and directing music, sound effects, etcetera and a lot more etcetera. It was all on my plate. The details took a long time, solid days in a row, even for a thirty-second spot.

A writer/producer project for a seven-minute video was the one that turned the tables for me. At the time, I didn't handle stress well. Rephrase: Stress interfered with my drinking and made me bat-shit crazy... and being bat-shit crazy erased my logic and detoured my sound judgement. My true colors would show soon, and change the essence of my career.

OUTTA HERE
Chapter 17

The client: Brindle County Chamber of Commerce, a big client from our satellite office in Brindle, Georgia, 120 miles away and just over the state line. The project: a seven-minute video for businesses... to convince them to relocate or start their business in Brindle County. It would require intense production, including open-door-helicopter aerial shots.

Despite the overwhelming amount of work the project represented, Barry had the traffic department continue to send me new projects as if I had nothing else to do. Working at least sixty hours a week already, a single mother and under a major amount of stress, I couldn't handle anymore. Miller helped me in all possible ways, picking up Bo so I could work late, but the end of my rope was visible and the light at the end of the tunnel was not.

I shared my frustration and anger with Miller. "This fucking job is already interfering with me having fun, and now it's interfering with my mental health, physical health, even my relationship with you!" The sound I made was a combination of a frustrated growl and a whimper. "And of course I'm seeing Bo less and less. This is not cool." Tears flowed as I sipped a double-strength vodka and tonic.

Miller didn't sympathize. "Work is work, Lela. Feast or famine, you know? You don't get to choose your client list or design your own schedule."

"But it's unfair! Too much! I can't hold up to this amount of fucking stress! And it's making me do bad work, just to get it done and off my desk. Is that what Barry really wants?"

I had worked up a bit of foam on my lips, so angry I couldn't swallow right. "Here's the deal: If they bring me another project tomorrow, I'm gonna give Barry a piece of my mind – a huge *chunk* of my mind, in fact. I'm gonna hurl all the fury I've bottled up in me. It's time he knows how this video project is affecting all the others... and how it's affecting me personally. I'm going cuckoo and if I hit a Bi-Polar spike, it's all his fault."

"Uh... you may want to think twice before you go off on Barry, Lela," Miller warned.

But I didn't think twice. I didn't even think once. Instead, I reacted like the flip of a switch.

The next day, the moment a job bag landed on my desk, I stomped into Barry's fancy office, not knocking and not closing the door behind me. I stood in front of his desk and shook the papers at him. The volume of my voice was at a crescendo. "Don't you know I can't do other jobs until I do your precious video? I'm neck-deep into it and I have a production deadline!" My hands shook with anger.

And, of course, I had to twist the knife a little. "If you were really in charge of this place, you could see what's happening."

I had startled him, for sure, but I wanted him to *listen*, so I re-grouped with a deep breath, determined to make him understand. With a lower volume and a little more calm, I proceeded with a verbal list of the other projects on my plate and how the deadlines piled up.

Barry seemed to think about it and flashed that famous toothy grin. He leaned forward, carefully pulling the expensive pen from his expensive desk holder, then silently doodling on his expensive blotter. Without looking up, Barry spoke to me. "With all those projects to do, Lela, I guess you better get busy." No emotion or enunciation, but calm and collected as if he was in a trance.

I exploded like Mount Vesuvius. "Are you fucking *kidding me*? *Seriously?* No way - you can't use me like that, Barry Sturbridge! I work over sixty hours a week, and I have a family! Plus I'm not stupid... I know how much money I'm making for you, dammit. I know my billable rate." Clenching my jaw, I put both hands on my hips and huffed a rush of air.

A new stance, less accusatory and more logical: "Give me time to do my job well or I quit," I said and I stared him straight in the eye. The tension increased by the semi-second.

Not looking at me, he shook his head back and forth, as in "no" or "damn girl, you're crazy" or as a father would say "what am I going to do with you, kid?" My heart beat double-time and pounded at my temples. "Barry, you're fucking telling me you won't re-assign the other projects?" No answer; he continued to doodle. "Are you saying I have to work *seventy* hours a week now and do a shitty job because of it?"

Barry leaned back in his fat executive chair, hands behind his head. And he smiled. "You must do what I tell you to do, Lela," he said, "And I'm telling you to do all the jobs on your list. No missing deadlines, no rest for the weary."

Furious, I stomped out of his office and hurried down the hall, breathing fire and muttering nonsense... not realizing I was at full volume. I rushed into my office and grabbed my purse, then thought better. "No, not yet."

I made a mad dash for the copier room and grabbed three empty boxes, put them in my office, turned off the light and closed the door. Still rushing as fast as possible, I went to Miller's office and blurted out my news. "I'm outta there, babe. I just quit."

His loud "Whaaaaaat?" brought the others into the hall.

"I love you a lot, guys, but I've had it. Too much work, too little appreciation. I quit." All in the group were wide-eyed and gasping. Maybe they were jealous or worried about their own future. I didn't care.

No radio, no humming, no air conditioner; I drove home in silence. Just the loud heartbeat pounding my head and my lungs screaming for air.

Twenty minutes later, I arrived home to the blink of the answering machine pulsing as fast as my heart. Six messages. The first was from Barry, asking me to come back. I screamed "Fuck you!" at the phone and hit the STOP button.

Then I popped a beer and sat on the sofa to settle my nerves. It took three beers to do the job, and for those thirty minutes, I thought I was unemployed.

Back to the phone, I listened to the rest of the messages. Two were from other Rockville ad agencies, offering me a job. Another two were from the owners of smaller agencies, asking if I would work for them freelance. The last call was from the marketing department of Connor Health about their annual report... "Now that you're a freelance copywriter," they said.

The calls kept coming, tons of friends and practically every agency in town. Flabbergasted by how quickly word had spread, I felt important and pleased that I'd made such a splash. Once again, my rebellion made waves. A knowing smirk held on my face as I took call after call.

The offers that intrigued me most were the freelance offers; there were eleven of them if my count was right. The agencies/potential clients described specific projects, and sometimes details of upcoming projects, assuming that I'd still be available.

One guy, known as Bones Bailey of Bailey Associates, said he'd pay me ten bucks more than the going freelance rate of $50 an hour. "You're worth even more, actually, but we can discuss it."

Another beer and another rest on the sofa. Excitement pulsed through my body, sending my heart rate into overdrive, yet I felt calm. *You're cool, Lela. You didn't fuck up, you just opened a zillion doors for yourself.*

In the fantasy world building in my head, I saw freelance working beautifully in my family life. Thoughts churned, focusing on practical details, too... like how the floor-to-ceiling windows in the empty dining room would make a great office wall, and about Miller's old business furniture and supplies in storage. Cool. It seemed too perfect to be a coincidence.

By employment contract rules, I couldn't steal Sturbridge clients, but I had refused to sign the no-compete clause, so working for another local agency would be no problem. "I beg you to sue me anyway, Barry-fucking-Sturbridge. Even your Old Man would tell you to back off." I popped another beer and assured myself I could get away with anything. After all, I was Lela Fox, Queen of Everything. Funny how a few beers made that fact so clear.

I knew with full certainty I could get away with stealing Sturbridge clients, too, if I wanted. *Wouldn't that be a slap in the face, Mr. Barry Asshole!*

As if on cue, one of the marketing managers from Shaffer Industries called, offering to hire both Miller and me to do his large-animal vaccine work. *How are these people finding out so soon? Seems like I should have left Sturbridge long ago and worked for myself. Hell yeah! Wwork for myself and manage my own schedule.* "No more sixty-hour weeks, you motherfucker!"

☀ ☀ ☀ ☀ ☀

Miller got home at 5:30, much earlier than normal. "What are you going to do now?" he asked.

"Well, it seems I have a mountain of options. In just a few hours, dozens of people promised me three months of freelance work. And *agencies*, Miller, not cheapskate small clients! It's the small agencies that are calling... like the Bailey Group. In fact, Bones himself called!"

Miller snapped a look at me, then nodded his head with raised eyebrows. "That's good. Bones would be great to work with."

"Also Paul Hogan, Cindy Bender... several others. It's almost too good to be true. Because with an agency, I can justify a high rate, right?" Miller nodded, still staring at the newspaper. "And still not have to kiss the client's ass! Let the agency do it, know what I mean? No long bullshit meetings or presentations."

"Yes, I know *exactly* what you mean! Bones and agency presidents have decades of experience in selling good creative, so you won't have to. Because... sorry, Lela, but you suck at selling your work.

"Because I get so nervous! And that makes me blurt out inappropriate things. I've done it all my life, business and personal. It's embarrassing."

"But... you'll have to sell it to the head of the agency. You're not scot-free."

"Right."

"And please listen... you know I worked freelance for twelve years in my studio..."

"Yeah, yeah yeah... and you've told me the problems with it."

"There are *lots* of problems with it, sweetheart... Including the freedom to do some pretty nasty extra-curricular things."

I stopped and shook my head, then wrinkled my brow. "Explain that."

The newspaper crunched on his lap and he stared at the ceiling for a second, thinking. "I had nobody to answer to, Lela. In the end, I hooked up with a client who had a nice stash of cocaine all the time and got hooked on the shit. I don't tell people this, but that's why I took the job at Sturbridge: to start again with a new group of coworkers and friends."

"What-the-fuck?" I spat the question like ammo. "Why haven't you told *me* this?"

"It's on a need-to-know basis."

At double volume, I shouted, "*Need to know?* We live in the same fucking house! We're engaged! Wouldn't that mean I need to know?" He didn't reply, continuing to read the damn newspaper. "And being an addict is something... damn, Miller!" Mouth wide, I stood flabbergasted. Did you go to rehab? What the hell?"

"I quit cold turkey and fought it like hell. Gripping the sides of the chair, white knuckles and all. Turns out, I'm stronger than the coke. So now, it's no biggie."

"Wow..." Shock had been my first reaction, then explosive anger that he hadn't shared this gem of info from his very-recent history. But after a few minutes of deep thought, feelings of respect came. *He beat it, so he must be strong and determined. And that might explain why he's kinda pissy sometimes... maybe that's where Mr. Miserable comes from. When he's all up in his head and thinking too much.* Intrigued now, I asked, "Aren't you afraid you'll go back to it? What do they call it... a relapse?"

"When I think about it too much, I just have a scotch and soda. That seems to do the trick."

"Well, that's good." Neither of us spoke for a long fifteen seconds. My mind was on overdrive, thinking of my own vodka version of "treatment" for my nerves being out of sorts. "That's good unless you get hooked on the scotch..." My laugh was hesitant, not wanting to implicate myself.

"Naw... don't worry about me on that! I only drink the good stuff and it's too expensive to drink all night."

"Duh... doofus, cocaine isn't cheap, and you did it all night long, right? So what's the difference?"

"In the end, I didn't pay for the coke. A lot of it was barter. I'd design a brochure for some blow, a logo for a line."

Exasperated, I made the most smartass comment I could think of. "Well, aren't you a clever young man?" A sarcastic *hhmph*, then, "Clever, but pitiful."

"But I don't want a thing to do with it now. I'm cured. Haven't had any in almost nine months, haven't seen my old friends... and now I have you and Bo. Happiness is the best rehab."

Though the discussion sent my heart rate to the moon and my radar kicked in high gear, I accepted Miller's explanation and believed he'd dropped the habit as he said. *Nine months is a long time – surely long enough to say it's no longer a problem. Maybe he has an addictive personality, but he beat what was beating HIM. I have an addictive personality, too, I guess. His cocaine versus my vodka... same thing, right? So all I have to do is go without for nine months, just as Miller did. Then everything will be cool. Yeah, that's what I'll do. And I'll start first thing in the morning.*

I'm still astounded that I didn't see the *enormous* red flag Miller's cocaine addiction represented, especially the easy substitution of scotch when the cravings took over. Perhaps it was the timing; when he told me, my total focus was on myself and my career. I didn't have much room in my heart to worry about other people's problems and issues.

I accepted this information and planned to go forward as planned. As if it was no big deal, as if he was truly cured, as if it didn't predict future behavior or point to the roots of his personality, as if there would be no wreckage from the past.

At the time, and for many years afterward, I justified my own addiction with the same kind of denial and naivety. I labeled myself "in control" because I didn't drink during the day (unless it was a beer, or a weekend, or a special celebration, or... any excuse would do).

With my drunken nose in the air and my head held high, I convinced myself I was functional, successful, and a happy mother with a smart and happy child. And I was never late enough to cause *real* problems.

I thought I had the achievements that no alcoholic could have and the good behavior an alcoholic could never pull off. Therefore, I couldn't be what I called "one of *those* people."

Alcohol worked for me. Until it didn't. Then all hell broke loose, like the kind that started the next day.

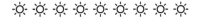

WILL WRITE FOR FOOD
Chapter 18

We swung by the EZ-Mart for a six pack and on to our errand for the night. I tiptoed, full of fear, but Miller seemed laid back and casual. The Sturbridge building was eerily quiet.

I popped the second beer and opened my office door, leaving it open for light. It felt strange to sit behind my desk in the dark but I still felt the joy within my "happy space."

At Sturbridge, like every work desk in my past, I had surrounded myself with silly bits of inspiration; I called each trinket a muse. Miller referred to them as pieces of junk, and it was a constant source of his teasing. But I firmly believed the silliness of the knick-knacks kept my creativity top-of-mind.

My trinket collection was about two dozen pointless mementos, weird advertising paraphernalia, Happy Meal toys, a rubber pig, and a miniature troll. Two dozen things that made me smile... lined up under a corkboard of pictures. I grabbed the first box and packed these memories with care.

"Surprisingly, I'll miss this place," I thought. For the past year, I had the opportunity to be creative to the max. Freedom to be me, a no-holds-barred me... no idea too bizarre. In all media, in both advertising and marketing, I had excelled. For that, I was grateful to Barry and his bulldog asshole attitude. I would always be grateful, but for now, I was still mad as hell. And my anger's resulting tears choked me as I packed.

Just as I began to question my soundness of mind for quitting a $60,000+ job, Miller peeked around the corner with raised eyebrows and a mischievous look on his face. "One last time?" he said through a half-evil, half-comical grin.

My own eyebrows rose, bringing a sunbeam of a smile. "I'd never say no to that!" Miller grabbed my hand and we ran to the conference room for one last love-making session on the monstrous table. Afterward, as always, I trudged to the janitor's closet and used the cotton-rag broom to sweep our pubic hairs off the table.

I didn't remember going to bed, so maybe I had passed out on the way home in Miller's black Jetta. But I remember sleeping fitfully and awakening early, hours before Miller's alarm was due to buzz. Carefully, I crawled out of bed and made a pot of coffee, then sat on the sofa with a notepad to process this job-changing/life-changing event. Two columns: "Freelance Pro and Con" and "Real Job Pro and Con."

Lost in thought, I stared at the paper for a half-hour without writing a thing. *I know the solution to this!* In the kitchen, I poured a glug of Amaretto liqueur in my coffee. *Oops!* I had forgotten my pledge to abstain for nine months as Miller had done with cocaine. It took a minute to justify it; I decided it was okay because Amaretto was a sweet *liqueur*, not *liquor*, and more like having dessert. Besides, it was daytime, and I didn't drink during the day.

Back to the sofa and my list... writing nothing. I was still thinking of the power move I'd made, the good it would do for me, and the slap in the face it was for Barry-fucking-Sturbridge. Thinking back, I realized I'd I never questioned the wisdom of my choice, never thought I could be wrong or that the snap decision might be because of an obvious and rapidly developing manic upswing in my mood disorder.

A compromise with Barry wasn't considered. It was a black and white decision in a contest of wills. And in my mind, I had won. The fact that he called and asked me to come back gave me even more of a thrill. I knew I'd put the sonofabitch in a bind and that made me happy. Revenge tasted sugar-sweet.

Yeah, mister, who's gonna do your precious Chamber of Commerce video now? Ba-haha! Who's gonna write about sheep diarrhea and make it sing?

Being so self-focused and self-righteous, it never occurred to me that I no longer had a way to support Bo or that I should have thought about that before I walked out. I believed what I did was normal and to be expected. *Stretched to the limit and I quit. Wouldn't anybody do that?*

Eased with a little Amaretto, I believed the problem would solve itself in a day. All I had to do was decide which direction to go. I filled my pad with pros, cons, and notes until my brain was full.

When Miller awakened, I rambled through a one-sided discussion that lasted until he left for work. He was silent but told me he loved me and he'd be thinking of me as I figured it out.

There were no home computers yet, but I had purchased a version of my own, what was called a "VideoWriter" by Magnavox. It's laughable to think about now, but then it was a godsend.

Like all "saved" documents, my résumé was stored on a 3.5-inch floppy disc. I set the machine up on the coffee table, inserted the disc, and used its crude cursor to open the document. I massaged the résumé a bit, made up new qualifications and accolades, and reprinted it on double-thick paper.

At eight o'clock, I began making calls. Job offers first, of course. I called in the order they had called me. Agency CEO Bob Clevenger said he would clear his calendar; he wanted to see me right away. My hands shook as I wrote the time on a notepad, one of many notepads that now surrounded me.

I couldn't call Miller at work to tell him the good news because I didn't want to go through Steamy. The busy-body would tell all, I feared, so I called my Mom to brag. I didn't tell her I had quit Sturbridge, only that I had an interview that afternoon. Confused, my mother spoke through a fog, "But you already have a good job, Lela. Why would you want another?"

Only then did it strike me that what I'd done may not have been smart. I would never tell my parents that I walked out, I decided, and would hide from them until I had my shit together and made *more* money than before. For the time being, I'd have to lie.

"Because I'm always in the market for a *better* job, Mom. All the awards I'm winning? All the new clients signing on?" She hummed an affirmative answer. "More awards and more clients equal more money and *more power*. I've got to hear what the new dude has to offer. Think about it... he called *me!*"

"But do you just... walk out of work to go to the interview?"

Think fast, Lela. "Oh, I'll just tell them I have a doctor's appointment." *One lie begets another.*

"Lela! It's not good to lie to your employer."

Not good to lie to your mother, either. "Mom, if Barry Sturbridge knew where I was going, he'd race to give me a raise before I walked out of the door."

That would've been a good tactic. Too late now.

"Oh, dear! I just don't understand your lack of loyalty."

"Mom, your generation has a crazy idea of employment loyalty. Barry Sturbridge isn't any more dedicated to me as I am to him. And, the deal is, Sturbridge is lucky to have *me*, not the other way around." *Yeah... keep thinking that way and you'll have a job in a heartbeat.*

"Lela, keep thinking that way and you'll *never* have a job. Try a little humility and appreciation."

After reviewing my résumé and portfolio and asking a few short questions, Bob Clevenger welcomed me as the Creative Director of Clevenger and Associates. "You can name your salary if you can sink a putt," he said, "A hole-in-one." He cocked his head toward a stupid office putting green in the corner. From the side of his mouth, he said, "Women can't do it."

Challenged, I chose a putter from a brass umbrella stand. As I lined up, shifting my weight right and left, the sonofabitch sneaked up behind me, reached under my skirt, and grabbed my ass. My instant reaction: I snapped in a 180-degree turn, putter extended at shoulder height; I smacked the hell out of him – busted his left ear with the stem of the putter. The wienie-ass groaned, cupping his ear. "You're fired!" he shouted.

"Fucking-A-right I'm fired, you sonofabitch!" I grabbed my portfolio from his desk and got the hell out of there.

Sexual assault lawsuits didn't exist at the time, certainly not for regular people like Lela Fox. Furious – at him and at myself – I intermittently screamed obscenities to the clouds on the way to the parking lot. I felt stupid; it was my fault. Like an idiot, I had left myself vulnerable, so of course he took advantage.

He's a sonofabitch but you're a dumbass! Because this skirt is too short... and you know these heels are too high! They make your legs look good... and you did that part on purpose! Fuck! Why did you wear this, Lela? Why? I felt hopeless, filled with shame and explosive anger. I had a special knack for doing feeling this way.

Bob Clevenger had a long-standing reputation for being an asshole but I never imagined I would become his victim. Humiliation and rage bubbled from my fragile ego, threatening to send me in a nosedive mood-wise, but it was the nosedive that saved me. The mania leveled out over the next few days as did the illusions of grandeur. In the long run, the degradation of sexual assault jerked me back to "normal" and brought a rare phenomenon: the ability to control myself and my actions.

I think the next twelve years would have been significantly different without Bob Clevenger's hands on my ass.

The first depressed day in bed, I concocted a plan to kill myself. The second day, I concocted a plan to kill Bob Clevenger. On the third day, I rose. It was time to pick up Bo for my days of motherhood and I pushed the pain down as far as I could.

I hadn't told Miller what happened. I knew he would want to avoid the outside conflict, believing the incident would change his spot in the tight community of the Rockville advertising world. Though he might "console me," he would encourage my shame to discourage me from telling anybody else.

Miller's focus would be on how our careers would be affected; somehow, his expected reaction didn't make me mad at him, maybe because I was ready to agree with all his reasons for keeping quiet. Besides, these days Miller wasn't the knight in shining armor type; defending my honor wasn't his style.

I sure as hell couldn't tell Mom what happened, no matter how much I needed her and her support. She wouldn't understand the slant of humor to it ("humor" for lack of a better word; that was the phrase in my head.) As far as the effect on my career... she would have no clue. And telling Daddy would be the first step in his murder conviction. Now *that* would affect my career big time!

So I kept my mouth shut; I told my friend Jilly but nobody else. Though I had two more interview appointments, I canceled them via messages with the appropriate receptionist. Interviews were too risky, I decided. Being alone in an advertising mogul's office was no longer exciting; it was dangerous.

There was only one agency in Rockville run by a woman. I called Kathy Craver to present myself as her next writer/creative director. "No budget, Lela," she said, "But I have a few projects that warrant your freelance fee."

No more interviews, I decided. Only freelance projects led by women. That's how my new advertising career began.

To set up my office, I lined the window-wall with Miller's old studio furniture. The main piece was an extra-long white laminate desk. Smooth and sleek, accompanied by bright-red file cabinets, and stern black accessories. To complete the L-shape, I added a round laminate conference table with folding red-metal chairs. It was on-trend at the time, austere and clean. Even though my office was in the living space of my apartment, it was nice enough for a client to visit, and many of them did.

The second day, I sat down to organize my notes of who had called and the projects they had offered. In total, it was an overwhelming number of leads. *Lucky or crazy?*

I found myself lost in thought and I panicked, suddenly feeling overwhelmed. *Wait – who called, who said what? Would that be with or without a layout? Who's the account exec? Was she the one that said call next week?* I thought I'd taken prolific notes but I soon doubted everything. *Maybe I hadn't talked to anybody at all.*

That's how the day ended. I made no phone calls, but organized myself and created a kick-ass office setup. That was plenty, I decided. Besides, it was five o'clock somewhere and Jilly was home. I grabbed the last three Budweiser cans, still in the grip of the six-pack's plastic rings, and walked two buildings down to my friend's apartment.

"Jilly, you're not going anywhere tonight. Let's just scoot up to my place and you can see my new office setup. Come on, *pretend* you care at least!" She waited until we'd downed all the beer, then agreed to go when I called to make sure Miller wasn't home.

I don't think she was pretending when she said, "Fantastic, Lela! You always wanted an office with a window, right? This is the ultimate!" I beamed with pride.

Only later did I find that the heat from the direct sun would send me running from the desk every afternoon. Scorching heat. Eventually, the sun melted a few things and fried my solar calculator and "VideoWriter" computer. In the winter, mornings were so cold I could hardly sit without double socks under high-top Sherpa slippers. The best-laid plans...

But I didn't know the downfalls yet; I loved my office setup and the arrangement of the creative trinkets that surrounded me. *You'll do your best work here, Lela. Here, you'll become famous.*

The next day, I woke with a vow to be more productive. At 8:01 AM, I called the marketing department of Connor Health, the largest hospital group in

Rockville. Turned out, I knew the woman who would be my contact, if I got the client. Alyson Harris was the beer pong lady who kicked ass on the patio of McHardy's Pub with the Hooligan gang. Hell, she was a drunk like me!

Over the next few months, I set up my client list exactly as I wanted and accepted only the projects that appealed to me. With plenty of freedom to say "no," I also had plenty of work to fill my time, easily forty hours a week... more if I wanted it, none when I demanded it. I dictated the deadlines, not the other way around. If my client couldn't work within my time frame... fuck 'em. Five minutes later, they'd call with a new timeframe.

Account execs seemed to appreciate my flippant approach and worked around my cocky attitude and inflated ego because "that's just the way Lela is." (I overheard a client say this to her coworker once.)

You'd think I'd be grateful for my success, and hopeful about the future... you'd think my pompous attitude meant I had a good opinion of myself, and the lifelong self-hate would abate with the calm of a stable home life. But, no. My self-worth was shit and probably why I walked around with my nose in the air. Pretense; I was good at it.

Because I could design my own schedule, I never planned a meeting late in the afternoon and began drinking before the workday was officially over. Not just sometimes, but *all* the time by then. And though I told no one, I worried about myself. I remember thinking the word "alcoholic" for the first time in a while, and it scared the shit out of me.

My gnawing thoughts brought a formal pledge that lasted more than five years, keeping me functional and financially sound, but more craziness was to come in my ping-pong life. More fun and sadness, more comedy and tragedy, more laughs and more tears.

I put my hand over my heart and stated the pledge out loud. "Forevermore, I pledge to never, ever, ever have a drink before four o'clock on a workday, so help me God."

I wrote it on a Post-it Note and tacked it to my desk.

☀ ☀ ☀ ☀ ☀

For the first time in my life, I earned more than I could spend, making almost twice what I did at Sturbridge. I arranged my own schedule. In fact, Miller would take Bo to daycare in the morning so I could get more billable hours in. They left, and I immediately arrived at work... in the dining room wearing my pajamas.

We all felt at home in a cute and cozy apartment. We were in love, had a picture-perfect family. *What more could I ask?* Then... even better! Miller got a kick-ass promotion, now Creative Director at Sturbridge. Two three-digit salaries in the same house.

I doubled up on contributions to my savings accounts and urged Miller to do the same, but he still refused to talk about money. In fact, he was so resistant to a discussion that I knew something bad was happening, or *would soon* happen.

No matter how tenderly I broached the subject of money or budgets or financial planning of any variety, Miller bucked. So I kept my head down and kept my worries to myself.

Everything will work out, Lela. Not to worry. Focus on the positives.

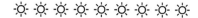

WEDDING PRETENSE
Chapter 19

We married on Weaver Farm in an ultra-creative, custom-designed wedding. The festivities flowed through various rooms and vestibules in a large A-frame cabin surrounded by three small cabins where the out-of-towners stayed. Views from the floor-to-ceiling windows were fabulous in November. Trees in all varieties of East Tennessee species brought every possible autumn color.

Drop-dead gorgeous, just as I planned.

For the actual wedding and dinner afterward, we invited only family and close friends. Then, the party folks would come later for the reception: hard-core dancing and drinking in the log-walled basement I had gussied up with autumn décor. The room was more than large enough to host our 100-or-so guests.

No bridal gown for me; I wore a sexy dress, of sorts. In contrast to the Chantilly-lace bodice, the skirt was metallic black, poufy and short, with a deep slit that showed quite a bit of leg. I carried a single red rose. The plan was for Bo, now in kindergarten, to walk me down the aisle of the A-frame's "library," in time with a jazz version of *Here Comes the Bride*.

As we stood at the mouth of the library's French doors, Bo's bottom lip quivered. "Mommy, I'm scared! I don't want to go!"

I had to think fast. "Let's pretend we're ice skating down this hallway-thing, going in slow motion with the music."

"Yeah, yeah, yeah!" He grabbed my hand, wanting to go first.

"But we'll skate side by side, okay?"

"Okay, Mommy."

We slid toward a fearful and angry-looking groom, standing beside the smiling Episcopal priest, my pal Smokey. His robe was silky and white. When I reached the halfway point skating the aisle with Bo, Smokey winked at me.

Bo would stay up front with us for the ceremony. He had the ring in the breast pocket of his little-kid navy sports coat. My hell-raising friend Jilly Jameson served as Maid of Honor; no bridesmaids.

Episcopalians kneel several times in a wedding service. In my planning, I'd tried to rent a snazzy kneeling bench but there was no such thing. Miller and I had talked about it but he knew I didn't really consider myself an Episcopal. "You just know Smokey kept you away from a murderer."

Beyond that snarky comment, his input on the rented bench was zero. Or so I thought. Miller had a plan to make the kneeling more interesting. When he mentioned it, I thought he was joking so I blew it off. Turns out, he was serious.

The first kneeling prayer was early in the service, and tittering laughter from the audience confused me until I remembered my fiancé's silly threat. *Oh, no! He really did it!* I snapped a look at him and he smiled. Yep, he had written, "Hey Y'all" across the bottom of his shoes with a Sharpie. In response, the small crowd laughed, especially Karen and Daddy. But I later learned my mother shrank, mortified and embarrassed in front of her sister, Aunt Jolene. I knew the whole creative-wedding thing didn't agree with her... she believed weddings should be solemn, held in a church with a reception serving only white cake and fruit punch in glass cups with saucers.

Her conservative, restrictive rules doubled for second marriages as if there was something shameful in it. While I had let her dictate every detail of my first wedding, I decided this would be the opposite. After all, Miller and I were paying the tab with a few key exceptions.

The invitation we created won a regional Addy award, a fold-over card with a front cover featuring a fuzzy-focus photo of a garter and two champagne flutes. The caption read "Join us on our Wedding Night." Suggestive, maybe, but classy. That, too, offended my Goody-Two-Shoes mother, and she asked me to print just one "proper" invitation for her sister.

While Mom was uptight about the wedding she called "deviant," Daddy and his appreciation for creativity loved it. He made a point to compliment me. Paraphrasing, Daddy said it had been the most fun and most meaningful wedding he'd ever seen. Aaah... my sweet father.

Before dinner, I dashed to set up the bedroom where we would spend the night and readied myself for pictures. My mom and sisters gathered around for a toast. I dared not tell anyone why I was upset; shame shrouded me.

Bo jumped on the bed with his older cousin Lizzie. They jumped and chanted in time with their leaps. Sweating, Karen took off her blouse to sit in front of the fan, wearing just her bra. Bo changed his tune. He now sang, "I see boobs! I see boobs!"

I glossed, powdered, and preened before going out for pictures.

"You look like a princess," my mom said, pressing her hands on my checks and kissing me on the nose.

"Thanks, Mom. That means a lot."

Both of my sisters squashed against me and tittered similar compliments. Jennifer said, "You may have hit the mark this time, Lela. That man will be a good father to Bo." I mumbled agreement but wondered if he would also be a good husband to *me. Yeah, what about ME? Don't you guys see what's happening? Isn't it screamingly obvious, especially today? Help! What have I done?*

Miller came in from the weathered deck when I arrived in the center court. It had been twenty minutes since being officially married. We had gone separate ways immediately after the ceremony, with no kiss. He gave Bo a high-five, but nothing for me. The guys whisked him outside to smoke a cigar or do whatever men do. I felt left out as if he didn't think being married was a "couple thing."

Miller and I were independent people with our own identities and successful careers, but this was our damn wedding day! He should focus on me, the bride. *His* bride.

"You happy, honey?" I asked, praying for a loving answer.

"As a clam," was his response. He flashed a sincere smile. "We're married, you and me, babe." He wrapped his arms around me for a full-frontal, eyes-open kiss. *Ah! The loving Miller is in there somewhere.*

By this time in my life, I had become an expert at convincing myself I was happier than I really was and more stable than I felt. As a lifelong expert at pretending all was well despite the chaos, I could also ignore his mother's odd behavior and act as if this wedding was exactly what I wanted it to be.

Pretense was my specialty, especially on my wedding days so far.

I remembered having the same feeling when I walked out of the sanctuary when marrying Andy. *Another one, Lela? Really? What the hell are you going to do now?* Catching myself thinking these self-critical thoughts, I knew what I would do... the same thing I'd done with Andy: Fake it, but this time with Miller.

Don't get me wrong... there were plenty of joyous things in our relationship. We camped, we traveled, and we loved baseball. Both of us worshipped Tennessee football and fought the crowds at the stadium every Saturday in season.

Not only that, our combined talents made kick-ass advertising. We won a plethora of awards and the creative community still considered us King and Queen. Together, we volunteered at the Boys and Girls Club. (I taught crafts to the girls, and Miller coached sports with the boys.) But most of all, we made picture-perfect parents to my son. We built our relationship on Bo.

I needed Miller to make my son's life whole. He taught Bo to play sports, mostly baseball, something I could never have done on my own. We made a happy family, and I celebrated that.

Bo's smile was full-face wide. He shouted, "Say cheese!" just before the photographer snapped each picture, appointing himself the signal-giver. The photographer was a friend of ours and played good-buddy with Bo. He told him a joke that Bo still tells, all these years later.

The photographer teased him. "Hey Bo, when I take pictures of cheese, you know what I tell them to say?"

"Pictures of *cheese?*" Giggles. "What do you say?"

"I say, 'Listen up, cheese... say people!'"

There were pictures of Bo laughing with his head back and slapping his knee in response to that silly joke. Nothing like a happy kid to make a parent smile.

☼ ☼ ☼ ☼ ☼

Wedding pictures showed incredible fall colors in the background of the posed shots and an odd mix of guests at dinner. When we entered (the last to arrive), all the people I loved raised a glass to us. "Here's to a happy marriage!" they said in unison.

The only problem was Miller's mother. She wore a gaudy, electric-blue dress that sparkled, and over-did it with flashy jewelry and thick eyeliner drawn to make a diamond point on the outer corner of her eyes. Flat-out frightening. I had told everyone the dress was "semi-formal," yet she was outfitted for a royal wedding. Beyond her typical odd-bird personality, which was enough to make me uncomfortable, her nerves this evening added to my own anxiety.

I saw Miller stiffen when his mother squealed at our arrival. Not exactly estranged, they weren't close and rarely spoke. She was just too weird for Miller to accept. That night, the more he ignored her, the louder her pleas for attention grew.

Miller looked mortified, reluctant to acknowledge her presence. He averted his eyes as much as possible, embarrassed. Obviously, she had thwarted his entire bearing; he grunted in one-word answers and became "Mr. Zero-Personality" again. *Please! Not on our wedding day! Dammit, Miller!*

The party guests began to arrive around seven o'clock. Almost eighty friends gathered as champagne corks popped and glasses clinked. The traditional first dance was far from traditional, but instead, a family affair. I held Bo on my hip and, together, we danced with Miller.

☀ ☀ ☀ ☀ ☀

The next day, we dropped Bo off at his dad's and took a pile of gifts home to our underground apartment. The rest of the weekend was for sleeping and making love. Miller was a voracious and sweaty lover; we joked that we had sex under the canopy of a rainforest.

Wait, listen! There's that sound again. It was the fourth time I heard a dull thud coming from the ceiling. *It must be the upstairs neighbor, stomping on the floor. You'd think being underground would muffle sounds, but maybe not.*

"Do you think the neighbor is hearing us having sex or something?" I asked.

"Naw... don't worry about it. We're not that loud, surely. I mean, have we ever awakened Bo or anything?"

"No, but–"

"Chill out, Lela. Our secrets don't float to the upper floor."

"I'll just try to find a pattern. Sometimes there are stomps or whatever when we're *not* making love. What's up with *that?*"

Sex had been a constant with us, sometimes kinky and sometimes straight with slow and sincere loving care. I teased Miller, "We go both ways." The week after our wedding was a sex-fest, loud, long, sexy, and several times a day.

A few days into the week following our wedding, the apartment manager called. "Uh... Lela?"

"Barbara? Yes! What's up?"

"I need a face-to-face with you."

What the hell? "Well, Barbara, I'm officially on my honeymoon, so I'm not–"

"Well, that may explain it. Your honeymoon..."

"What are you talking about?" My brow was knotted in confusion.

"Well, your upstairs neighbor has called to complain about some loud noises in the bedroom."

"Oh. Shit."

"Yeah. Screaming, she said."

"Oh hell, I'm embarrassed. So so so embarrassed."

"I trust you'll take care of it, right?"

I didn't answer but hung up and fast.

SAME ZIP, SAME PIZAZZ
Chapter 20

The underground apartment began to close in on me. My office was too hot, even after I moved the desk from the window wall to the interior wall. I fried like a chicken leg from eleven AM throughout the afternoon. I needed a more comfortable place... a larger place to spread out my multiple projects... and room to add an assistant's desk.

The rent was going up with the next lease; the traffic had doubled with a construction project on a nearby thoroughfare; Bo's friend had moved out; the storage space outside was full. It was time to move, I decided, though Miller disagreed. My response to his grumbling wasn't nice. Pissed, I screamed, "You just don't want to have to deal with it... that's why you want to stay."

"Guilty as charged."

"Again, why can't we *buy a house*, dammit? We're both making tons of money!"

"*Again!* I don't want to talk about it! How many times do I have to tell you that, Lela? Go away, you nag."

"But rent is like throwing our money away, honey. We can *afford* a house... a nice house. All it take is to just work with me on a simple money management plan."

"Forget it, Lela. Mind your own business."

I paced, huffed, sighed, but Miller said nothing more. Reading the fucking newspaper again, like he always did... reading the paper and watching sports on TV. I tried to think logically, move forward with the issue at hand. "Then I'm looking for a rental *house*. No more apartments... too small and too many rednecks. I want a neighborhood, a nice one."

"I don't really give a shit. Just leave me out of it."

"No! You will be involved in all aspects. I demand it!"

"You *demand* it? Who the hell do you think you are?"

"I'm your *wife,* dammit! Your partner, the mother of your best friend, you Fuckwad! All three of us will live there and all three of us will be involved in choosing where we live. And yes, I demand it. Understand?"

No reply meant agreement, I thought. I didn't bring it up again but made him add appointments to his day planner. "Miller, we're scheduled to see a house out west on Thursday night. Seven o'clock. I'll meet you there. I was convinced he'd change his tune and get excited about a new start, but he simply grumbled agreement to everything I decided.

What an asshole. But I got it done; I got what I wanted.

It was a Monday when we toured the rancher in Westford Hills. The owner gave us the tour, stepping away to give us privacy for a discussion. "This is the best I've seen, Miller. And the landlord! Not a slum-lord like some I've met. He's a county commissioner, you know."

"Whatever you think, dear."

"Well, he's here personally and seems to care about the house. And with the interrogation he's given *us,* he also cares about the quality of tenants."

"Seems that way."

"It's in perfect shape. New carpet, a new stove... and a free washer and dryer."

"Yeah..."

"Fuck you, Miller. Have an opinion, would you? Grow a pair and speak up."

"Up."

"Fuck you."

Neat as a pin, our Westford Hills home was on a level lot in the curve of a quiet street. Two extra feet in the one-car garage for a mini-workshop, a full bedroom for my office and, at last, privacy. The backyard was at the edge of the woods, a perfect playground for a seven-year-old boy.

The back deck was as long as the house, accommodating an eight-chair outdoor dining set with room to spare. The fireplace was a bonus; Bo loved to carry the logs from the deck to the hearth. He said, "It's my job and I do it good."

I called Mom to tell her we were in and give her our new phone number. There was no such thing as transferring a phone number in those days; if you moved, you had to change your number. It was a pain in the ass and risky for my business.

"Miller, you know I'll lose customers because of the phone number change. I'm going to do a mailer. Can you design it for me?"

"Certainly, dear. Let's shoot for another Addy between us."

"Sure. I call a meeting in fifteen minutes."

"No. I'm playing golf."

"Today? We just moved in! I need your help!"

"But... it's the weekend. And you know that's when I play."

"*Every* weekend, Miller? Even a weekend when I need you so bad? I can't do this all by myself."

"But you packed it all by yourself."

"*Exactly.* Jesezus! Participate, huh?"

"Don't be a bitch. I'll be back before dark."

"Asshole."

"You can wait to unpack, can't you?"

"You know I can't, Shithead. Things must be in order for me."

"Then you're on your own, Lela. I've made plans already. What can I say?"

The pressure between my ears thudded with the beat of an angry drum. I burned with rage, clenching my jaw and my fists, feeling the top of my head ready to blow. After lighting the first cigarette in the new house, I threw the lighter across the room and blew a long stream of smoke. "Well, dammit... I was going to ask you to vacuum the apartment because I have to drop off the keys first thing in the morning."

"No can do."

"You always leave when I need you most."

"Quit whining. Grow a pair."

I couldn't afford to let clients lose the ability to contact me. Phone calls announcing the phone and address change would have sufficed, but I decided to make it a big-deal official campaign, sending an oversized postcard to clients, potential clients, and vendors. The headline: "Same Zip, Same Pizazz." Clever, I thought, because only my zip code was the same; everything else had changed. My name (now McKeown), my phone number, and street address indicated a move up in life circumstances; at least that's what I hoped they'd think.

The mail campaign worked. Four more clients signed on the week the postcards hit.

Miller was also increasing his authority within Sturbridge Advertising as Barry landed client after client; their growth plan was going gang-busters. The copywriter who replaced me used perfect punctuation and proper English (always bad for an advertising writer), and was "minimally talented," according to Miller. I had to admit it made me feel sneaky-good inside.

We sat at the new dining table; we'd split the cost of a massive table in Scandinavian-modern design, with eight sleek chairs. Miller usually sat across the table from me when he got home from work, and what time he got home would always be a mystery. He worked scads of overtime. Most perfectionists do; so do those who have doubts about their abilities, and those who have something to hide.

After the "how was your day, blah blah blah" pleasantries, I opened the subject I hoped wouldn't send Miller into orbit. It was time for a discussion. Past time. "With a higher rent payment, honey... and more expenses altogether now, we need to finally bring our money together and create a joint account."

"You know I'm not really cool with that."

"I still don't understand why you're so secretive about the money thing, Miller. Aren't we supposed to be equal partners? Partners don't zip their lips about the important things."

"But Lela, it's been working so far... just splitting the expenses."

"But now I'm making more money, too, Miller. Lots more, and so are you. I want to put our money together to save for a down payment on a house. Long term, rentals are for losers, right? It's time we moved up. We've earned our place in life. We can afford a house."

"Uh... maybe so, maybe not."

"But I've done some research. We *can* afford it."

"Well, still... maybe not."

I ignored his continued resistance. "And combining our savings earns more interest. The more we save, the sooner we can start a family, too."

"A family... another sore subject, Lela. Are you trying to ruin the *whole* night?"

A long, frustrated sigh burst from my lips. "If you didn't have such a secret, it would be a normal husband-and-wife discussion. So spit it out. Tell me the secret. It's time, babe. When do I get a baby and when do I get a house?"

Miller took off his glasses and squeezed the bridge of his nose. "It has to do with the cocaine."

We hadn't talked about his former cocaine habit in many moons... mostly because I had failed to abstain as he had. To talk about it would be to admit my own weakness. "But... that was months ago, Miller. Guessing you haven't had any coke in over a year now, right?"

"Fourteen months, eight days."

"Oh. You keep such close track. I guess that's good. But... what does that have to do with buying a house and having a baby?"

"Mostly buying a house. Requires a credit rating."

"Huh?"

This time the angry sigh belonged to Miller. "Dammit, Lela. You're going to make me *say* it?"

"I can't read your mind! What the hell is it?"

"Okay..." His deep breath in through his nose seemed to take a full day; the breath coming out of his mouth smelled of scotch. "Okay, my business went belly-up, but I didn't declare bankruptcy. I still owe a shitload of money to a shitload of people."

"Whaaaa?" My voice was two or three octaves higher than usual.

"In debt up to my ass. Printers and photographers, a bunch of vendors who won't forgive the balance... plus Visa, American Express..."

"Credit cards?"

"The first time I took you to dinner? At the Cellar?"

"Yeah... what about it?"

"Zoomed me over the limit on the Visa. So they cut me off. I'm making minimum payments and getting nowhere."

"I thought you were doing great with money, Miller! You make the big bucks! And you certainly spend it like you're loaded... out to dinner, all the golf Sundays, clothes, damn – this dining table! What have you done with your money? Why haven't you paid off debt first... recreation later? Like normal people do!

"I guess I'm not normal."

"What the fuck?"

"Sorry, Lela. Now you see why I didn't want to tell you."

"So your credit rating is in the tank?"

"No way anybody would approve me for a loan. Not even an easy loan at one of those rip-off places."

I didn't know I'd been crying until three drops hit my silky purple shirt. They had dripped off my chin. "Oh, God, Miller."

"Jeezus, Lela. Please don't cry. That pisses me off so bad. Don't you think I feel like shit already? I don't need you whining about it, too."

Though I had struggled, my mother had taught me the rules of money management. I had a budget and stayed within it. I was organized, thrifty, and thought only tacky losers were irresponsible with money. How could Miller fit in that category? A mass of emotions passed through me. Fury, concern, embarrassment. Then, determination. *By God, I can fix this! I'll be the one.*

After a few more vodka-tonics, I dared to broach the subject again. "I have an idea, Miller, if you'll let me be in charge."

"No."

"No? No discussion, just 'no'?"

"I'm not letting you dictate how I spend my money. Maybe it's a man thing, but I know your nickel and dime attitude and I won't do that. Ever."

"I can help you pay off the debt if you'll let me. If you tell me the totals of who you owe and how much."

"Ha, ha, Lela. That's not going to happen."

"What? You're telling me I can't pay it off?"

"You? *You* paying it off?"

"That's what I was thinking. You pay all the bills and I spend all my earnings to pay your debt. Can you afford to pay all the bills?"

"I have no idea."

"Then we need to talk."

"No."

"Another 'no' with no discussion or explanation."

"Get off my back, Lela."

I thought about it, pissed and feeling ashamed. "No. I won't get off your back. Because your debt is now my debt. Your credit rating affects *my* goals, *my* future, the very center of *my life* and I won't let you keep *me* down. Your secret is out... now let me fix it."

More clipped comments from Miller, more misunderstanding of my goal to "save him from himself," and, from him, more requests to shut my trap. But I wouldn't let it go. I quit asking and started telling.

"Here's the deal. Take this notepad. Write your creditors names on it, line by line. Can you do that?"

"I don't want to, Lela. It's like facing my failure, looking it right in the eye."

"You only have to do it once because I'm taking it off your plate. I'm going to pay your debt. Write it all down. Get me one statement or some way to contact each of them. All my money goes to the debt and I bet I can have it all paid off in a flash."

Miller blew a doubtful *hmmph*. "Not in a flash, Lela, more like a decade."

"Well, how much is it?"

"I don't even know."

"You don't *know?* How could you let it be so out of control?"

"Just shut up and do it. Never mention it again."

I did rescue Miller, paid off his debt (nearly $50,000, which was exorbitant at the time). He would have been much better off declaring bankruptcy, but he was too proud.

Either way, I felt it was my responsibility to bail him out. He was, after all, my husband, and I had vowed to take the good with the bad. For richer or poorer, right?

I didn't see the red flag of his refusal to discuss money with me, or maybe I just didn't want to see it. I avoided conflict with Miller, hoping to keep the off-putting "Mr. Miserable" at bay. His anger made me nervous.

And his anger made me sad. I knew the marriage wasn't strong. I knew he shut me out of his life in almost every way, refused to go 50/50 emotionally, and refused to take the slightest responsibility for the house and our lives.

While I had demanded the sole responsibility in my marriage to Andy,

I yearned for a partnership with Miller. But it seemed the more I pushed, the more he pulled away.

Our shared joy was Bo, and that part of the relationship was 100 percent awesome. He was a caring and giving father, teaching Bo about "guy things," as they called them. More and more, they partnered as one and left me as the disciplinarian, the bad guy.

I thought of keeping a notebook of red flags going on in the marriage but decided it would be too depressing. On the outside, it was the ideal marriage; we were an example to many.

Things would look up soon, I believed. Maybe I wasn't getting what I wanted personally, but I thrived in the family atmosphere we had created, pretending it was enough.

The power lay in Bo's happiness. If he was happy, I was happy. So I endured, pushing through fears and keeping the shame and disappointment to myself.

DEAR LELA
Chapter 21

We spent almost two years in the Weston Drive house, living through a series of dramas and traumas, some created by our own stupidity, some brought on by others, and some caused by plain ol' bad luck.

Bo had a bike wreck, a chin-into-the-curb crash that required plastic surgery to repair his chewed-up face. The day of the wreck, I fumbled with the phone before the call went through. "Miller, hurry! Meet us at Westpark Hospital. Bo had a *bad* bicycle accident."

They didn't put Bo to sleep to sew three layers of stitches in his chin and let us hold his hands in the procedure room. The suddenly white-faced Miller had to sit down before he fainted. All the medical people laughed about it, even the doctor himself, teasing about "the big brave man fainting." But Miller couldn't laugh with his head between his knees and his stomach swirling.

I whispered to Bo. "I'm with you, sweetheart. Everything's going to be okay." I was calm, collected, and emotionally strong throughout the procedure and during his stint in the recovery area, purring assurances and telling silly jokes. But Miller, even in the recovery area, remained nauseated and quiet. By the time Bo was released, Miller was fine. That's when I collapsed in the lobby of the emergency room and cried for the following 24 hours at home.

The two banded together to tease me. "Mommy's afraid of invisible blood!" they joked and squealed in laughter. The jokes didn't stop my tears, nor did the vodka.

To this day, seeing Bo's scar makes me shake with nerves.

< < < < < < < > > > > > > >

Those years also put me face-to-face with nearly a hundred Sundays of being alone as Miller played golf with his buddies. At first, my comments were typically things like, "But... the family!" or "We need you!" and "Bo and I will miss you too much, Miller." My objections didn't change a thing; he played no matter the weather or circumstances. Once he played in the snow. Not only that, I discovered just how expensive golf could be and that twisted my spirit per our financial arrangement. Miller groaned about my attempts to discuss it, calling me "a nag" or a "controlling bitch."

Eventually, I gave up and found a way to take my Sundays to a new level. My attitude flipped like a fish out of water. On Bo weekends, we would travel the almost-two-hours to see my parents, who Bo called Nonnie and G-Daddy. Never exposing my alcoholism, I thought, nor the shame of our marital finances, I built a strong relationship with my parents during that time. I still wouldn't take their advice, but I listened without bitching them out.

On non-Bo weekends, I relished being without Miller so I could go to the lake with my friends, drink all day, and stay out late. If not on the lake, I was in a bar... playing the vixen, laughing inappropriately, pretending to be French or British, acting flat-out stupid. During that time, I got so drunk on vodka that I got kicked out of a bar. So I switched back to beer, and all was well for a while.

As I grew more and more disabled by alcoholism, I resented Miller's absence because I couldn't function well without him. Yet my anger would cause me to reject his help. Once I stumbled and slurred when demanding that he leave me alone. I said, "I don't need your input, Asshole. I can handle this myself!" and slid down the doorframe to the floor. Miller laughed; he hooted, in fact.

"Why are you laughing, dammit?"

"Because you said 'I *can't* handle this myself.'"

"See how much of an asshole you are! You can't even hear right!"

Yet Miller seldom challenged me about the amount I drank. And I never noticed that he drank almost as much as I did. Alcohol was innocuous in our life, not an issue. It had no bearing on my life, Miller's life, or our relationship. I actually believed that shit.

One vendor at a time, I paid all Miller's debts. Thanks to me, he was finally debt-free. Then I called all three credit agencies and demanded an update of his credit rating. Two months later, he was looking good on paper.

I felt no resentment, only relief and hope, and I was proud of myself for doing my "job" so efficiently. So now it was time to move forward, I thought. On the day I wrote the last check, we sat in the living room relaxing after work; I was at the top of the world, feeling free and optimistic. I said, "Okay, dear darlin'... it's time for the big talk!"

"Big talk? About what?"

"About becoming parents."

Miller huffed a sigh and smashed the sports section against his lap. "Lela, how is it that you have such a knack for choosing the wrong time for your fucking talks."

I felt shocked; I thought Miller was just as thrilled about our next adventure as I was. In the snottiest voice I could muster, trying to imitate his own, I asked, "Why is it the wrong time, Asswipe?" No response from the recliner. "I thought this would be a happy talk. You know your debt is paid, and if anything, I'd expect you to kiss my ass. I covered yours to the tune of more than fifty-thou."

"Yeah, I owe you for that. I really do."

"Is that a thank you?"

A ten-second stare at my exaggerated smile finally brought a smile to his face. Surprisingly, it was a genuine smile. "Yes, it's a thank you. Now what it is you want to say about babies?"

My fear disappeared and my mood instantly lightened, back to hopefulness. "I got pregnant easy with Bo the first month we tried, in fact, so it will probably be the same with another baby. Name your day 'cause I'm ready to go off the pill again. Tomorrow would be good for me."

"It's not quite time."

"What do you mean? We best not wait. Bo is getting older, almost too old to be a big brother. Not to mention that *my* biological clock is ticking, too."

"Let's talk about it later."

My stomach fell as an alarm bell rang in my head. "Okay, you say when later is."

"What?"

"When is later? Later tonight? Tomorrow night? Friday night? Saturday morning? I want an appointment time like 'later' is a date and time."

"Lela! Jeez..."

"I'm not putting this conversation off or letting you get out of it. I'm nailing you down, Miller McKeown. Miller-Daddy!"

"Oh, please stop."

"What? That upsets you?"

"Lela. Just accept 'later.' Later means 'some other time.'"

I paused. *Am I being pushy? It sounds like how you "talked" to Andy about having a family. It's not just your decision this time, Lela McKeown. It will be a joint decision, so chill out. Go slow.* "Okay... how about later this month?"

"That's good."

"So I'll wait... even though I feel like I'm getting dissed."

"You're not getting dissed. Relax. I'm reading the paper. You know I need time after coming home from work. Just... back off, okay?"

Breathe, Lela... in through your nose, out through your mouth. Again... again. Don't let him get to you. You're still important, still his wife, it all okay. Those thoughts argued with the others that screamed for his attention, his loving care, and the kindness that used to be his daily M.O. "No problem, hon. I'll back off."

"Good. So what's for dinner?"

Though I was on edge for the rest of the month, I said nothing to encourage having "the talk." I had started to believe he was putting me off, backing out of the promise he'd made when we married. But I was desperate for a child, desperate to the point of tears.

And why? Maybe it was that underneath, I knew it was the last thing I needed. The marriage wasn't stable – I knew that. But I was still stupid enough to think a baby would solve that, bringing us closer together instead.

By then, I was sure I was an alcoholic, which I why I wanted a baby so badly. The only other time in my life I didn't drink myself to oblivion on a daily basis was when I was pregnant and when Bo was a newborn.

I would use a baby to sober up. A smart, responsible woman like me would welcome such a sacrifice, right?

Three weeks after the first discussion. On a golf Sunday, Miller left a letter for me on the new dining table. "Awww... it's a love note!" I said. But it was definitely not a love note.

"Sorry if I've misled you, Lela, but I had a vasectomy six years ago. I never wanted children until Bo. And please don't start on the adoption thing. I'm not into that."

BATTER UP!

Chapter 22

It took two days before I could talk to Miller about the note. As I feared, he couldn't repeat the words, saying, "Why do you think it was a note? I can't *say* what a fuck-up I am. And I find it hard to apologize, even to you."

"But, Miller... you fucking *lied* to me. Lied to my *face!*"

"There's nothing I can do about it now, okay? So please don't make me feel worse." His voice was a plea, but he didn't ask to be forgiven. And I'm not sure I could've or would've forgiven him anyway. Within the week, when the initial hurt had subsided, the reality of not having another child hit me as a better idea. What drunk needs a baby? Doesn't a drunk end up neglecting a baby? Does a drunk even deserve a baby? Because a drunk is despicable, a loser, a bum, and eventually, a homeless drug-addicted scumbag in the gutter. Why would I want to take a baby into the gutter with me?

I'd have to make up a good lie for my family, who expected Miller and me to have another child, or at least that's what I'd told them. What if I just didn't say anything more about it? Can I get away with that?

The moment Miller walked through the door after work, I announced my news. "Husband! Wa-hoo! I did our taxes today and guess who made more than you did? Almost $10,000 more, in fact."

Miller emptied his pockets on the foyer table as he always did. "No shit?"

"No shit."

"That's great, Lela. I'm proud of you. Very proud. And if anybody deserves it, it's you."

"Ah! That's nice to hear. Thank you." *Wow. You best celebrate comments like that, Lela. "Cause you don't hear them often.*

"But remember that's the *gross* amount, Miller. I have expenses."

"Yeah, printer paper. Big deal. But no worries... you'll go down pretty soon."

"What?" I wrinkled my brow. "What do you mean? And where did that comment come from?"

"Vodka has become pretty important in your day, Lela. I think you're addicted to it."

I laughed. "Yep, it's important all right! But I don't drink at *work,* for God's sake!"

"You will."

"No, Miller, I won't. I have sense, and I'm not *addicted* to vodka, for God's sake. It's nothing like cocaine."

It was Miller's time to laugh. "Yeah, riiiight."

"Quit it! You're wrong and you're pissing me off."

"But it's just a matter of time, Lela. Trust me."

My stomach turned, but I didn't dare contradict him. I felt attacked and the worst part was I knew he was right. But I'd never admit *that* kind of truth. *Asshole. He doesn't know you, Lela, or how dedicated you are. He doesn't see your professional side. But why doesn't he see how good of a mother you are? He's not seeing the entire picture, so you're not in imminent danger of anything. You're cool. Addicted to vodka, my ass!*

Then a thought jarred me, clogging the pipes from my brain to my heart. *How can you be addicted to vodka when you also drink a lot of beer?*

I stood from the sofa and leaned far into his face. "Fuck you, by the way; I'm not cooking tonight. Call in a pizza or whatever. Goodnight."

After that night of accusation, I slowed down on my drinking. Maybe to prove Miller wrong, maybe to prove something to myself. I was hell-bent on being the kick-ass woman I had imagined I'd be.

Careful as hell, I purposely stopped at three drinks in the evening... though I made them doubles. The craving for the third drink made me shake, and I found the only way to fight it was to go to bed.

On weekends, I limited myself to a six-pack of beer during the day (but if Jilly or someone else offered me one, I justified taking it because it would be rude to refuse such a gift).

Though I'd paid all the debtors, Miller continued to pay all the household bills, and I socked my money away like Scrooge. I opened a special savings account for the sole purpose of building a down payment for a house, determined to save and save fast. I figured we wouldn't need much; it was a time when mortgage loans were easy to get.

Ten months later, the down payment money was there, and we bought a house in a neighborhood called Echo Valley – or as Bo called it, "Echo-Echo-Echo, Valley-Valley-Valley."

The backyard cinched the sale. It seemed in the cards... the perfectly level yard of smooth grass would be a baseball field. Impeccable dirt-spots in the center and at the mouth of its triangle shape. Bo had become adept at hitting thrown balls, with our fat dog Murphy always eager to waddle around fetching the balls and returning them to Miller, pitcher extraordinaire.

Though it was another way to leave when I needed him most, Miller offered to "get Bo out of my hair" on the afternoon of moving day and took him shopping for his first real-leather baseball glove. I took pictures of Bo that day and clearly remember the twinkle in his eye when looking so lovingly at that glove. He seemed so grown-up, much older than the sensitive almost-seven-year-old he was.

"And I want to sleep with it, Mommy. Then I'll be a great baseball player forever."

"Oh yeah? Then, of course! And–

"Miller says snoring on it will make me hit home runs." Bo's eyes still sparkled as he tucked the glove under his chin. His hand hadn't been outside of it since dinner. I bribed him to remove it long enough to eat the Happy Meal that Miller brought home.

So on our first night in the new house, he snuggled down with the glove, refusing the series of bedtime stories he usually demanded.

The next day, I made a pledge to spend more time with Bo... no matter how much I wanted to alphabetize the spices in a new-house cabinet. The first order of business was to explore the neighborhood, on an adventure to find kids around Bo's age. My crazy friend Jilly had given me a junkyard bicycle so

I could ride with Bo.

The handlebars were twisted somehow, and I had to hold them at a seventy-degree angle to go straight. This caused a shitload of laughs with the two of us as we pedaled the bottom street.

There we ran into two boys, one that looked seven, and the other maybe five. Not shy, the dark-haired older boy said to me, "Hi! I'm Bryce Thomas Everett Jones Junior. I have four names and a 'Junior' because I'm *important!*" Cracking up, I threw my head back and cackled. Bo circled back to our meeting point and, with surprising confidence, introduced himself.

"I just have three names, but I'm important, too!" His eyes were animated, excited to meet this new boy. The younger blonde boy, I assumed the brother of Four-Names, joined us. "Who are you?" Bo asked him with hopeful eyes.

The boy mumbled with his head down, looking painfully sad. "I'm Roy, but only my Momma thinks I'm important." I tried to smooth it over, saying he must surely be important to his dad and everybody else. He wasn't buying it. Suddenly, he snapped a look at his brother. "But Mom says I'm *precious. So there!*" He looked satisfied as only a young boy can. The expression screamed that he had successfully one-upped his brother.

"I have a loose tooth," Four-Names boasted, "See?" He wiggled his front tooth, and, yes, it swung easily. *Gross.* Without pause, he said, "Hey y'all, call me Bryce for short, so you don't have to say all my names."

Just then, a woman dressed in sweats and a t-shirt stepped on her front porch about two houses down and yelled "Bryce, Roy, dinner!" I waved and limped my bicycle toward the house. Her name was Debra, she said. A cute woman about my age, maybe older, with short hair in a wedge-cut, wire-frame glasses, and a genuine smile. We chatted for a few minutes and friendship was immediate. The two of us had much in common, beyond the age of our children, and we could have talked more, but it was dinnertime.

Debra and I exchanged phone numbers and vowed to let the kids play together anytime. She told me that Bryce would soon start in a little-kid baseball league and shared the contact information with me. Bo could join the league, too, she said, "Ages six and up."

"It will be exactly what he wants to do, Debra. Thanks. And he can be on the same team as Bryce?"

"It's early so I'd say so. Then we can do some carpooling. I don't have chauffer help and it's hard with two boys."

"Oh... sorry but I just assumed you were married."

"Sadly, I am. Let's just say he's not much of a family man."

I winced and her eyes glassed over with tears. My heart broke for her but I had no idea what to say. I stammered. "Well... see you around, Debra. And surely around the baseball field!"

On the way home, as Bo rode circles around my sideways bike, I asked him if he'd like to be on a baseball team. He stopped his bike and screamed, "Yes, yes, yes, yes, yes! Can I, Mom? Please? Please! Please!" He cocked an imaginary bat over his shoulder and swung. In a voice loud enough for the whole city to hear, he screamed, "I want to knock it out of the park!" I laughed at his exuberance.

"Bryce and Roy's mother gave me the number of the man in charge of the league. Maybe I can call him tonight."

"Tonight! Tonight! Tonight!" He kept up the chant for nearly twenty minutes. I had no choice but to pick up the phone. The boy was obsessed, and Miller's excitement nearly matched Bo's.

"It's an adult-pitched league, very casual," Vann said, "We have three spots left, and I'd love to have Bo join us."

"The same team as Bryce Jones, right?"

"Yes, ma'am. And baseball friends seem to stay close friends, lifelong friends sometimes." Bo sat at my feet while I was on the phone, jerking my pant leg up and down. I grabbed a scrap of paper and wrote the details Vann spouted. The pre-practice meeting was the following week, and I told him we would be there.

Miller said he knew Vann, the league director; they were both Sunday golfers. Surprisingly, on the day of the pre-practice meeting, Miller left the office early to join us at the field. It was a small field, bare of bathrooms. There wasn't a concession stand or a back fence, either. The entrance was down a steep hill from the boulevard in an upscale neighborhood, home of the famous Dogwood Trails. The streets were chock-full of big, fancy homes, flower gardens and flowering dogwoods... and a stone's throw from the park where my ex-divorce lawyer had tried to seduce me.

The other parents were better-dressed, higher-class, and snootier than we were, except for Debra Jones. *More reason for us to be friends.* I met her husband that afternoon, too. Paul, a homely man who staggered like a drunk and mumbled like a drunk. I supposed he *was* a drunk and my heart went out to Debra and the kids. Underneath, he disgusted me.

At the time, I could still stay sober when Bo was around, or most of the time, anyway... which I thought made me better than the low-life, full-time, sleazy-ass-drunk Paul Jones. I judged harshly.

Vann Carter opened the meeting and began by saying he had bad news. The coach had backed out. "Would any of you like to coach these fine young athletes?" Miller's hand popped up in an instant. I knew he had coached teenaged kids in his past, but it was shocking to see him willing to commit to something that would interfere with his work schedule.

Miller stood up. "My son is Bo, here... Bo Winston." He pointed, prompting Bo to jump up and run around the group. "I've coached kids before and know the mechanics of the game. So I'll just..." He pulled on his belt loop to straighten his pants. "I'll have to learn how little to expect from little kids. But my wife, Lela..." He stared at me as if encouraging me to raise my hand. I did. "Lela can help, and she'll make it fun for the boys from the touchy-feely side." *What the hell is he talking about?*

Vann spoke up. "This is awesome. Good deal, Indians, I know your coach Miller McKeown well. We play another kind of game together. With a white, dimpled ball."

I couldn't keep a loud hoot of a laugh inside. It sounded like a "Wahaaha!" Nobody else laughed. Looking around at the other parents, I said, "Get it? White, dimpled balls? A game?" Again, nobody laughed. It seemed like nobody breathed. "Okay, never mind... just my twisted sense of humor." I could feel the crimson of my face burning from jaw to forehead.

Though I knew he'd be glaring at me, I sneaked a look at Miller. Yep, his mouth was agape and his eyes penetrated mine like daggers. He stuttered in trying to explain, or at least I think that's what he was trying to do. Obviously, his tactic wasn't working because all that escaped his mouth was, "She is... but we can... maybe you will–"

Vann interrupted. "Golf. We both play golf." The parents nodded, along with a few of the boys. Without taking my eyes off Vann, I saw him wink at Miller. But the long pause remained.

Miller broke the silence. He squatted in front of the group. "Look at me, boys. Do you know what commitment is?" A few boys shouted pint-sized versions of the definition. "Right. It means you'll be here no matter what... all the practices, all the games. And you'll always play your best. That's commitment."

He extended his hand. "Stack of hands! Team Indians... commit to be your best." All the boys participated in the symbolic team ritual, with the ending shout, "Team!" I felt I was watching much older boys, men maybe. Thrilled with Miller's presentation and attitude, I beamed with pride. *This will be a fun spring. As long as he's not an asshole to the boys. Surely he won't be. Oh, God, I hope not. What would I do THEN?*

Vann shared my pleased smile, I noticed, then led the boys to the run-down shack that stored team equipment. Bo's face lit up like a 400-watt bulb when Vann handed him a maroon uniform shirt, Indians, number 45. The smallest available pants looked two sizes too big, but I reasoned I could alter them for temporary wear.

Vann and Miller talked for twenty minutes after the meeting ended and, during that time, Bo and Bryce played catch with the ball and gloves they had brought to the field. Though he whined about not having Murphy to run after the stragglers, I had never seen Bo so excited about something, even more excited than about seeing Santa Claus the past Christmas.

The ride home was a happy one with all three of us talking "we're gonna this" and "we're gonna that." Seeing Miller as animated as Bo sent me to the moon with happiness. Thoughts that the marriage may work better with this shared hobby filled my mind.

☼ ☼ ☼ ☼ ☼

Thanks to self-employment, it was easy to get Bo back and forth to practice. Miller met us at the field, just five miles away from his office. He often went back to the office while Bo and I went to Mickey D's or out with Debra and the boys.

The first practice was chaos, but the kids paid enough attention to garner Miller's instruction on the first lesson: batting stance. The older players swung and missed a few, but overall, our killer batters shined. Among the six-year-olds, Bryce was in the upper echelon, with Bo not far behind.

I scampered like a squirrel, carrying a clipboard, to meet with each parent. There was much to do and say; I gathered contact information, assigned snack days, etcetera. "Team Mom" wasn't a job for wienies, I realized, or at least not the way I was going to do it.

The only girl on the team, Lucinda, who shared a birthday with me, had a terrible batting stance and Miller worked with her one-on-one to correct it. No matter what he told her to do, she would switch back to the "wrong" posture when Miller wound up to pitch. He stopped a dozen times, finally giving up. Lucinda knocked the hell out of the ball. It sailed far into middle field. "Way to go, Lucinda, you did it just like I told you! Perfect!"

Her mother came to where I sat on top of the grassy hill. "Lela, you have no idea how much I appreciate what your husband just did. And please tell him I like what he's doing overall. He seems like the perfect coach."

"Why don't you tell him yourself, Anne? He'd like to hear it. There will be an after-practice meeting, for kids and parents, top of the hill."

"I'll tell him." And she did, making sure everybody heard it. In fact, she gave a mini-speech, singing praises of Miller and urging the group to do the same. A round of applause ensued. Bo didn't know why people were clapping, but stood and yelled, "Hooray for our side!" It was a line he learned from my dad, his G-Daddy, and it became our special team cheer.

On game day, though we needed to be at the field at two o'clock, Bo awoke early and donned his uniform before breakfast. His new glove hadn't left his hand since breakfast and, again, I had to physically pull it off for him to eat before the game. He checked his bat bag four times and was in the car waiting alone for fifteen minutes before we left.

I felt sorry for him; it's not in a child's nature to wait.

Miller had spent a fortune on bags, gloves, balls, caps, and bats for himself and Bo. He bought a scorebook and taught me how to keep it. During the games, I would sit in the dugout with the boys, keeping the book and trying to keep them calm and focused.

Debra met me going in. She brought a t-shirt: TEAM MOM on the front and GO INDIANS on the back. A touching gesture, I thought, and the kids loved it.

When I ran onto the field to take the new game ball to Vann, the pitcher, the Indians' parents cheered, shouting "Hooty-hoot!" and "Hooray for our side!" We were a tight-knit bunch.

I left the field with a burn in my throat, hoarse after screaming all those cheers and shouting instruction to the boys over the noise.

The Indians won the game 15–10. Bo made it to first base on his third at-bat. He concentrated so hard; I could see those seven-year-old wheels turning, waiting for the perfect time to run to second base.

The vision of his snaggle-tooth grin from third base brought a cheer from the dugout. As he crossed home plate, Miller picked him up and threw him in the air, joyous.

Miller's after-game pep talk to the team was on-target, praising the good and mentioning the bad only to say they would work on those things next week. Bo marched to the car with his glove held high, beaming with happiness, happy and filthy like all little boys should be.

I was proud of Miller and of Bo. A gleeful Team Mom drove the van home as we sang the victory song.

Seeing Miller as such a strong advocate for the players, successfully playing a maximum-support coach and mentor roused new hope in me. Hope for us as a couple, and us as a family.

Maybe he *was* a kind man in his inner soul... maybe we can live the dream most folks think we're living already.

Seeing Miller in such a giving mode, humble and honest, moved me. My first thought was "He's acting like my Daddy," and it instantly erased dozens of resentments I held against Miller.

Long-held resentments began to fade away. Of course, it didn't take much for me to push the reset button; I hungered for a fairy tale and hung my hat on the man and the marriage I'd dreamed we'd have.

But, alas, Miller was a moody and two-faced man, nice as hell to boys and their uppity parents on Saturday afternoon, then an asshole to me on Saturday night. At times, he'd be kind and humble for seven days in a row... just enough time for me to relax, followed by a slam, a cruel joke that sliced to the core of my being.

I lived on his roller coaster, happy for the happy days and drunk on the bad days.

CUCKOO, ROLY-POLY & DODGE
Chapter 23

Stepchildren and dual-home kids have it rough on Christmas. It's nearly impossible to split the holiday for equal custody, but with Andy and I both in Rockville and my parents less than two hours away, we worked it out with a half-day split.

Seeing Miller's out-of-town family was another issue, especially because he didn't want to see them. Holidays were stressful for my poor husband because he'd run out of excuses to not make the trip.

The year Bo was eight, we spent an early Christmas with Miller's family near Atlanta. We traveled to his mom's on the twentieth of December to spend two days, then a day with his father, who lived in Marietta, just north of Atlanta.

As already established at our wedding, Miller's mother Lorraine was a genuine cuckoo bird. She flitted around screaming words not related to anything at all, had zero social skills, and the irritating hum of a helicopter-mother from hell. Her obvious anxiety pulsed tension throughout her tiny house; you could feel the walls bulging out and sucking in, timed to her breath. And it seemed she enjoyed re-hashing details of Miller's childhood, vomiting guilt-trip-worthy comments... like when he killed a bird with a surprisingly well-thrown baseball.

To say it was difficult to visit her was a grave understatement.

When we arrived, she ran out to the car in her pajamas, saying, "I never get to see you!" *Why would she say that when we're here? Sorry, but you can't guilt-trip me, you crazy bitch.*

She squirmed around on the sofa as I opened the Christmas gift she had chosen for me. "Oh, Lela, I hope you like it! I know Miller will!"

Pulling back the tissue paper, my eyes flew wide and I prayed to sink into the floor. A feather "whip," lacy, red crotchless panties, and a squirt can of Redi-Whip. Shocking and inappropriate, even for her!

Miller reddened, darker than the red of my new panties. Bo was clueless about everything but the Redi-Whip, which suited me fine. I squirted a dose on his arm. He asked, "But why do you get this for *Christmas?* All wrapped up and stuff?" I had no answer, only the buzz of embarrassment humming in both ears. It seemed loud enough to fill her minuscule living room, now made smaller with a six-foot plastic tree and ornaments in the hundreds.

Miller turned stone-faced, silent, and sullen. Mr. Miserable, but this time I understood. For icing on the cake, his mom gave him an impersonal Walmart gift card, and for Bo... an adult blow-dart gun. The rule was "no violent toys" at our house, and further, the gift was far beyond his age group. *How could she think this is okay?*

At least Miller's brother Chad was normal, and he didn't react to her inappropriate gifts or anybody's reactions to them, placating the crazy woman on the sofa. I saw a look pass between the brothers that showed equal disdain for their mother's craziness.

I felt sorry for the guys; my whole life, the only issue with *my* mother had been her extreme Southern-Lady morals. She considered ninety-percent of things people did as "inappropriate" and spent most of her days embarrassed because Daddy had been "too friendly" or made some other horrendous mistake.

So the evening with Crazy Lorraine was foreign and disconcerting to me. Bo didn't know what was going on, I think, but he obviously felt the tension and jumped around like a monkey, bellowing dinosaur calls and vying for all the attention he could get. Acting like a rotten kid in general, he created even more tension.

I escaped the craziness by taking a shower in her miniature bathroom. Dressed and back in the living room, Lorraine shouted at me, "Dinner in twenty! And don't you dare come to the kitchen, Lela! I don't need any help." Though relieved, I didn't know how to respond. *Thanks? Hallelujah? You're damn right I'm not coming in there!*

☼ ☼ ☼ ☼ ☼

After spending two horrific nights and gulping down a quick breakfast, it was – thank God – time to go. Lorraine started her famous whining. "Can't you please stay a little longer? I am so lonely at Christmas. I have nobody but you guys." Whine, whine, whine. Her bottom lip stuck out a full inch, pouting like a child.

As we backed out of the driveway, she hung onto the driver's side mirror, crying and begging us to stay. Her mascara and hideous eyeliner streamed down her face in a river of tears. Like a pitiful child, she put her hands under her chin and pleaded, "Please stay... I beg you."

Miller backed out of the driveway, taking advantage of his mother's momentary release of the mirror. From the main street, he shouted, "I'll call ya, Mom," and gunned the engine.

☼ ☼ ☼ ☼ ☼

The half-hour trip to Marietta wasn't enough time to ease Miller's anger and upset, so we drove around a bit. He was furious and needed to vent. But, of course, he did it silently. As usual, Miller didn't allow me in his emotional life, especially if he needed to share bad stuff.

I should've talked about the weather or anything except his family, but I grumbled about how his mother had complained about our next destination. She discouraged Miller from seeing his father, or "the bald-headed asshole," as she called him.

I said, "Miller, is it just me or don't you think she should be over the divorce after 22 damn years?"

"She holds grudges like life preservers."

"Did she... uh." I feared the answer wouldn't be what I wanted to hear; I hesitated but persisted. "Did she teach you to do the same? I never know how you feel about those who wronged you. I know of a few already and I've never heard you mention them at all."

"They become non-people to me."

"Non-people. That sounds scary."

"My brand of revenge is none of your business," he said, turning left into his dad's driveway. *Great. None of my business. And said when it can't be discussed, like the beginning of a fight we can't have. What an asshole! And, of course, I need him right now! Doesn't he know his family makes ME just as nervous?!*

The long driveway included a signal that rang a bell indoors and the elder Mr. McKeown met us at the end. He boomed words of welcome, smiling ear to ear and distributing bear hugs to the three of us. Miller's father was a mammoth of a man, tall and solid behind his roly-poly wife of twenty years.

Without a prompt, they both bitched about Miller's mother, said they hated her "bitterly." Again, I thought this was juvenile. Their comments made me uncomfortable and I could see Miller squirming. Bo was obviously feeling the tension, too, because he held back instead of going crazy about the trampoline in their backyard.

Inside, his dad and stepmother began a tirade about Miller's former wives, telling tales that humiliated him and infuriated me. Another set of freak-a-zoids on the other side of Miller's family. *What does this say about him? A peek at what's to come? Certainly a look backward – growing up with these four would screw anybody up. Poor Miller.*

When we sat down for dinner, I remembered they were both diabetic, so the food was "healthy" but simple and without seasonings, the opposite of what we ate at home. Bo, with the good manners I'd taught him (truthfully, Ella was the best teacher), said nothing about the food. When Roly-Poly asked, he agreed to a cookie, and I didn't interfere.

"You had two good bites of broccoli, so you're okay, Bo-Bo," I said, "A cookie for you!"

Miller's stepsister had stayed silent through dinner until she suddenly boomed a comment to Bo. "Besides, it's Christmas! A boy needs a cookie. Two cookies!" Her name was Dodge, the late-in-life child of Miller's dad and Roly-Poly. She was roly-poly herself, almost six feet tall, with a neck the size of a rhino. Her short haircut and padded football jersey screamed that she was gay. Not a problem... until she started talking.

As Bo munched the Oreo, Dodge offered gory details of her girlfriend and their sexual relationship. Her parents didn't flinch, but I was appalled and so shocked I couldn't respond; I didn't even try to stop her.

Bo asked the girl pointed questions and her answers were just as "adult." *Don't these people know how to act around kids!*

"So you don't have a husband, just a girlfriend?" Bo asked.

"I don't *want* a husband. I'm gay, a woman who likes women. Never heard of a gay person?

I interrupted. "Dodge, he's just nine."

174

She snapped a look at me, daggers for eyes. "So? What does age have to do with it?"

I had no answer, didn't want to rock the boat because she scared the hell out of me. And to cross her would be rude to Miller's father, I thought. I looked away while she continued to glare at me and realized everyone had darted from the kitchen, dishes left undone. I watched their last steps from the screened porch to the backyard.

They mean to leave me alone with her; they must know something worse is coming. Determined to put a plug in it, I said in a friendly voice, "Dodge, hon, I'm thinking he's too young to hear this. It may confuse him, you know...?"

"No, I don't think so." Then she turned again to Bo. "See, kid, there are women who like men and they're called 'breeders.' Your mom is one. Then there are women who like women and they don't have kids. They usually have more fun and don't worry about life's bullshit. Get it?"

In her only pause for breath, I scrambled to interrupt. "Okay, Bo, let's go outside and–"

As if I had said nothing, Dodge continued, first touching Bo's chin to turn his head back to look at her directly. "And there are men who like men and men who like women. Same thing. Whatever it is, it's cool."

Bo didn't hesitate. "I have a friend, Bryce, and I like him.

"Then maybe you're gay."

I stood up and shouted, "Okaaaay! That's enough now, Dodge! I see your point but Bo doesn't. So stop. Now." My heart beat rat-a-tat, torn between protecting my young son and pissing off a woman twice my size.

She looked at me and sat back her chair, raised her glass to pass a cube of ice between her lips. As she chewed the ice greedily, she spoke to me. "Sure. No problem. Raise a homophobe. You'll be sorry. I should kick your ass, just for fun."

Silence.

Bo only heard "kick your ass," and jumped from his chair to, literally, kick Dodge's ass. "Oh, don't do that, Bo. Let's go jump on the trampoline, okay?" Thankfully, the mention distracted him. He snatched two more Oreos from the package and ran out the back door.

Not caring if I pissed anybody off, I had my say. "Don't you ever, *ever* speak to my son about your personal choices! Do you understand me, Dodge? You have no right."

"So you're a homophobe, too."

"Quite the opposite, in fact! Goodbye."

To my back, she shouted, "You're probably just playing the breeder 'cause your momma taught you. Come here and let me make you scream, make you a wet, horny bitch. Rub my clit, Lela. Suck on it, bitch!"

She shouted to my retreating figure until I slammed the screen-porch door behind me. I knew I'd have a hard time telling Miller what had happened... and how much I needed his help in keeping her at arm's length. So I breathed a relaxed sigh when Miller's dad pulled Bo aside for a game of whiffle ball.

I pulled my husband aside, still shaking with anger and... I guess it was fear. "Miller, it was awful! She told Bo he might be gay and, in the end, yelled at me to suck her clit! What should I do?"

A chuckle began deep in his belly, growing in volume as my eyes widened. "Why are you *laughing,* for God's sake? This is serious! For Bo and for me both! Help, honey, don't fucking laugh." I pled to him, feeling desperate, overwhelming, threatened... so many emotions.

"Lela, it's not the first time she's done this. Why do you think we all left? All you can do is ignore her."

"But how? She's a crazy-ass in my face! Help me!"

"I'll keep my eye on both of you, babe, but I can't exactly wrestle her to the ground. Who knows what she's capable of? She's crazy as a loon!"

Dusk came; we went inside only to find Dodge with her legs spread wide on the sofa, watching a TV police drama. She eyed me and placed her hand on her crotch. *Why doesn't somebody say something? Are you people blind? Are you going to let her be so cruel to me? Let her show her crotch to my son?* Dodge stayed past everybody's bedtime. Eventually, Roly-Poly asked her to leave.

The guest bed was too soft and the pillows too plump, so neither of us slept well. But Miller and his Dad had helped Bo build a fort in the *huge* Master bedroom closet. When the exuberant nine-year-old jumped in bed with us just after dawn, he said he slept "like a sock."

"I think you mean a rock."

"No, a sock. That's what Bryce said."

We all laughed though Bo didn't know why.

Anxious to get out of there and, as soon as the breakfast dishes were done, we piled into the Jetta and took off. Nobody hung onto the mirror or threw guilt trips like scalpels.

☼ ☼ ☼ ☼ ☼

As soon as we found the interstate ramp for the drive home, I summed up the past three days. "Well. That was a weekend I'll remember forever!" I said, trying to lighten the mood in the Jetta.

"That's why I don't visit my parents, Lela. Do you understand now?"

Before I could answer, Bo spoke with enthusiasm from the backseat. "I had fun in the tent! I like Mr. M!"

How cute! I asked, "Mr. M? Is that what he told you to call him?" Miller's dad was the only normal one of the bunch. The word "normal" was a stretch, but if I had to pick one, it would be him.

Miller's smile was wide. "He's an M-Three like me, Bo. Because I'm named after him. I'm Miller Michael McKeown the Third."

I huffed, "I never knew that! I've filled out legal papers for you without adding 'the Third' to your name! Why haven't you told me this gemstone about you after four years of marriage?"

"Need-to-know basis, I guess."

Though I rolled my eyes, I was pissed. "You're a sonofa–" I stopped, not wanting to cuss in front of Bo.

Bo finished the sentence. "You're a son of a M-Three!"

AUGIE HIGHFIELD
Chapter 24

I gashed the side of my van's interior while loading the pipe scrap. *Dammit! But... another business expense.* The pipe wasn't long; about five feet, but would have been six feet in diameter if I hadn't asked them to cut it in half length-wise. The pipe was heavy corrugated steel, used for under-the-road culverts.

I cussed as I struggled to get it in the van. My deadline for prop-gathering was that day, and I'd been lucky to have found it, especially for free. The pipe was for the next day's TV shoot I called "Baby City," a commercial promoting Connor Health's obstetrics expertise.

The set for Baby City would be a winding road of curvy-cut gray carpet with a line of dashes stenciled in the middle, suggesting two lanes. The half-culvert became a hump in the road. Then, a dozen-or-so babies would crawl on the road as the announcer talked about how a birth at Connor Health would put your baby on the road to a better life, blah, blah, blah.

I hired the town's best videographer/director, Augie Highfield. Tall and bald, with a mullet ponytail formed from the bottom fringe of hair, he looked like the consummate artist. And he *was* an artist. We had worked together a dozen times over the years and, together, had a reputation for doing the best local work.

Our relationship was one of mutual respect at the time of my life when being respected didn't make my skin crawl. Maybe I felt comfortable with Augie's respect because I no longer had Miller's... and now I *needed* to be held in esteem from others in the business.

Inside, I felt an ounce of self-esteem for perhaps the first time in my life. My meds and my moods were stable. The only problem was... well, you can probably guess.

The Lela/Augie relationship would later change dramatically, but for now, we made a powerful combination.

My intern came to the Baby City shoot to be a "baby wrangler," and I had hired four more. Each of them took armfuls of babies into the studio to crawl on the road, plucking them out when the baby cried. It was a crazy, exhausting three-hour stint but Augie had captured tons of good shots on 35mm film. (Long before digital media and much more expensive.)

As a joke, I brought vodka-tonics in baby bottles for the wrap party.

I raised my bottle. "Here's to a kick-ass baby shoot!" A dozen crew members toasted to good times and good work. "But no more babies for a while. Too loud. Next client I'm going for is a nursing home."

The sound man said, "Or a home for the deaf and mute." Laughter rippled as the next set of baby bottles came out of the fridge. More suggestions for the client list included the morgue, a library, a monastery, and a cemetery. We laughed and acted stupid; it was exactly what a wrap party should be.

For everybody else, the drinking ended at four o'clock and the party was over at five sharp, the end of the workday. But just before five, I'd dashed to the liquor store for a bottle of tequila and two shot glasses.

Augie Highfield and I drank tequila and more tequila, nearly emptying the bottle. By ten PM, we had run naked around the building, done some heavy petting on the sofa in the editing suite, and created ridiculous videos of ourselves in the studio.

Around midnight, I realized I hadn't called home. "Well, I guess he knows I'm running late," I said through a cackle of laughter.

"Will he call the police or anything?" Augie asked, suddenly concerned. His paranoia threatened to kill my buzz, but I was too far gone.

"No police, But he may call Jilly or my sister, looking for me."

"Call them. Say you're sick or something."

"Well, Augie, you don't quite understand. Our marriage isn't exactly what you'd call 'open,' but we don't necessarily report our whereabouts to each other. Not anymore. And since I found out he'd *lied* about wanting children, I don't see a reason to be a loyal doormat for Miller McKeown. But he's a good father for Bo, earns a good income, so whatever..." I danced a soft-shoe circle around Augie. "But his income is less than mine – ha ha ha ha."

"Good for you, big bucks."

I breathed a defeated sigh. "There's more to it, I guess. Miller's good for appearances' sake. There's not much more to it now. But the reality still makes me cry now and then."

"Damn, Lela. I had no idea."

"I don't tell many people. As you might imagine."

"Maybe you should, maybe... go to a therapist or something?"

"I see Dr. Vodka on a regular basis. Best therapy there is."

"Unless Dr. Tequila is on call!" Augie poured two shots and raised his glass. "To therapy!" I nodded and threw the tequila to the back of my throat.

"So where does your wife think you are?" I asked.

"I told her I'd be working all night. It happens often, so she's not alarmed." It was Augie's turn to sigh. "And I've got a secret for you. About me. Maybe the opposite of yours."

"Do tell."

"Before Connie and I got married... only four years ago, right?"

"Right. It was a damn good party, Augie. Your wedding, I mean."

"Yeah-yeah." He brushed the comment away like a pesky bug. "Anyway. I made it clear that I didn't want any more children. I mean... my oldest is in high school and I sure as hell don't want to start again."

"Gotcha."

"So... Connie turns up pregnant. She's two months along."

"But... but how? You're not... snipped?"

"Nope. Maybe that was selfish on my part, but Connie just stayed on the pill... until she stopped taking them, *on purpose*, without telling me."

"Oh, God, Augie, I'm sorry."

"Yeah. Total betrayal. But what do I do? I mean, it's a baby. *My* baby."

"What a shitty thing to do to you, Augie." A long silence ensued; we were too drunk to talk about such deep issues. "So, Augie, like me... you either need therapy or another shot."

"Another shot. Hit me, José Cuervo."

As I poured, I lamented, "Well *my* baby is ten years old, and I'm so old now that the docs would consider my pregnancy high-risk. My now-or-never has come and gone. And I hate Miller for it." I stopped with my shot glass in midair. "Oh shit. I forgot about Bo, too. It's my weekend. Fuck!

"Uh-oh."

I continued. "So the daycare would've called Miller to get Bo. And let me guess how pissed he was about *that*. Daycare pickups are my job. And poor ol' Bo felt... dejected and ignored I'm sure."

"He's a big boy. He'll be–"

"But this isn't the first time I've done this, Augie. What a crummy mother I am!

"Give yourself a break, Lela. You just told me that your family life is shit. That's an easy way to explain your...uh..."

"Say it... my 'bad behavior.' Yep, I'm a shitty mother. I gotta go, Augie. Drunk or not, I gotta go."

☀ ☀ ☀ ☀ ☀

Five days after the shoot, Augie and I were in the editing suite, reviewing the footage. Always hard on himself, Augie grumbled and mumbled things like "That would have been perfect if I had only..." and "I wish I had zoomed in on that shot." He was a perfectionist.

It was hard to listen to him trash himself because I knew that tactic all too well. No matter how much I asked him to stop beating himself up and move on, he continued. It took three hours to edit the first five seconds.

Finally, I said, "Time is money, Augie. If you keep wasting time, I'm pulling back on the budget." I was half-teasing, but he slammed his fist on the desk and changed his approach from hot to ice-cold. Like a snotty child, he rushed through marrying the announcer and custom music with the video... frame-by-frame, with minimal input from me; he didn't even ask if I agreed with what he had already done. It was like he was playing Mr. Miserable, Miller McKeown.

"Jeezus, Augie. Quit being an ass. Compromise, please. It's will never be perfect according to you, so take the best of what we have and move on." But he said nothing, slamming on the keyboard like he had a deadline in five minutes. Again, I asked him to quit being an ass, but he never said another word.

What could I do? Give in to him... losing face and wasting time and money, or relinquish control and feel distant from him? Neither was a good choice. And though I trusted Augie to make the best possible decisions, I knew our mutually creative relationship had changed.

It did.

The elevator shaft was tiny; an exact fit for the two of us, laying side by side at the bottom. Augie held the camera, and I clenched my jaw, watching the elevator box free-fall from five floors above us. It slowed a few feet from our heads, then eased down to rest on the three-foot pole between our bodies.

Pneumatics. Magic. The brand of magic that made me scream out loud and piss my pants. I was glad I wore a panty-liner pad.

"Dayum! What a rush!" Augie was ecstatic. "And I got it! I got the shot! That's *if* I held the camera steady enough... because I was scared, man. Dayum!" He struggled to rearrange himself, gaining room to turn toward me. He saw my face and his face fell. "Oh God, Lela! Are you okay? You're white as mountain snow, girl!"

I fought to answer. My blood pressure was off the chart, surely, but I was determined to keep a straight face and be brave. After all, I wasn't *required* to lie in the elevator shaft with him. I had volunteered to do it. For the rush, for bragging rights, for another cool thing to share with Augie. "That was... uh... exactly what I feared it would be. But perfect, the perfect shot," I was speaking staccato, trying to be professional and hide my fear.

"You can't fool me, Lela McKeown. I heard your scream," he teased. "I think that's what vibrated the camera, as a matter of fact." He grinned at me. Our friendship, both personal and professional, had just clicked up a notch, I knew, and just in time. The Baby City editing debacle was in the rearview mirror.

Augie must have felt a relationship bump, too, because he said, "That was cool as hell! *You* are cool as hell! Your strange scripts are a godsend to my career!" He continued with similar comments as I rearranged my head, knowing we would have to do a second, third, and fourth take, maybe more.

I heard the assistant director's voice outside of the shaft, asking if we were okay. Augie yelled, in my ear, to tell him we were. "Damn, Augie, you kill me *and* make me deaf!" Augie and his assistant helped me get out of the shaft as they discussed details for the next take.

We were shooting a TV spot for Connor Health, again. This one was for the alcohol and drug recovery program. The elevator and the man inside represented an addict's downfall, with an announcer who said Connor

Health's program could help an alcoholic stop before reaching the bottom and/or help them rise from the bottom.

Great metaphor; great advertising. And more appropriate to my life than I could have imagined at the time. The irony wasn't lost on me.

Augie and I stepped outside to smoke a cigarette. He told me he'd been thinking about what Miller had done... that "the sonofabitch" had lied about having a baby, one of life's most important choices, as he put it. "You don't deserve that, Lela."

"Well, nobody does, Augie. But you were betrayed, too."

"So we should have a whine party?"

"Nah. I don't whine anymore. Turns out it might have been for the best. Would have cut into my party time... I guess you figured out how much I treasure that, huh?"

He ignored my point, gushing with anger toward Miller. "Well let me tell you one thing about Miller-fucking-McKeown... he's not the hot shit this town thinks he is. He's an asshole first and foremost and much better at being a snob than a creative director. King Creative, my ass!

I was flabbergasted... shocked that Augie, or *anybody* in the business, would dare to question Miller's talent or position as King, I felt great relief. "Oh boy! So *now* I can tell you what I've wanted to say for years! I agree with you whole-heartedly!"

I told Augie how Miller treated his "underlings" along the creative hall at Sturbridge, and why I'd quit working with him on projects of my own. "He thrives on one-upmanship, Augie, and honestly, I think he's hiding his own feelings of inadequacy. He thinks he sucks deep within. The whole thing makes me sick."

Augie continued to bash Miller's lack of talent, social abilities, and approach to life all around. Though I agreed with every comment, it was hard to hear. I interrupted. "Enough about Miller. How's the baby?"

"Oh, good..." A smile built by tiny fractions on Augie's face. "I've pissed you off?"

"Do you want me to trash Connie?"

He looked at the ground, kicked a pebble. "I see what you mean." Augie took an exaggerated hit from his cigarette, the brown, long, and extra-skinny brand. Few people smoked those weird things, especially not men. But the oddity of the cigarette fit Augie's quirky personality and it made me smile. "So... let's talk about us instead."

"Us? What about us?"

"You know it's going to happen sooner or later..."

"Uh... let's make it later, Augie. We have work to do." I looked away, trying to escape the tension his comment brought, but when I looked back at Augie, his eyes were still drilled into mine. "What? Come on! The reality might mess up the fantasy."

His glare was serious. Then his left hand reached to touch my face; he ran his thumbnail along my jaw and ended by cradling my cheek in the palm of his hand. It was a touch that sent a chill down my spine. It wasn't a "normal tease"; the touch was overtly romantic. No, much more than that; it was sexy, caring, loving.

That approach wasn't our deal.

For all the years we worked together, there had always been tongue-in-cheek sexual comments between us, keeping a bit of friction and titillation. It seemed to work with us, but underneath, it made me feel... dirty. Like a whore, a "fake vixen." A reminder of my rapes, maybe. Or the sad knowledge that I held power over men only because of my sexual prowess.

Though supposedly innocent, I had always felt uncomfortable with it. But I kept my discomfort to myself, justifying it... after all, his attraction to me motivated Augie to do his best work. But the dirty feelings were getting worse.

Augie laughed, still caressing my cheek. Eerily, I felt something sinister from him. Something threatening and demeaning. He stared at me for a full thirty seconds and maintained his gaze when his assistant yelled from the side door, announcing the next setup was ready. A tick at a time, his face contorted into a knowing grin. "Do you want to climb into the elevator shaft with me again?" he asked.

I grinned, too. "You know I can't say no to you. I've always said: If I'm ever gonna be crushed by an elevator, I'd like to be with Augie Highfield. It's like having a... crush... on you. Get it?" Augie groaned. I cackled. The crew told us to stop screwing around and get back to work.

☼ ☼ ☼ ☼ ☼

I didn't know what exactly changed between us that night but change it did. Augie's sexual teasing became more obvious. I caught him looking at my boobs, joking about my "nice ass," and pushing the jokes just a bit too far. It had built so slowly, I felt stupid to tell him I was uncomfortable.

The one time I dared to say something, he blew me off. "Oh, cut it out, Lela.

You know I'm a timid little boy underneath, teasing you because I can't have you."

Two months later, creating a three-minute video with intense together-time required, his teasing continued, and I tried again. "Augie, back the hell off, dude! You say your flirting is innocent, so keep it innocent, dammit."

He repeated his innocence. "I don't mean a thing by it, Lela! It's just the way we work together."

"Well, not anymore. Because, to me, it doesn't *feel* timid and innocent, and I don't appreciate you trying to shame me when I'm telling you I have boundaries.

"Oh, you're just overreacting! Come on... let's get to work."

Dammit! I hate men! All of them. They just don't get it! I have emotions and I am NOT overreacting!

But his comment smacked the shit out of my pride. I felt dissed and shrank away. *Maybe your ideas ARE stupid, Lela. You're not all that, ya know. Maybe you're good, but maybe Augie is better.*

In the weeks that followed, I let Augie make me feel stupid and inadequate all around. As if I had lost my spark, my creative edge. *You're past your prime, Lela. Hang it up.*

Though I tried to believe in myself, to push hard against the doubt, I gave in. I fought to hold my ground, but Augie had created a mudslide under my feet. I turned down a rocky road where inadequacy was a constant marker. I had lost the battle. I had to write off my friend as bad news for my psyche.

The talented and revered Augie Highfield would re-enter my life as a client in Lifetime Number Eight and accept that I had radically changed in the interim. He cheered me, in fact, and urged me to jump back into the advertising world again with both feet.

But it was a time when doubts about myself were all I had, and he seemed to enjoy adding to my misery. A new and unhappy Augie had emerged and teamed with the wretched dry-drunk Lela Fox, we were a toxic combination.

In Lifetime Number Nine, when I finally found what Alcoholics Anonymous calls "a new freedom and a new happiness," Augie Highfield got his due.

But that's getting ahead of the story.

☀ ☀ ☀ ☀ ☀ ☀ ☀ ☀

BETTER LATE THAN NEVER
Chapter 25

I had fretted for years about the *one* class needed to officially graduate from college. On a day I felt both guilty enough about disappointing my parents and brave enough to admit my stupidity, I called the TSU Guidance Center. "The class I missed was a computer class, back in the day when computers were hardly in existence." The woman was young enough to accept the half-truth as correct.

"Oh, I see."

"I mean, it was a decade before HTML! I suppose programs were written in DOS, for God's sake! You're too young to even know what I'm talking about."

"You're right."

"So do you have a general elective about intro to computers now?" She mumbled through a list of classes.

"There's intro to programming, of course."

"Yeah, but that's for computer science majors. This was just a Mickey Mouse thing, a three-credit-hour class, and actually, that's the other half of the problem."

"A half a problem?" she asked.

With a sniff of a laugh: "When I graduated–"

"Wait... I thought you *didn't* graduate."

"Right, sorry. I'm just used to saying it that way." In my mind, I saw her brow screw into a question mark. "Anyway, in 1982, the university wasn't on the semester system, but the *quarter* system."

"Oh... wow. That *is* a problem. I'm not exactly sure..." As she trailed off, I confirmed I needed someone in charge, not this underling. My problem was above her pay grade.

"Look, can I speak to someone else who–"

"Yes," she interrupted, "I'm giving you to Janet. She'll figure it out."

Four minutes of on-hold music later, a woman answered without a greeting. Her voice was perky and filled with a cheeky smile. "Ms. McKeown, I know the *best* way to solve this!" Obviously, the original counselor had filled her in on the issue."

"Okay, great." No reply and a pause long enough that I thought she'd hung up. "Hello? Are you still there?"

A giggle. "I'm right here, ma'am. The noise you hear is my typing. It's an email to Dr. Spade, the handsome Dean of Communications. I'm suggesting that he design a project specifically for you, like a mini-thesis kind of thing. Computer-based and tied to advertising now that you've been in the industry."

"Well, it would be great to do something at home, and–"

She interrupted. "And Dr. Spade is a good friend of mine. Smart as Einstein. Here's his number, Lela. I'd call him later this afternoon or early tomorrow."

☀ ☀ ☀ ☀ ☀

Dr. Spade was young, a redhead with a scruffy beard and albino-invisible eyelashes and brows. But the advisor had been correct; handsome and smart were perfect words to describe him. Together, we "invented" a project for me to earn the needed credits. Working at home, I would design the paperwork and *describe* the tracking system for pie-in-the-sky software designed for an ad agency... following ten projects in different media from inception to completion.

I wouldn't write the code, just design the sequence of tracking and "inciting events." Things weren't so complicated back then; mostly, computers generated the paperwork and data entry came after the fact. There would be a lot of forms to design, plus a thesis to explain my concepts and solutions. The challenge was huge, but one that used my experience in the agency business and the idealism I still held.

And the OCD anal side of me looked forward to it.

"Miller, I need your help for part of this graduation project. Tell me how Sturbridge handles client changes. I need details." I sat down with a notepad to record his descriptions.

"Dammit, Lela! There you go again, demanding my time when I'm relaxing. Besides, why do you need your college degree now? I mean, now you're self-employed, so who gives a shit?"

"*I* give a shit. My *parents* give a shit. They paid for four years of school and they want to see my name on a diploma. And I do, too. Miller. You have your degree and I want mine."

"Yeah, my diploma meant nothing beyond my first two jobs. You're way past that, Lela."

"You know what, Miller? Fuck you. Fuck you *twice*. Some partner you turned out to be, ya know? Boil it down and you're worse than Andy."

He jumped from the recliner in a heartbeat. "*Never* say that! You bitch!"

A small voice raised in a scolding song, echoing from the top of the steps. "I heeeear you! Don't arrrrrgue in front of the chuuuuuldren!"

Though I tried to fight it, I couldn't hold it in and burst out in laughter. Thankfully, Miller did the same. The fire in his eyes when he pounced from the recliner had scared me. Turning to go, I couldn't help but snip a smartass remark. "Thanks for your help, dear. I truly appreciate your time."

I had worked on the project for four months before our traumatic December home robbery. I had completed a fleshy outline, designed a dozen spreadsheets, and created about 20 intricate forms, from project sheets to invoices.

The big, bad robbers stole my computer, *of course*. Another *of course*: I hadn't been very diligent with back-ups. The third *of course*: the big, bad robbers also stole my printer... and the replacement printer threw off the margins of every form I had so carefully designed.

After many starts and stops, I accepted having to start anew and planned my new approach. I dedicated two hours each morning with vodka-laced coffee – head down, focused, and typing like a fiend. Those were the days when I could still be productive, creative, and anal at the same time.

The final printout totaled 138 pages, housed in a custom binder. I made an appointment with the dean to present my project. He agreed and let me know his assistant would attend again this time.

The professors asked few questions. I sensed they would have approved the college credit even if my work had been substandard and sloppy. But it wasn't; it was perfect. No shit.

The dean called that afternoon. "Congratulations, Lela. At long last, you're a TSU graduate. And with Honors, they tell me."

Yippee! Better late than never, I graduated with a Bachelor of Science in Communications. I wouldn't have to lie on my résumé anymore. Mom and Dad wanted me to "walk," but I refused. In my mind, I had graduated in 1982.

I checked with several TSU departments to arrange a name change on my diploma. I wanted it to read "Lela Lynn Fox," but everybody said it was impossible to change to the original name after two name changes in between. Officially, I would have been "Winston" at the time of graduation, but that name left a bad taste in my mouth.

The mailman brought my diploma two weeks later, but I never took the diploma out of the tube.

I found the orange and white TSU tube when unpacking the attic boxes in Lifetime Number Nine. Though rolled tight for almost thirty years, the calligraphy name in the center was perfectly flat: Lela Lynn Fox. Just the way I wanted it.

By that time, I had framed hundreds of TSU diplomas in my fourth career as a picture framer. And by then, I had zero money for things as luxurious as custom framing.

Funny how my life had twisted around, again. And again, and again, and again...

TOO MUCH SUCCESS
Chapter 26

A change in management at Connor Health stopped the fun stuff in its tracks. A new, uptight CEO took charge and Marketing Manager Alyson passed the problem to me. Matching the CEO's approach, she forced me to be increasingly conservative in my ideas, leaning on me to write without exclamation points or "frivolous themes."

"So you want me to write like a robot?" I asked, shaking my head in frustration. "Don't you know that I'll no longer be writing to the audience, but only to answer the new CEO's request? Doesn't that make you want to fight against him, Alyson? Or are you a pussy?"

"Lela, don't make it harder for me. All I can do is quote his directive: 'Don't make waves.' I know it sucks but it's just the way it is. My hands are tied."

Disgusted... with the "new approach," with Alyson, with the other marketing managers, with the CEO, even the receptionist of the department. I hated the change and spent days grumbling, disgusted with anything and everything in my work. *I deserve better than this... I'll show them how right I am! I'll just do their work half-assed. Then they'll know they're dead wrong. They'll see that my ideas are what's making the whole damn group of hospitals successful. It's all because of me!*

So self-important!

To make the point, I treated the next few projects like poison. I gave them less than half of my normal care and attention but billed the same amount as before. *Alyson wants an advertising robot? I'll write like a machine. Who* cares if it makes an impression on the consumer? The dumbass CEO wants ideas with no creativity? I'll barf out perfectly punctuated headlines along with words that make the reader skip the rest of the ad. Who cares? Obviously, not the client.

Fuck 'em! Fuck 'em all!

I spent three full therapy appointments discussing this slap in the face. I was livid! But my therapist, in all her damn calm wisdom, talked me around. Yes, I promised to give my best to the client who put shoes on Bo's feet. I didn't like it, but I put my heart back into my work. They deserved that, I thought, and I deserved to continue the relationship with my long-term client. That attitude lasted a few miserable months.

Then, in early March, I wrote an ad for the Sleep Center with the headline "Snoring is Annoying but Silence is Deadly." Good stuff; Miller agreed. Alyson requested a full rewrite, per input from the CEO. Take out the "is" words and insert "may" or "might." She shared the quote from her boss. "We don't want to offend anyone."

This watered down the message to be unnecessary, in my opinion. The headline, as they re-wrote it: "Snoring May Be Annoying, but Silence Can be Deadly."

I threw a fit and called Alyson flaming-mad. "Why don't you grow a pair, huh? You know what they're doing is wrong!"

She tried to calm me down, saying she understood and... "Don't tell anyone, Lela, but I agree with you 100 percent." Yet I wasn't satisfied with that comment, nor would I back down when she reminded me I was still being paid the same amount of money. "Lela, you know we pay you well, and you deserve it... because you're talented and responsive."

A rational person would have rolled back on their heels, accepted her flattery, and shut the hell up. But I wasn't rational any hour of the day, especially that day... after two afternoon vodka-tonics. I wanted to be right. And I wanted them to suffer for such a bonehead move. *By God, you show 'em, Lela! Tell 'em how fucked up they are!*

Instead of accepting her flattery and understanding, despite her efforts to appease me, I screamed, "If you want bad copy, hire a bad copywriter!" Then I hung up and sat back in my chair with a huff. I felt important and 100 percent justified... for about sixty seconds.

With a sinking feeling in my gut, realized it was a knee-jerk reaction and a horrendously bad decision. Had I thought of the repercussions? I had not.

Yes, this was an emergency that earned me another early drink, I believed. I reminded myself to stop at three drinks because I was due at the daycare by six o'clock. At 4:52, I had my fourth drink, hoping I'd be sober by six, ready to drive the five miles to get Bo.

Deep in thought, I sat at the kitchen table and drank with purpose. I felt my stomach churn as shame moved up my spine.

I had tremendous pressure to be creative, yet I was forced to do substandard creative work. It felt like a royal slap in the face. A Catch-22 for my now-questionable success... a task for those beneath my station.

The truth is, this disagreement gave me an out. I quit because I wasn't able to be a success *and* a drunk. I'd like to say the choice was mine, but Mr. Smirnoff had taken my choices away.

MOONLIGHTING
Chapter 27

I suppose I could have called my best client at Connor Health right back after I hung up on her. I could have apologized for my outburst, or made a joke. Alyson would have certainly forgiven me if I'd called right back. Instead, I laid drunk for ten days, ignoring client phone calls and missing important deadlines. I also missed important family times. Miller was totally responsible for Bo because I couldn't drive or function well enough to be a mother or wife. But he hadn't complained; I think he liked me out of commission, thus out of his hair.

After days and nights of drunkenness, I had to lie to Bo. I said, "Mommy is sick." The next day, he ran to the den and asked to go play Putt-Putt. When I refused, a look of deep disappointment melted his sweet face. His own mother had hurt him. *Oh God, Lela! What are you doing! GET UP!*

Flashbacks of my weeks of depression during my marriage to Andy formed a vision of danger. The result of that had been Andy's infidelity and our subsequent divorce. *Yikes! Do you expect a different result, you Bi-Polar piece of shit? Get up! Sober up! You're ruining everything!*

The rest of the evening and the next day, I didn't drink. I made it through the second day, too, but I was shaking, craving vodka, wine, anything. The need for alcohol was deep and all-consuming, scaring the hell out of me. It took four days to feel normal, a Herculean effort, but thank God, I was able to stop for my son's sake, for the sake of my marriage.

It convinced me I didn't really have a problem... because I could quit on my own.

But as alcoholism took over my days, my judgement became more and more absurd. To "solve" the problem of losing Connor Health as a client, I decided I hated advertising and wanted to do something else altogether. Yep, I threw away what had made me a vibrant success and the career I'd dreamed of since I was twelve.

The truth behind the change: I couldn't continue drinking and be accountable to my slew of clients (After so many unreturned phone calls, I wasn't sure which may still be clients but I fantasized they were hungering for me.) So I quit. Just... quit.

LelaWrites, the company, was no more. My six-figure income was gone. Too much pressure had done me in, I thought. What I didn't know was *any* job that demanded my presence and attention would have done me in at the time. Work interfered with my drinking, or "my lifestyle" as I innocently called it.

A fresh start was the answer, I believed, with no clients, no deadlines, and no demands.

To quit drinking permanently was not an option, but I pledged to cut down on the vodka for a while. A few days later, I breathed easier... and I had an idea. Selfish, but an idea.

Anne, the mother of the girl on Bo's baseball team, had an interesting job, I thought. She made t-shirts with ribbon accents and traveled to craft fairs and arts festivals across the southeast, selling her wares. I decided to follow her lead. She was t-shirts; I would be jewelry. Making jewelry was the perfect way to combine my creativity with a passion for the unique.

Company name: Moonlight Jewelry. To prepare, I did zero research on starting a business or living as a traveling crafter... no preparation at all. Another snap decision. But I asked Miller to design a business card and brochure for me and he seemed happy to do it. Maybe he thought traveling would keep me out of his hair, let him get closer to Bo and farther from me.

I reveled in my creative designs. All the earrings were long and flowing dangles, made with cast-pewter charms from obscure and inimitable vendors. I lied to customers, saying I had carved the molds for each charm and poured the molds with pewter. A Moonlight Jewelry brochure detailed my carving and casting processes, but I had purchased stock photos and written flat-out lies.

My design focus was to have no focus at all: variety was my shtick. I bought wholesale charms to match any special interest a customer may have – from Scottie dogs to grasshoppers to garden trowels, and all between. Together, I spent a fortune on an over-abundant inventory and dozens of tools that weren't needed. There was no capital set aside and budgeted to cover my business expenses... no organization, no rhyme or reason... I just bought the shit I wanted.

At first, I made earrings only but soon branched out to bracelets, necklaces, and elaborate lapel pins - which required more hardware, more tools, and pounds of beads and baubles. Thousands of dollars of supplies came via UPS and Fed-X... two or three packages a day.

Each design was christened with a clever name, like a headline. For instance, I called the garden trowel "Diggin' It." One of the celestial designs was dubbed "Moonlight Madness." The dachshunds boasted the name "Wieners are Winners," the armadillo was "Killer Armadiller."

The witty names made customers smile and helped my designs sell. Thinking up the design names was the only writing I did.

Mostly, I spent tons of time organizing storage systems and micro-managing the "background bullshit" of a business. I ignored the important stuff, like figuring out how to make money. I never figured that part out.

Some business people can get away with flying by the seat of their pants for a while. But I never had control of the business... or the business owner, for that matter. I wallowed in vodka and irresponsibility, taking stabs in the dark about what might work to make money.

Oh, yeah... money. Mostly, I just kept spending it.

☼ ☼ ☼ ☼ ☼

"Daddy, can you help me make a traveling display for my jewelry? I have a good idea, but I need your input, your tools, and your joyful smile." Daddy agreed in a heartbeat. The two of us worked well together, sharing the ability to jerry-rig things behind the scenes.

I had always loved being in the workshop with Daddy, starting at a young age. The giant palace of a workshop at the farmhouse was like a step into the happiness of Daddy's soul. It boasted the full gamut of power tools, tins and bins to hold every variety of hardware, and 24 feet of pegboard to display hand tools.

The basement was his manly handyman fortress, and it made me smile to see Dad's eyes light up as he walked down the steps. But on this day, his sweet face fell as the afternoon progressed. My shame stained the basement floor and it could have been a disaster. I drank four beers and came close to drilling a hole into my left index finger. Daddy got aggravated with me and took over the use of power tools before the three o'clock hour arrived. There was tension in every corner of the basement.

I stayed for dinner. Tipsy enough to forget my parent's feelings, I asked Mom to grab another beer for me. "You drank it all, Lela," Daddy said. "At least sober up to drive." I looked down at my plate, awaiting a lecture. But Daddy just shook his head. "One more time, baby... we're worried about you. You drink too much, *way* too much. Let us help you."

"No, I'm okay, Daddy. I don't need help! It's just... Saturday, ya know?" I flashed a fake smile and squirmed in my chair. After the first taste of alcohol, stopping was a problem. A *big* problem. On days that fact hit me between the eyes, I felt lower than a snake... worse than a loser, and I could only ease those hateful feelings with a drink. The vicious cycle had begun.

TEAM MOM
Chapter 28

After two years in Tiny League, Bo and Bryce moved up to Little League. Miller followed Bo's rise and coached the new team, the Cardinals, sponsored by Third Tennessee Bank. Bo wanted number 45 again and sweet-talked Vann, in charge of the equipment, to grant his wish. Lucky kid; Vann went to the extra mile for Bo Winston, perhaps his secret favorite player.

By the last practice, Bo was a strong third baseman. He knew the third-base techniques and terminology but was confused about the jargon of the schedule. Getting ready for the first game, he ran halfway down the steps and asked, "Wait... who do we verse today?" It took a minute to figure out what he was asking... he meant, "What team do we play?" Cardinals "versus" who?

The question became a family joke each week when discussing the schedule but it took Bo all season to accept that we weren't making fun of him. Such a sensitive child... the product of an insensitive, no-holds-barred mom. Go figure.

Just as she did in our first and subsequent baseball seasons, Debra made a TEAM MOM shirt for me, this one with GO CARDINALS on the back. Again, I sat in the dugout with the boys, organizing them in the lineup and keeping the scorebook. Being "Team Mom" gave me a little control over the booze on Saturdays; one of the many benefits of our family hobby.

The Cardinals kicked ass. We made it to the championship game in the tournament, but lost by one measly run, leaving the bases loaded. It was a heartbreak for all of us and the boys cried. I cried watching them cry and Bo got mad at me for that. But the dirt in the dugout was wet with tears.

The boys kicked the dirt and stuck out their bottom lips. A pissed-off Jordan Lawson threw his batting helmet into the lake, screaming to the sky. But Miller's pep talk after the game was masterful. "We should all be proud! We're the best! We had a bad day at a bad time – that's all. Hold your heads high, boys!"

We loaded the car with bats, bags, and totes, and as Miller closed the trunk, I saw a tear trickling down his cheek. I nearly choked; I was so moved. Until that day, I had never seen Miller McKeown cry. His emotions were non-existent, I'd been told, but he cried the entire way home.

Bo cried and cited things he should have done, errors he made... shaming himself. I spoke up immediately; the "shaming yourself" drill was all-too-familiar with me and I would *not* let Bo go in that direction. As I bragged on him, telling him he was a fantastic kid and an awesome player, I cried, too. I felt crazy-sad about Bo being upset in the first place and the fact that I couldn't make his life perfect tore at my heart. Soon I sobbed; Miller didn't even roll his eyes.

We left the baseball gear in the car and dragged our feet walking inside. With no words or a plan to do it, we simultaneously sunk to the floor. As a family, we laid together, clinging to each other. And all three of us cried until we laughed.

The end of that baseball season was the last time I could fake a happy time in my marriage. Even the idealistic me realized it couldn't go on as-is. And I knew the change had to be within me.

See, I didn't want Bo to suffer through a divorce. I refused to take away his father-figure, a man who truly loved him. So, I'd just back off, lower my expectations, and re-refocus.

I knew Miller wouldn't question me because he didn't want to deal with me in the first place. The less of me, the better. So I became a headstrong, bitchy woman. My "new focus" would be all-night parties and alcohol. I said yes to anything that might absorb my loneliness, shame, and disappointment.

Another failed marriage... what the hell? Another drink!

Another insult from the man I loved... of course! Another drink!

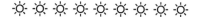

THE GEOGRAPHIC CURE
Chapter 29

"Believe me, Miller. We *can* afford it! There are three reasons we should move. Do you want to hear them?"

"Jeezus, Lela, I'm sure you've listed them already, during this thirty-minute, jaw-flapping speech you've got going."

I ignored him. "The middle school in this zone sucks. Bo needs better; he needs to be in *Skylark*. So we either use his dad's address to place him there... that's dangerous because it gives Andy a leg up in stealing custody, right? You know what he's been trying to do... fucking with us?"

"Yeah, but I think Andy's just–"

"Miller, don't you want the best for your stepson?"

"Well, of course, but–"

"And, most important – he could ride the bus to *both* of our houses if we lived in Skylark, too. Everything will fall in place, and the neighbor kids will be more... our socioeconomic level."

Miller threw his head back and laughed. "Lela! Why are you suddenly saying snob shit?"

"Oh, you know what I mean..."

"No, I don't. Don't you think Bryce and Roy are good playmates for Bo? Are they really..." He gestured air quotes. 'A lower socioeconomic level?'"

"No, I don't mean them! There are others here..."

"Sorry, I call bullshit on this line of reasoning. And I think it's a bad thing to take Bo away from his friend Bryce."

"Friendships like that last. Don't worry. The main reason is the school district, but there's also your new station in the community."

"What the hell are you talking about?"

"Just hush and listen. Buckle your seat belt, Miller. It's happening. *I'll* make it happen. We're moving to Skylark."

"So close, but so far, far away..."

"What do you mean? It's what... five miles away?"

Miller folded the newspaper and slapped it against his thigh. "I'm not talking distance, Dumbass. Everything is upscale out there, Lela. The farther west you go, the more expensive everything is. Surely we can't afford a house out in Skylark!"

"For the *new Vice President* of Sturbridge? Ha! Miller, we can afford *anything!* And you *want* to live in a kick-ass neighborhood, Miller. To match your new station. It's good business, ya know?"

"But you sound so damn uppity. Is it really all about appearances?"

"A lot of it. But ask Barry if he'd rather you live in Skylark... making a statement about how well the agency is doing."

"But Barry Sturbridge isn't paying the mortgage for that statement!"

I huffed a sigh. "Miller you have no idea what our financial situation is. I've been keeping the books since I got you out of debt, you ass. Don't worry... we've earned a lot of equity here and the timing is right. Besides, I need more room for my jewelry studio. And I need to hire two people... at least one... to help me."

"Help you do what? Lose money?"

"Ha, ha. Shut up. You don't know a thing."

"Moving is a bitch, Lela." Then his voice became a sing-song list of predictions. "You'll expect me to help you and we'll argue because I won't help. Because I can't. Moving makes me crazy."

"Shut up! Yes, you will help me and you won't go crazy. Trust me... everything's fine."

"Trust you? That's a scary prospect, Lela."

"Miller, you and I need a nice, new start, anyway. Why not start again in a beautiful new house?

We moved to a huge, contemporary tri-story on top of the hill in one of the toniest neighborhoods in Skylark, a high-end suburb in the coveted Meadow Ridge area. Though he resisted the concept at first, Miller enjoyed his new status symbol. He enjoyed showing the town how important and successful he was. I matched his enthusiasm at first, decorating the house in the grandest of styles. Anything but traditional, nothing "off the shelf," nothing that matched... creativity reigned. I reveled in the freedom to create a happy place. *Now if it could just be as happy as it looks...*

Upstairs was a loft sitting room and two bedrooms. The main level was huge... a foyer/mudroom entry and great room with a two-story ceiling... square kitchen with an oversized island and countertop bar, and the massive Master bedroom and bath, with just-as-massive connecting closets and a utility room. It was a killer layout, way ahead of its time.

The full basement was unfinished, with only roughed-in plumbing in the kitchen and bath, and studs to divide it into two large bedrooms and extra-large dining room/den. It was a self-sustaining two-bedroom apartment with a separate entrance.

At the time, I didn't know how important that apartment would become to our lives.

Our first job was to hire a contractor to finish the basement so I could put my studio down there. The first step happened quickly; when the sheetrock was up and the carpet down, we added a ping-pong table to the great room.

The next weekend, Daddy came to build a kick-ass studio in the basement. "We're going to need countertop measured in yards, not feet, Lela. Might be illegal to have something stick out of the back of the truck that far," he said.

"You'll make it work somehow, Daddy. Because you always do." By Sunday afternoon, I had a super-sized studio with a built-in workbench, special exhaust fans, and two walls of custom-designed shelving.

"I love you, Daddy. Thanks for your help. Can I get you a beer? Maybe get you a sign that says 'Will work for beer'?"

"No, dear. I'm driving. Unlike you, I don't drink and drive."

"Don't start on me, Daddy!" My defenses were on high alert.

He looked at me with pain in his eyes, then cradled my face in his hands. "I love you, baby. Be well. I pray for you, Lela. Every day." I didn't understand why he cried but it sent me into a rash of sobs.

We held onto each other, both sobbing, for several minutes. Seconds before I felt myself melting into an emotional puddle... ready to let myself collapse into his strength, he let go of me. Daddy lowered his head, and walked away. He sat behind the wheel of the waiting Buick and backed out of the driveway.

Crying in earnest, I had never needed a drink so bad.

When my hangover ceased on that Monday morning, I drove to the *Skylark News* to buy a classified ad. It was a tiny rag of a newspaper with an equally tiny sales office and rates so cheap that I bought a triple-size ad.

> Part-time assistant needed for home-based jewelry business. Detail work in hand-crafted production design and assembly, inventory management. Work in sales booth at art festivals, local and traveling in the southeast spring and fall, all expenses paid but the days are long. You choose work hours (no early mornings). Higher than average pay.

Where did I get the idea I needed help? By that time, I couldn't do much at all. "Functional" was a stretch. The "help" I needed was somebody to run the business for me. But I'd conjured up a helper who would be more like a friend... somebody I could party with at the end of the day. Besides, I didn't want to be lonely down in the basement and knew I could buy a friend if I held out for a good candidate. Pretending my sales justified a payroll, I told nobody the real reasons.

The first to answer the ad called the afternoon it ran. She sounded about my age with a smoker's cough like mine. I liked that; my smoking wouldn't be an issue. We set an appointment for the next afternoon.

She loved the studio setup, she said, gathering a bushel of thick black hair into a ponytail. "Part-time with travel benefits? Is that right?" The woman wanted to confirm the too-good-to-be-true offer."

"Right. I go to art festivals as far north as Indiana, south to Birmingham, up in the north Georgia mountains sometimes... and I've just now applied for shows in Charleston and Savannah. We'll see how it goes. I need a lot of help."

"And the hours are...?"

"Choose your own, but I don't do mornings."

"And what's the pay?"

"You can pretty much choose that, too. What do you think is fair?"

Her face froze with a half-opened mouth. Five seconds of silence, then she carefully said, "Are you serious?"

"What's the going rate?"

"I'll do four hours for 25 bucks."

"Sold." I reached to shake her hand. "But can I ask something personal?"

"Uh..."

"No, not *that* kind of personal! Just trying to figure out how you got that beautiful complexion. And all that hair! Because you're a striking-looking woman, Lola. Where do you come from?"

"Well..." Silence.

I jumped to take back my words. "Oh! Uh... never mind. I didn't mean to offend you. Please don't answer. Don't worry about it–"

She interrupted. "I'm half Cherokee Indian. I don't tell many people. Some don't like it."

"Oh, I like it! A lot! But how does a Cherokee get a name like Lola? Makes no sense."

"It's not my legal name. My mother used to sing to me... Lo-lo-lo-lo-lah. The 1970s song?"

"Yes! So your mother was a rock-and-roll Cherokee?" We both laughed.

"I'll see you tomorrow... one o'clock?"

"That's fine. I look forward to working with you, Lola."

"Lela and Lola – we'll make a good pair."

"I think we do already."

Lola and I would be friends for many years, much longer than Moonlight Jewelry lasted.

I had hired a friend, an enabler, a companion... but ended up finding a soulmate of sorts. She offered me more than I deserved and I gave her nothing but the worst of me.

GLUE GUN GIRLS
Chapter 30

The Meadow Ridge newsletter delivered to our mailbox showed promise of friends and fun, I thought. Living in a large and congenial neighborhood for the first time, I looked forward to joining the Women's Groups and taking part in the progressive dinners scheduled each month. The second week of living in Meadow Ridge, I called to RSVP for the evening Women's Meeting, set for the following Tuesday.

"I'm an up-and-comer in the neighborhood, Miller, so what makes you think a women's group would be out of my reach?" I argued. But he just shook his head and went back to the sports section.

I wore jeans and a nice top, thinking that would be fine, but when I arrived at this *gorgeous* but traditional house, the woman who greeted me at the door wore a little black dress. "Oops. So sorry... I had no clue about the dress code. Thank you, but I'll come to the next meeting, not this one."

"Oh, don't be silly! Come in and have fun, dear. How would a newcomer know? Come on... I'll introduce you around." The room reeled with three dozen women, dressed to the nines. Party outfits with wide sparkly belts, palazzo pants with ruffles and bows. The makeup was thick and perfectly applied. I was so stunned that I forgot my own lack of dress. With the first look of disgust thrown my way, I knew this wasn't a group for me.

These are the kind of women who go to charity balls and shit. I don't belong here! But what the hell... I'm here, so I'll have a quick drink and slip out. I scanned the room; there was no bar setup. A man in a tuxedo stood by the mahogany dining table and poured a flute of champagne for me, filling it only half full. Soon I saw that all the ladies carried half-flutes of champagne. No wine, no beer, no cocktails, only half a drink. *What the hell? What kind of party is this?*

Nobody would talk to me, the fidgety, underdressed newcomer. The hostess breezed back by and shouted to the pudgy brunette behind her, "Jennifer, say hello to our newcomer, uh... Lorilee."

I reached to shake the new woman's hand. "But I'm Lela, not Lorilee."

She stared at my extended hand with wide eyes... as if it was diseased. It didn't take long for me to bring it back to my champagne flute. "Oh. And I'm Jennifer. Jennifer Clayborn, wife of Jim... Rockville's premier businessman? I'm sure you've heard of him. And he'll soon be running for mayor!"

Though she was my height, I could see up into her nostrils; this bitch looked down at me as if I was scum. *Fuck you, bitch. I'm not here to impress you. As they say, "I'm just here for the beer."* Her face fell as if she had heard my thoughts. I smiled, gesturing a toast. Then it was her turn to fidget; Jennifer's discomfort was palpable as her eyes searched for someone to save her.

I decided to make her even more uncomfortable and started a conversation. "Is this a regular meeting of the Women's Club? Do you always dress so... formally?"

"Oh... you don't know, do you?"

"I don't know a thing, and I don't know anyone here. We moved to Meadow Ridge two weeks ago."

"Oh... that explains a lot. Well... this is a special meeting. It's Mrs. Meadow's birthday... let me introduce you." She turned and walked fast, zigging and zagging through the crowd, obviously trying to lose me. But I kept up with her, maybe just to piss her off.

Her destination was the throne of an elderly woman sitting high atop an overstuffed chair next to the grand piano. "Emma is the widow of Albert Meadow, she explained, who used to own the farm where our neighborhood now stands." I shook Mrs. Meadow's hand and saw her struggle to see beyond her cataracts. Women had gathered around her chair as if to worship her.

"Good to meet you, ma'am," I said, *No more! Please get me out of here!* I turned away from the group, hoping to see the hostess to tell her I was leaving. She wasn't there. *Fine, I'll just take some champagne for the road.* I dashed back to the waiter and held my glass for a refill.

"No refills, ma'am."

"What? Why?"

"At the request of the hostess."

I turned the flute up to get the last drop, set it down on the nearest table and escaped. *These women are the opposite of me. I live in too fancy of a neighborhood!* I drove home and put on my pajamas, poured a glass of wine and tried to pry conversation from Miller. He was reading *Golf Magazine* and ignored me, merely grunting now and then.

What the hell? I poured another glass of wine, which led to another. I went to bed drunk. Again.

But I had not gotten drunk alone. I did have rules.

☀ ☀ ☀ ☀ ☀

A different group, the Creative Club, met the following week. I called to RSVP, hoping it would be a casual affair with more casual women. The invitation said to bring a project to work on, so I brought a spool of copper wire and my special "wrap pliers." I was working on freeform wire rings and getting damn-good at it.

"This time it's surely more casual, Miller. A group of women talking while doing their craft." He rolled his eyes again and made a snide comment about a stitch-and-bitch meeting.

The hostess met me at the door of a contemporary house like mine, with a welcoming foyer and two-story ceilings. I stepped into the living room where twelve-or-so chatty women talked over each other and laughed hysterically. *This is more like it; maybe this is the group for me.* Ugly fake flowers covered the extra-large, round coffee table, and each woman had a glue gun in her hand. They were making wreaths. Ugly wreaths.

"Welcome to the Creative Club, Lela McKeown!" the hostess shouted to the group. Most of the women shouted back words of welcome: "Good to see you... Glad you're here... Thanks for coming," blah, blah, blah. The hostess urged me forward, stopping about ten feet from the coffee table.

The woman wearing an argyle sweater spoke first, friendly and upbeat. "We were just discussing the features of Aileen's brand, Lela... you can break the tie – what brand of glue gun do *you* have?

"Uh... I don't own a glue gun." Silence. A long, uncomfortable, thunderous silence.

I continued. "I mean... uh... I work with wire... to make jewelry and stuff. That's the project I brought today. And I... do other crafts and things, just not... glue gun stuff." The speed of my words slowed as I realized they fell on deaf ears. Twenty-four dead eyes stared back at me; the women remained mute, mouths agape as I stammered to fill the deafening quiet.

The hostess was the first to speak though achingly slow. "Well, girls... we should remember that *some* people have *other* interests..." Again, no one else said a word.

The dark-haired overweight woman said, "We make wreaths. You must bring your own glue gun." There was a sneer in her voice. I heard disdain. The other women joined to support her with another simultaneous reply, "Yeah, your own glue gun... we only make wreaths... we've never had a newcomer before... why are you here?"

I stepped back. "I'll just go, then. Nice meeting you!" I backed up from the spot where the hostess and I stood side by side. Expecting a rush of comments to encourage me to stay, I dawdled, but nobody said a thing. I let myself out.

How could they be so mean, so... clique-ish and rude? What's the big deal about wreaths? Why exclude new people with new ideas? On the way to my car, I justified my self-worth in the best way I could. *They probably didn't have wine, anyway.* I went home and worked on wire-wrapping as if my feelings weren't hurt. As if I didn't feel like a square peg. As if I was A-OK.

But I wasn't A-OK. *I want and need friends! This neighborhood is not for me. I want to move!*

After trying those two groups and finding the "socioeconomic reality," I never took part in Meadow Ridge functions again. When Bo joined the swim team, I sat away from the crowd, on the far side of the pool, drinking beer and reading a book. Nobody ever talked to me, but I saw some women pointing and whispering. Probably about the beer at their pristine, puckered-up community pool.

There were no kids Bo's age who lived on our street, but a group of ten-ish-year-old boys gathered at the field beside the pool on weekends. One brave day, Bo rode his bike to the pool and tried to get in on the soccer game. They snubbed him.

As a family, we decided to keep to ourselves and tell the snobs in Meadow Ridge to go fuck themselves. When it was our turn for Neighborhood Watch, I never responded to the notice, never picked up the "supplies."

That was the weekend that seven houses were burglarized.

I was definitely living above my station in the Meadow Ridge neighborhood. The odd thing is that I truly believed I would fit in with those women. I didn't know other people considered being drunk as a shameful thing... because for me, being drunk was the only way to *avoid* feeling shameful.

And I'd never heard a person turn down a drink because... "No, dear. I'm starting to feel it."

I thought everybody drank as I did. And because I could tell a funny joke and act silly, I thought I was 100 percent acceptable to others. The delusions of a drunk...

I compare that high-falutin' neighborhood to my residence in the first part of Lifetime Number Nine and laugh. Settler's Ridge wasn't high on a hill, didn't have a women's club or a creative club, or any such social groups. I was in the same boat as my neighbors, desperate people living paycheck-to-paycheck. What a different Lela I was by then... what an odd place for happiness to begin.

THEN THERE WAS JENNA
Chapter 31

Each weekend when Bo was with Andy and Ella, and any possible weekday, Jilly Jameson and I hit the lake in her shiny-new ski boat. We drank a case of beer between us, skied, and floated with the "Lake People," a twenty-strong group of Hooligans with boats or a connection to those who did.

Jilly stored her boat at Starshine Marina on Norton Lake, about forty miles from Rockville, the farthest and sleaziest of Norton's twenty-plus marinas on the eastern shore. She could have afforded the biggest and the best, but the powers that be had kicked her out of most of them. It seems Jilly (or me) would be too drunk at the end of the day and cause some kind of ruckus.

Once we spilled gas all over the decking and into the water. Another time, I grabbed a handful of bait fish from the tank in the marina store and threw them at her, thinking it was funny as hell... but not thinking of the dire repercussions. Laughter was constant when we were together; we had no interest in being upstanding citizens. Drunk from beginning to end, it was like Jilly and I starred in our own "Girls Gone Wild" video.

My friend/employee Lola and sister Jennifer were in the boat with Jilly and me one particular day in July. The sun was hidden behind thin clouds, making the usually oppressive Tennessee humidity and heat tolerable; it was a rare beautiful day in mid-summer. I specifically remember it was a "girl's day" because our claws were out with catty remarks about the overall stupidity of the male species.

We were on a mission to join more women on the lake for an all-day party and the plan was coming together beautifully. Jilly's childhood friend had bought an old SeaMaster boat, also docked on Norton Lake, but at the nicest marina closest to Rockville. We were going to meet up with them at two o'clock.

On the water, it was almost ten miles to the far-north Starshine Marina; it took hours to get there by boat unless you hauled ass the whole time. And Lake Norton's choppy water made that a roller coaster ride. Who wants that? So we had planned to meet at a marina in the middle.

On the way, we took turns playing the figurehead ornament on the front tip of the boat: tops off, mouth open and screaming at the wind. Freeeeeeeedom! Like in the movie *Braveheart*.

That day, and in that time in my life, I thought I had the world by the tail. Single (so to speak), a business that somebody else ran (for the most part), and a son who only needed simple, part-time care. Oh yes, I had it all. And here I was with the wind in my face... on the sparkling lake... under a warm sun with the best friends I'd ever had.

So why was I crying?

I knew there was a gaping hole in my soul... miserable for the same reasons I was supposedly happy. Single when I wanted a happy marriage, ineffective in a business based on lies and going broke, and a son growing up too fast. And, of course, the ever-present need for alcohol and more alcohol that scared the hell out of me.

"How much longer?" I asked Jilly as we bumped along the lake.

"Like a kid! How much longer, Daddy?"

"Seriously, I'm anxious to meet everybody."

We were meeting Jilly's childhood friend, Lori, a successful gay businesswoman in a long-term relationship with a woman named Camille, Jilly told us. "And they're bringing friends. Lori said 'Jenna, Jodi, and Janet.' Hilarious! The three J's."

Our boat arrived at the dock before Lori's crew and we smoked cigarettes on the dock, waiting. A half-hour later, a worn-out boat puttered toward us in the marina's no-wake zone. "Yep, it's Lori," Jilly announced.

A girl in a white bikini stood up and waved to us; I almost dropped my beer. She was the perfect specimen of a woman. From a distance, I saw mocha-cream skin wrapping the figure of a Barbie doll, voluminous blonde-highlighted brown hair surrounding a perfectly smooth heart-shaped face. My eyes locked on her and I exhaled in a moan. "What's wrong, Lela?" Jennifer asked, "What's the moan for?"

"Nothing. I... uh... stubbed my toe on the decking a little. No big deal."

If there's such a thing as love at first sight, that was it. Like a teenager, my heart took a leap and landed in her arms. I'd always suspected that I was a bi-sexual... the idea planted at age 18 when a woman first romanced me.

As the boat came closer, the woman removed her sunglasses to show emerald green eyes, glowing as if lit from behind. A flash of a smile showed ultra-white, faultless teeth. One odd fact: she wore glistening, almost-red lipstick.

Lori docked the boat next to Jilly's. Ms. Luscious Lips was the last to climb onto the decking. Oh, God! Her legs were strong! Taking Camille's hand to pull up, she rose from the boat with no effort, in one stealth movement. Defined muscles; her body screamed: "physically fit." Even with the lipstick, I thought she looked like a badass, a feminine badass. But the words running through my head were "Beautiful Goddess."

Jilly, always the social butterfly, introduced everybody. My heartthrob's name was Jenna, and I would soon come to know there was a subgroup called "Lipstick Lesbians," not so literal that they wore lipstick all the time, but the very opposite of butch. Whatever it was, I felt lightheaded with... what was it, exactly? Lust, need, awe, hunger, desire... aching thirst for the woman in the white bikini.

Without even talking to her yet, I knew I wanted to be with her. The familiar question came to mind as I again questioned my true sexual orientation. My first gay partner fed me grapes – no shit; she fed me grapes. Then Sara, the woman of threesomes with Vick Belford... she was hot, but this... this goddess... she was something altogether different.

The attraction to Jenna was so intense and happened so instantly, I knew it was God's reminder of my true preference. Just as Miller's half-sister Dodge had said, I'd only married because it was expected of a Southern girl; it was the softer, easier way.

"Hi." She was coy, flirty, but in a mixed-company, socially acceptable way.

"Hi." My eyes were saucers, and I wasn't sure how to be cool when my body buzzed with three-inch-thick vibrations. The situations with women in the past were one-on-one with nobody else around. I swallowed audibly, nervous.

Jenna laughed. "So I make you nervous?" A velvet voice, with just a touch of a twangy accent, more than mine but like many of my Tennessee friends.

"Uh... yeah. You *do* make me nervous. Because I can't seem to stop looking at you."

"And that scares you?"

"Hell yeah! I'm like... mashed potato legs."

Jenna laughed, cocking her jaw to the left. "I won't ask what that means..."

"Good, because I have no idea either."

"Lori tells me you're what we call "curious.""

"I've heard the term. Does it still apply if you've tested the waters?"

"Depends. Did you *like* the water?"

"I was young... then I was just drunk as hell."

"But... was it bad? Or good?"

"It kinda freaked me out at first, but if I had to choose between saying good or bad, I'd definitely say good."

"And there were more?"

"A few."

"Then go with the flow. No reason to be afraid of me. I'm harmless."

Laughing through the words, I said, "No way you're harmless! I don't think so!" Then I whispered, "I'm afraid to touch you because I'd never be the same again."

Again, Jenna laughed. "Silly girl!" The innocence in that childlike comment sent chills down my spine. Then she touched my arm and sparks flew. Amazed, I looked at the throbbing spot she touched with blinders on both eyes. *This is a scene in a movie. Whatever it is, surely it's not happening to me. This is a fantasy, a dream, something not real. What should I do? Run? Kiss her? Marry her?*

Jenna turned and leaned over to pick up her towel; I could hardly stop myself from touching her perfect butt, pulling her back against my hips. I closed my eyes, fighting to keep my legs from swaying. *Surely you're not going to faint, Lela. Get your shit together!*

When Jenna turned to face me, her face flashed concern. "Are you okay? You're white as a marshmallow!"

Fighting the forces that made me dizzy, I laughed. Then threw my head back and roared. "White as a *marshmallow?* That's a new one. Wouldn't a normal person say 'white as a ghost' or 'white as snow' or–"

She interrupted. "What makes you think I'm a normal person? And maybe

I like mixed-up metaphors. Like you and your mashed potato legs."

"Oh, I see... you're a feisty one, then."

"Guilty as charged." Another of the J-girls joined our conversation, handing Jenna a beer. Luscious-Lips didn't take her eyes from me nor try to hide our connection for the benefit of her friend. The other J-girl said to me, "You're the curious one, right?"

"What the hell? I guess Jilly told Lori my deep, dark secrets."

"Doesn't have to be a secret, Lela," J-girl said. "I see your interest in Jenna and that's cool. It's *all* cool. Because you're among friends."

The plan: anchor the two boats together in a cove further down the lake. Somehow, I arranged to ride in Lori's boat with Jenna. The boat was laughingly crowded; the two of us were squashed together at the thigh and shoulder. Heart rate on high, I was going insane with desire, trying to stay cool because I feared my sister would freak if I let my lust for Jenna show. My plan was to stay as far away from Jennifer as I could while staying as close to Jenna as she'd let me.

I'd set it up somehow... and see her that night.

☼ ☼ ☼ ☼ ☼

I dashed home only to shower and change clothes. In a rush, I threw a handful of airline-sized vodka bottles in my purse, said goodbye to Miller who hadn't acknowledged my entrance, then swung by the grocery store for a few bottles of tonic. Jenna and I met in the side lot of a gas station on her side of town. I followed as she zigged and zagged through a neighborhood and turned into a deep gravel driveway.

Nervous as a cat but happily excited to be with such a gorgeous woman, I talked to myself in a silent, but scolding voice. *Don't screw it up, Lela. Be cool. Don't tell her she's bowled you over. Don't let her know that you'd follow her to the ends of the earth.*

Her apartment was like a movie set: the "bachelor pad" over a garage, outside steps added as an afterthought. The front door opened into a tiny kitchen with half-size appliances. Jenna said, "I hope you don't need ice because my freezer space is zero."

"No ice needed," I lied. Further into the apartment, I wondered how someone so beautiful could be poor enough to have to live in a place so small. The ceiling was seven feet high if that.

Jenna led me to the "den," perhaps eight by eight, with three bean bag chairs and a TV on a funky-cool entertainment center. Nothing more. But art filled the walls; the focus was a round mirror, four feet in diameter with a "frame" of cactus plants. Stunning. "Did you make this amazing mirror, Jenna?"

Her little giggle peeped through a smile. "Yes, I did. I figured even *I* can't kill a cactus. And there's plenty of sun in the afternoon." She cocked her head and smiled like a coquette. "Have a seat, baby. This one's big enough for both of us."

"Yes, it is," I said, easing into a neon-blue bean bag. "I haven't sat in a chair like this since I was a kid. They're still cool, though." I patted the empty half of the chair. "Come to me, baby. Let me make you feel good."

When she cuddled next to me, I felt my stomach rise to my throat. *Don't screw it up, don't jump in her pants yet. Be cool. Be romantic. Don't let her know how eager you are.* With as much normalcy as I could muster with a throbbing crotch, I said, "This is nice, Jenna. Small, but nice."

"I'm hardly home and it's cheap. Cold as hell in the winter though and, as you can tell, hot as hell in July. I don't think there's any insulation at all."

Small talk. I hadn't learned much about her during our lake visit. I knew she worked for a company that managed organ transplant issues for kidney patients. She personally managed a staff of two, she said. Jenna was three years younger than me and had recently broken up with a woman she'd dated for more than a year.

Lori, Camille, and the other J-girls had teased her, saying she was "better off without that butch." The comment surprised me for two reasons. I assumed the term "butch" would be an insult among lesbians; a straight person's derogatory term. Second, I was confused about how she could be interested in me if she preferred a butchy girlfriend.

So, within the first few minutes of being in her apartment, I asked how she would feel about dating a married woman after having a "masculine partner" for so long. Her answer wasn't what I expected. "Lela, I don't try to paddle up-river. Years ago, when I let go of the '*rules*' of who my partner should be, I found myself attracted to all sorts of people... purple, green, blue, men, women, masculine, feminine... whatever. I have an open mind, I guess. What I love, basically, is love."

"Love?"

"Lovers who love."

"That would be me," I said with a satisfied smile. "But... and men, too?"

"Sometimes."

"I've been married twice, and this one is going down the tubes as we speak."

"Let's talk about that in bed."

"You won't have to twist my arm, sweetheart." My eyes were still saucers, my heart beating double-time with lust, yet I was fearful, not wanting to do anything "wrong" in this situation I didn't quite understand.

She kept the topic going. "So, your husband?" I nodded, taking a swig of my drink. "Are you sexually attracted to him?"

I made circles on her belly with my finger as I answered. "Well yes, but no. It's too quick and... too sweaty and I always feel maybe half-satisfied, if that."

The vodka bottles were still in my purse; I was too busy to bother with them and perfectly happy with what was happening now. So though I'd been drunk all day, I was instantly willing to become un-drunk. That hadn't happened in a few decades! But that night, my priorities changed a thousand percent.

Hours later, I drove home sober and smiling like a Cheshire cat.

☼ ☼ ☼ ☼ ☼

The next day, Sunday, I wished I could have picked her up in my former red-hot Miata, but I'd traded it for a van to haul my jewelry display to art festivals. "Sorry, Miss Sexy. Only moms drive mini-vans, right?"

Jenna said, "Moms and hot mommas like you."

"You don't mind? Not that I give a damn about cars... that's what stupid men care about. I'm much more interested in who's inside the car with me."

"Ditto doo-doo."

"Doo-doo?" I laughed, one hack... then two... then a loud chortle. "Jenna, you crack me up with your girly stuff."

"Well, I *am* a girl. And much younger than I am old."

Cocking my head, I thought about the profound meaning of that comment. "That's the best way I've ever heard to describe 'young at heart.' Can I steal that quote?"

"No stealing required. It's a gift." Traffic was heavy, and I had to turn left on an obscure road to get to the softball fields. Jenna pointed and directed me, and each time I squealed, thinking a crash was imminent, she laughed.

"So danger makes you laugh?"

She laughed through a "yes" answer. "*You* are dangerous, Lela, and you make me laugh."

"Sure you don't just like me because I'm head over heels about *you?*"

"Are you?"

"Head over heels?" As I navigated the gravel road to the softball fields, I contemplated the safest answer. *Why not be honest? What do you have to lose?* "Oh, yes, babe. I think you have me wrapped around your finger. Some kind of voodoo love-at-first-sight magic you've thrown on me."

"I am not a voodoo doctor, silly."

"I say you are!" I tossed my curls over my shoulder, deciding to let go and say what was on my mind. "I suppose I should be more secretive about it, but... what can I say? Jenna, I'm clear on what I want to do for the next year or so... I want *you.*"

Jenna giggled and I smiled from deep in my heart. "You want me even though I'm a bad softball player?"

"Yep, even if you strike out six times, you're as hot as lava, babe. And you make me hot, just thinking of you. Wet as a waterfall."

"Oh-so-poetic, my dear writer-lover. You say the nicest things!"

"It's easy to sweet-talk you, Jenna. I've never had anybody who deserved it as you do."

"Oh, stop! You're just trying to get me in bed again."

"Not just 'again.' babe. Always."

We spent the afternoon at the softball fields, and she introduced me to her friends as if she was showing off a trophy. Jenna bragged that I was unhappily married and she had made me "see the light." A sneaky-happy-horny feeling ruled my afternoon; her bragging about me swelled my heart.

How long had it been since a "mate" had taken pleasure in introducing me to their friends? Decades; certainly not since Miller and I had been married.

The two of us spent all afternoon and evening together, in and out of bed, and it seemed she didn't want me to go, even though she'd stated a "no later than" bedtime. "I have to work early tomorrow," she had said.

We kissed and cuddled and shared a few vodka-tonics. She finally kicked me out around midnight, promising more and more "later."

I pulled into my driveway with a hole in my heart, like I'd just left all the happiness in my life on the far side of town. Miller wasn't home, so I went straight to bed. With my mind on overdrive, I couldn't sleep and when he came to bed, I immediately moved to the sofa.

The morning startled me; I awoke when Miller walked into the living room.

"Make coffee, will you?" he asked.

"At your service, my King."

"Oh shut up."

I took my coffee down to the studio before Miller left for work and completed my first task before nine o'clock: Skylark Florist. Jenna called me at noon, hiding in the conference room, she said. "Lela... baby... don't send flowers with a card like that. My coworkers don't know... uh... anything about me and assumed it was from a rich, older man... I guess because it was so big and gorgeous. Thank you, darlin', but they've been teasing me all morning."

"Oh, I'm sorry if I've embarrassed you. But I did it to make you feel good... if only a fraction of how good you made me feel this weekend."

Giggle.

"And can I have another chance to make you feel good tonight?"

Another Jenna-giggle. "Remember I'm house-sitting at Lori's. Doesn't she live close to you? You two were talking about it in the cove."

"Well, she's not in Skylark but just east of me. Can I spend the night with you at her house?"

"Maaaaaaybe," she teased.

"Oh, baby, I'd give my right arm to cuddle with you all night."

"I want you to bring something."

"What's that?"

"Your husband."

"*What?*"

"Don't freak, Lela."

"What do you want from my husband?"

"Remember I said I love all kinds of people? Green, purple, and blue?" It was a whisper, but I couldn't respond; my mouth was wide open in shock.

"Okay, babe. People are coming in for a meeting. I have to vamoose." She said that word with her cute twangy accent and I smiled. *Damn, she's a doll, perfect! Hang on to her tight, Lela. Whatever you do about Miller, don't let go of Jenna.*

After she hung up, I listened to the dial tone and stared into space. *Bring my husband? To share? Hell no! I don't want to share! And I don't want it to only be about sex, I swear to God I'm in love or some real-life bullshit. I want to take care of you, Jenna, guide you through the big, bad world.*

"Fuck!" I threw a notepad across the countertop in my studio. "I don't want to share!" But I also wouldn't deny Jenna anything. I justified it, thinking maybe she just wants him to watch... *that can be kinda sexy.*

But I had to be sure, so I left a message with her receptionist for her to call me before she left for the day.

Jenna defended herself with her badass side front and center. "Don't jump to conclusions, baby. I just want him to watch."

"That's what I hoped you'd say, but... Jenna, I have... I don't... I'm..." I threw up my hands. "I can't say it."

"Can't say you don't want him there? Or can't say *why* you don't?"

"It's just... I can't tell you how much I'm into you. You and only you. And it's not just the sex, sweetheart. I can't explain what's happening. Like a teenager with a crush. Butterflies are flying around my head and out my butt."

"Whoa there, Lela. Stop right there." I thought she would laugh; butterflies coming out of my butt was quite a visual. "Lela, Don't do this, baby. The lesbian thing is just new for you. A weekend doesn't make it true love. So stop the crap."

"Oh shit, now you're going to break up with me," I whined, dejected.

"How can I break up with you when we're not..." She blew a sigh, pausing for ten seconds before continuing. "I want to play with you, Lela-baby, see what happens when other people get involved."

"What do you mean 'involved'?"

"You worry too much! Just you guys come for dinner. Say... 6:30? We'll keep it light and just see what happens. Does he even know about us, anyway?"

"I don't tell him what I do."

"Then he may not even want to come. You never know."

"Miller, this is Jenna... Jenna, meet Miller."

My husband's eyes didn't leave Jenna's as he spoke to me in a dreamy voice. "Yes, she's as beautiful as you said she was." Jenna stared him down, then looked at me and winked.

Jenna purred to Miller, "Look at those muscles, big guy. Your chest just screams 'climb onto me!' You're a protector, aren't you, Miller?"

I guffawed, thinking nothing could be further from the truth, and knowing that was a classic woman's pickup line for a man. "Oh, Jenna, sweetheart, you don't have to act charming around him. Look at his pants already."

Beautiful Jenna stepped back to look and giggled behind her hand. Miller's erection pressed hard against the crotch of his pants, his eyes rolling like the Fisher-Price telephone toy. He breathed out a lungful as he fought the need to conceal it. "Girls, both of you... give me a break. What do you expect?"

I spoke immediately, pissed. "I, for one, expect a little restraint, Miller. It's not like this is some perversion or something. Control yourself, for God's sake!"

He dismissed me, scanning Jenna's body as if seeing through her tank top and shorts. Then Miller reached to kiss her, and I swallowed hard. *No, no. No way. I don't like this.*

I tasted bile and thought my heart would explode, so I ran away, so to speak, dashing further into the living room. I picked up the remote nonchalantly, watching Miller and Jenna from the corner of my eye.

"Come back over here, baby," Jenna said. She stood with Miller in the kitchen where we started, peeking around the bulge of his bicep.

"No!" Full emphasis and full volume.

Miller, whining. "Come on, Lela. I thought this was for all of us."

"None for me, thanks. I just lost my appetite for you, Miller McKeown. And I don't want to watch you with her – you'll hurt her! And for sure you'll do it wrong!" I was near tears, feeling a gamut of emotions. Sadness, fear, anxiety, rage, disgust, remorse, gloom, but mostly I felt like I'd been deceived. I tasted bile and felt my knees wobble.

Jenna put her hand on a cocked hip. "Don't be pissy, Lela." I'd never heard her speak in anything close to a hateful tone, and she'd said it purposefully hateful. A shot through the heart; I'd been dissed. She continued, "We had this set up already! And he'll do fine. Don't worry and don't be mad, Please play with us."

"Play?"

"It was supposed to be fun, remember?"

I pressed the channel-up button, keeping my eyes on the TV. "Tell ya what... y'all go on upstairs to bed. I'll watch HBO with this damn cat." The cat jumped on my lap and a halo of yellow-orange hair swirled. "What the hell? What kind of cat is this, dammit?"

"That's Pussy," Jenna said.

"Figures."

Miller dared to speak. "Lela, are you serious?" I looked at him with a slack jaw as if I was bored. "You're seriously not making love with us?" He stood behind her, his hands on her hip bones as she bent forward a bit. As he spoke, he pulled her backward to grind into his crotch. "I really want you to be there." The motherfucker's breathing was already ragged.

"The hell you do! I can't watch you! Neither of you! Jenna, please be with me, baby. Don't do..." I searched for a word as she twisted backward and reached to unbuckle Miller's belt. "Jenna, please don't! I want you and I'll take care of you." She didn't respond, focusing on the huge snake she'd found in Miller's pants.

"Goddammit! Miller! Let go of her! Take me home! Stop it, motherfucker, and get your hands off of her." Neither of them seemed to hear my objections. I continued to shout, "Listen to me! This is absolutely *not cool.* Jenna, I thought..." Tears rolled now as I tried to look into Jenna's now-cold eyes. "And Jenn-Jenn-Jenna," I hiccupped, "You *tricked* me! I'm hurt. So sad, baby. I thought... I thought we really..."

I'm not sure I planned to finish the sentence, but Miller acted before my pause. In one quick motion, he scooped Jenna into his arms and bounded for the steps. Jenna hooted with laughter as they scaled the narrow staircase. "We'll be back, she shouted from the top. "Have a piece of chicken, sweetie! And salad's in the fridge..."

I heard her giggles fade as a bedroom door closed upstairs.

Deceit. Rejection. Trauma and the bitter taste of heartbreak. And this time, it wasn't 100 percent my fault.

Miller and I got home around three in the morning and I slept on the sofa, waking around seven when he dropped the coffee decanter and screamed when his bare foot stepped on the glass. I took my swollen eyes downstairs to my studio, not saying a word.

When the clock struck eight, I called my old therapist, Brenda Cole. I'd seen her off and on since I divorced Andy but I hadn't seen her in a few years. It was time for a check-up from the neck-up.

I felt like a shell of myself. Bewildered, beaten down, hopeless, depressed. It would take a lot of vodka to get over this one, I knew.

With Jenna, I thought I'd found love and its truth. Not just the confirmation of my own sexuality, she also represented freedom from the Lela that had been holding me back.

Before Jenna, I'd never met anyone I found more important than vodka.

Without pause for caution, I gave my heart to Jenna and she deceived me when I was at my most vulnerable. "Poor pitiful me" hit like a rocket, and the medicine for it came in a clear bottle and paired well with anything at all, lime optional.

Now sober, I have options. Drunk, I had none but to continue the suffering.

YUCATAN PENINSULA
Chapter 32

The only nine-to-five job my friend Jilly Jameson held was when she worked at Riverstone Services as a social worker. It was the first job to match her degree, a Masters in Social Work. She made a pittance but had a fling with her boss, Jim Schultz. The three of us once had a picnic and I smashed the tub of potato salad into my face, drunk and trying to be funny. Despite smitten-Jim's objections, Jilly quit the job after seven months, citing its interference with her social life.

Her daddy bought her several jobs after that, financed several businesses that failed, and supported her otherwise. But her best job, for me, came when her dad bought a travel agency for her to manage. She landed a few corporate accounts, enough to justify keeping the doors open, but mostly she booked travel for friends.

She booked four girls' beach trips through the years, finding super deals on elaborate shore houses along the Florida Panhandle, mostly in our party-central town of Destin. True to her personality, Jilly became a specialist in adventure travel for trips far away from tourist destinations, including many international excursions for her and Lantana, her buddy or boyfriend; she would never specify.

The biggest benefit of being in the travel industry was a slew of "incentive" trips for the agent and a companion. When she dumped Lantana, I became the willing hanger-on. Things were going downhill fast for the Norman Rockwell family who lived high on the hill. I had written him off after the Jenna debacle but still, crap came in continuous waves with Miller. There was no hope for a future with him, but I couldn't leave. I didn't have the money and I wouldn't deprive my son of his beloved father figure.

Leave it to Jilly to send a pick-me-up exactly when I needed it.

"Oh, Lela! I have exciting news!" She called earlier than normal; from work, she said. I was downstairs in my jewelry studio. "We're going to Mexico!"

"Mexico? Tell me everything!"

"There's a new resort and they're inviting travel agents to go... for free, of course, so that we'll later recommend it to our clients. An incentive trip. Are you in?"

"I'm there already."

"It's a new area, or soon to be, anyway. They're trying to make it a twenty-square-mile tourist area, lined by resorts along the shoreline. It's on the tip of the boot of Mexico, the Yucatan Peninsula. They call it Cancun. Five nights at a five-star, all-inclusive resort."

"Oh wow. Fucking-A, Jilly. Just tell me when and where."

"The promo even includes *first-class* airfare from Rockville!"

☀ ☀ ☀ ☀ ☀

We drove to the airport just after dawn on a cloudy day in early March, singing loud and laughing long. Jilly and I were never at a loss for silly. Once in the airport, Jilly used her blonde hair and patrician looks to fake being French, keeping a straight face despite my horselaughs.

Though there were several stops on the flight and one plane change, we landed in a tropical paradise less than five hours later. Paradise was on the other side of the large windows of a ratty-looking airport, which smelled of dead fish at intervals along the walk. But Jilly's continuing French persona made the grossness funny, too.

We were about twenty yards from the baggage carousel when Jilly stopped, arms wide. "Ooh-la-la!" she whispered.

"What?"

"Don't you *see?*"

Looking straight ahead, I spotted the divine being. A fine specimen of a male guide with a sign at his feet. There to meet us. "Oh, wow, what a dude! And bringing us drinks! He's hot, Jilly!"

"Not just hot, mi amiga! *Caliente!*"

"You're switching to Spanish now, mademoiselle?"

"Sí, sí!" And with the same crazy-funny aura, Jilly transformed from a French bitch to a sexy señorita. She rushed toward the man, carefully taking one of the coconut cocktails he held with her left hand, and squeezing his chest pecs with her right. "Ooh-la-la, señor! Me like-y!" She shimmied, bending her knees and swaying her hips. "Sí, sí, sí! Señorita like-y!"

The man turned red despite the rich-mocha complexion beneath. His reaction, so innocent and endearing, urged Jilly on. Her flirting was so obvious and ridiculous – completely over-the-top – that others in the airport stopped to watch. Some applauded.

The surprising thing: we only had two drinks on the plane. Barely buzzed, at best. Laughing and acting silly was the main benefit of being with Jilly. She was the yin to my yang... bold and irreverent, daring and courageous. And she made it okay for me to do the same.

Few friends "got me" as Jilly did. And I understood her, too. Underneath, she was a wounded child like me, self-medicating with raucous humor, impulsivity, and unending alcohol. Together, we were a cute couple and considered it our job to embarrass those who could handle it. As we phrased it, "We were born to make waves."

And here we were... anonymous in a foreign country and ready to be romanced with luxury, rapt attention, and free, unlimited drinks. There was no better combination.

I had stepped forward, at first thinking I should calm Jilly's exuberance, and then the man turned to look at me. A heady smile began with the upturn of sexy lips and grew to encompass his entire face. Bushy black eyebrows raised, he handed me the second half-coconut drink and bowed. I instantly fell in love.

Latin men would be afraid of blonde American crazy women like Jilly, anyway. Me, a not-so-shabby curly brunette... I'd be their choice. For the first time in my life, I'd be more attractive to men than Jilly was. I didn't know how she would handle that; humility was not her strong point, to say the least.

"I am Pedro," he said in heavily accented English.

"Of course you are," I answered, nibbling on the stirring straw in my drink and looking through my eyelashes at his now-redder face. An intense, five-second gaze. Then, never taking his eyes from mine, he reached down to grasp the handles of two screaming-pink canvas bags, emblazoned with the white logo of the resort. "For you, my friend," he said, extending his arm to pass the bag.

Jilly couldn't stand it anymore. Still in character and using large body language to speak, she said, "Señor, I am the travel agent reviewing the cinco-star resort." She put her hands on my shoulders, "Mí compañera es... my sexy girlfriend. No touch-y, por favor."

She had made it clear she was the V.I.P. but it wasn't a slam on me. On the contrary, it was to protect me for what she feared I would do. She knew I was already in bed with him in my mind and that would be a bad thing. Yes... a bad thing for our trip, for my lacking self-worth, my sense of confused sexuality... for all the reasons in the world.

We entered the trolley for transport to the resort. There were six other travelers – three agents and their companions, and all of them were puckered-up middle-aged couples. One lady had a beehive hairdo like a 1960s matron. Weird. Most had seen Jilly's performance inside the airport with Pedro who was now at the front of the trolley with a microphone, facing the group.

He shouted over the noise of the construction equipment outside the airport and the motor of the open-air trolley. Pedro motioned to the driver and the trolley moved forward. His speech began. "You all have a yellow sheet..."

Granted, his accent twisted the vowel sound, but Jilly wasn't going to let him get away with it. "Yellow... shit?"

I blew a loud "HA!" and all but Beehive followed suit.

Not to be outdone, Pedro's retort was, "Señorita, you need more drink! Pronto!" He poured an airline bottle of rum into another hollowed coconut shell. "You no need... juice, sí?"

Back in Tennessee character, she snorted. "Bring it on, Pedro!" Jilly wobbled her way to the front to get the drink, turned, and raised her cup. "To Cancun!"

I joined in the toast, then stood myself, "And to Pedro!" I winked at him with a sly smile that screamed, "Find me later, baby."

"I'll drink to that!" Pedro shouted, and the trolley-full cheered. Even Beehive. The ride took about fifteen minutes, max. The scenery changed from impoverished villages, through construction sites, and to a gleaming palace of pink stone. The Cancun Royale. Wow. I'd never seen such opulence!

We were encouraged to take advantage of all the attractions and amenities at the resort. We took scuba lessons, sailed to a deep-sea fishing excursion, spent an afternoon in the luxury spa, and ate decadent meals in a half-dozen of the many restaurants on the property.

But mostly, we drank rum and tequila. And we laughed. And laughed. About nothing, about everything, about the silence and the noise, the peace, and the chaos. With our giggling and inclusivity, we made and lost a string of friends, including other tourists and, especially, the hotel staff.

The first morning, we crept to the pool early, hoping the sun would burn our throbbing hangovers. But the more I sweated, the worse I felt.

Around ten o'clock, a "native" strolled by. He wasn't dressed in the resort uniform but faded floral-print shorts and no shirt. Rough-looking with dreadlocks reaching his mid-back, he looked like he hadn't had a bath in a week. Over his shoulder hung a dirty wooden drum, bouncing off his leg as he walked. He beat the drum slowly, achingly slow and with a single bang, and sang just as slowly, a syllable a second at the most. "It's... time... to get... drunk... again." He was taking drink orders, yelling the specifics to the bartender at the swim-up bar.

"Two tequila shots, two rum and pineapple," I said, and he smiled. Three teeth glowed against his dark skin. Moments later, a swimsuit-clad waitress brought our drinks. They always added cherries and some type of umbrella or tropical accent, even for shots. I threw back the tequila in one swallow and started on my rum-and-pineapple. *Ah... there we go! Hangover cured.* We were up and ready to party again before the sun was completely overhead. Oh, the magic of alcohol!

The staff at the hotel knew us well by the end of our stay, teasing us about wanting a drink and a steak. (I had a T-Bone and tequila for breakfast two days in a row.) Jilly was a never-ending repository of jokes and funny antics. It seems like we had laughed for the full four days.

"Jilly, I'm not sure what hurts worse... my sunburn or my belly, from a whole lot of laughing."

"You're hanging in there pretty good, Lela. Not bad for a country girl."

"Look who's talking Ms. Kentucky."

We took a cab into town, such as it was, buying trinkets and t-shirts. But the city was dirty and full of beggars. Plus, Jilly's blonde hair made her a target. There were no young, white, American tourists... only sneaky-eyed Latino men who made us nervous.

On the cab ride home, Jilly complained, "They'll never make this is a resort town! Too dirty and stinky, too many sleazy people who want 'a dolla, a dolla, gringo!' I'm pretty open-minded, you know, but Cancun sucks. And that will be in my report."

"But the resort itself is awesome. A traveler would just have to stay on-property. I feel safe here. And... Jilly... what about your report? I thought you said you were going to do it while we were here and take pictures, all that. But I've seen no camera and no pen and paper. What gives?"

"Too distracted. And actually, *Miss Writer*, I was hoping to hire you to actually write the article... just taking good notes for you and maybe an outline or something. What... a hundred bucks?"

"A hundred bucks!" I said this with such emphasis because I thought it was a huge amount.

"Okay, a hundred bucks, a steak dinner and a bottle of tequila."

"Along with the free trip, right? What a deal for me, my friend. What's our next destination?"

Jilly and I stumbled through a dozen more promo trips, some close by and some far away... some for a week, some just an overnight. We partied 24/7 while away, never coming up for air.

A few times, we would promise to "stay sober tonight," but it never happened. It was always chaos, though at the time I called it crazy-fun... the best time I'd ever had. My words are different now.

I increased my fee for Jilly's written reports and put the money straight into my personal savings account, which had been lonely for quite a while. I didn't know how much I'd need that money later... how *could* I have known? There's no plan for shit like that.

MIDDLE OF THE EARTH
Chapter 33

Though the core of Jilly's travel business was commercial, her adventure-travel specialty blossomed with safari bookings, rainforest excursions, and journeys to third-world countries. Plus, she had been on a dozen such trips herself with boyfriend/buddy Lantana.

To be ready for more such trips, Jilly enrolled in a two-week Spanish-immersion trip to Ecuador. Compliments of the Ecuadorian Department of Tourism, a bonus came with her confirmation: a travel voucher for a week's stay for two in the capital city of Quito.

Of course, my BFF called me. "We're going to Ecuador!" she said. "A whole week! Then you'll leave and I stay for the immersion class!"

"Hell, yeah! Jilly, you are the best friend to have ever! When?"

"Three weeks. Get ready. And brush up on your Spanish, Lela. No half-ass on this trip. It's not 'an American city in disguise' like a resort... ya know what I mean?"

I studied the language meticulously, hurrying beyond the basics, though I never mastered proper sentence structure. Bo helped me study, quizzing me with the flash cards I bought at the bookstore. I think he learned as much as I did, with much less effort. Smart kid.

We had two side trips planned, and with her "inside information," she had booked a dozen activities ahead of time. Jilly marveled at the ease of planning. "When a travel agent calls, doors open," she said. And for me, once again, I basked in the benefits of being Jilly's bestie.

Our flight from Rockville was non-stop to Houston, and from there, a direct, first-class flight to Quito. The weather was bad; there was a dangerous thunderstorm inland.

The captain spoke over the intercom, first in English: "Attention passengers, the storm over northern South America is widespread and dangerous. Lightning and limited visibility have forced a re-routing of our flight. We will land in Guayaquil, on the coast, and the airline will pay for a night's hotel stay for each of you. Please tell your flight attendant of any special circumstances."

"Fuck! A whole day of our vacation lost!" I was pissed.

"But the real problem isn't that, Lela."

"Then what?"

"Just wait. You'll see."

The problem: the hotel was a flophouse straight out of the movies. The smell of sex permeated the staircase for the three levels we climbed to arrive at our room. Behind the splintered hollow-core door, a grim room with one bed, no bedspread, and used condoms lined up carefully on the window sill.

I felt my mother's germophobia soar through my carefree drunken attitude. "Eeeew. I see what you mean, Jilly. What do we do?"

"You're the creative one. Think of something. All I know is I'm not sleeping on that sheet. It would probably glow like a lighthouse with semen stains if we used that blue light thing. I don't want to see it."

Oddly, there was a shower curtain rod suspended from the ceiling, placed at the head of the bed. We took pictures of each other doing pull-ups on the bar, which didn't break until I was on pull-up number five.

We unpacked the "largest" clothes we had and spread them on the sheet. Our jackets, a necessity for our planned trip to the Andes Mountains, became our blankets. We left the window open, allowing the condom-scented wind to cool the stagnant heat. Not that it would have mattered; the window glass was half gone.

Thank God for jet lag; I fell asleep without too much worry of bugs crawling on me and Jilly said she, too, slept soundly. Before dawn, even before coffee, we paraded onto the bus for a ride back to the airport. It was a twenty-minute flight to Quito and when we landed, my first reaction was a squeal of delight.

"Jilly! This city is white-glove clean! The whole place looks upscale! I mean, wow! The natives are well-dressed, well-groomed, and more than half of them have smiled and said hello to us! Quito is awesome!"

"I've read articles that said so, but seeing is believing. What a contrast to dirty-nasty Guayaquil. And thank God!"

"Yeah, Guayaquil is what my mom thought all of Ecuador would be like, I guess. She's still so freaked out I'm here."

"What did Miller say? You never told me."

"Because he never said a thing. Maybe he said, 'Have fun,' or whatever, but we hardly speak now. Or if we do, it's to talk about Bo."

"Sorry, chicka."

"But who wants to talk about that now? Not me, señorita!

Fantastic art and handicrafts lined the streets, sold by humble artists who welcomed American money. No beggars, no litter on the street. Quoting the article Jilly found, she said Ecuadorians were "proud people, hospitable and unpretentious," and the description was delightfully true.

I knew enough Spanish to get by, barely, but Jilly could converse. She negotiated an upgrade to the executive suite of a nice-enough hotel and ordered room service with a fluency that astounded me. The three-course meal was traditional Ecuadorian: lots of seafood and, always, potatoes topped by a fried egg.

Taxis were screaming-yellow with a checkerboard on the bottom half. Jilly used her exuberant Kentucky-redneck accent. "The Middle of the World, por favor!"

The Middle of the World is the park at zero-degrees latitude – the imaginary line of the equator. I stood in awe of the Aztec-looking graphics on the buildings on that gorgeous, sunny day. Even at point zero, it wasn't hot because of the altitude. The Andes Mountains had no foothills like in the eastern U.S.; the mountains rose straight up from the sea.

As we strolled along the path on Middle Earth Plaza, I asked Jilly about it. She said, "You've seen nothing but the Atlantic coast, Lela. Haven't you at least seen pictures of crag-faced beaches? I mean, the Pacific coast is rocky."

"How would I know? When I won that award and went to L.A., I didn't go to the beach. Pacific beaches? No clue." I thought about Jilly's upbringing as we walked. "So how does a girl from Kentucky get to see so many parts of the world, anyway?"

"Ask my dad. Maybe he was in the Mafia or something."

"Well, you're lucky."

"But no, Lela. What *you* got from your parents is much more important! You got love. *Love, girl!* And you'd still get it if you'd just let them in."

"I know. I'm blessed. But they're suffocating sometimes."

A hack of a laugh exploded from Jilly's mouth. "Oh, come on! You have no reason to complain." I didn't reply right away, watching my feet on the asphalt path. Thirty paces later, she asked, "Why don't you let them in your life, anyway? And what happened to Jennifer being your bestie? She never hangs out with us anymore."

"Jennifer told me I drank too much." I said it fast, thinking it would be less painful to hear, less of a soul-bearing confession to Jilly.

A long pause. "You drink too much, huh?"

"Yep... that's what she said." I sighed from deep within my lungs. "Said she couldn't watch me destroy myself anymore, or something like that." I tried to act completely unperturbed... flat and nonchalant. "Hey! Let's chill on this overlook a second." I sat on the bench and fiddled with the hem of my shorts.

We sat in silence for almost a minute. Then Jilly asked, "Did she use the word 'alcoholic' or anything?"

My breath caught. "Well, I don't really want to say."

"So she did, right?" My silence was an affirmative answer, I guess. I had told nobody about Jennifer's confrontation and how it cut me to the bone. She wouldn't stop talking that day, no matter how much I cried or how many times I told her she was wrong. Her voice shook with emotion, but no tears fell; she just sat there with lips so thin... like a pencil line. She must have said "I love you, Lela" a thousand times, and "I'm telling you this because I love you."

I stretched my back with an exaggerated "yack" moan. "Man! I'm getting stiff sitting here! Daylight's wasting, my friend. Let's go."

"You sure? Seems like you'd want to talk about it..."

"No, let's go get into something crazy instead. You up for trouble?"

"That's one way to deal with it."

"Oh, Jilly! *Hush!* I don't want to talk–"

She raised her hand to rub her chin, absent-mindedly. "But I'm thinking... I'm getting a little worried myself."

I sprang from the bench, narrowed my eyes, and shook a finger at Jilly. Rat-a-tat, I spit words at her, "Don't *you* fucking jump on me, Jilly Jameson! I am *not* an alcoholic!" I said it loud. Heads turned.

"Chill out! I'm not jumping on you! Dayum!" Then she spoke through a deep sigh, "I'm thinking... if *you're* an alcoholic, then what am *I?*"

It seemed my personality split into three parts with that comment. One Lela laughed heartily. The other Lela cried like an abandoned infant. The Lela in-between quaked with fear but refused to let the other two show their emotions.

It was like... my life passing before my eyes. I felt the ghost of Granny Liz on my shoulder, her bony finger shaking as if scolding me... yet she was smiling and, in her left hand, a pan of biscuits shined golden brown. In my mind's eye, I saw the face of my father, snorting a laugh as he does. And I felt the dual-sided breeze of balancing on the edge of a cliff - with five seconds to decide if I should jump.

All the while, one of the Lelas laughed, one cried, and one trembled.

I sat listening to the cacophony inside my head and watching Jilly's eyes twitch while looking into mine.

A decision. The laughing Lela won the contest. I ate the biscuits, laughed with Daddy, and jumped off the cliff. To me, it was freedom. I threw my head back and pealed hysterical laughter. "Easy answer, Jilly! It means you're an alkie, too! We're twins! Let's have a drink to celebrate!"

A slow smile built on Jilly's pale face as she threw a lock of blonde hair over her shoulder. "You think?"

"I *know!*"

"What the hell?"

"Exactly!"

"Ecuadorian wine?"

"A dozen cups. I saw the vendor on the plaza."

"Me, too."

We stood at the same time. Quick steps turned into a race-walk pace, which sparked a competition where we tried to trip each other in trying to win. Laughter, the easy kind that Jilly and I had always shared. She was as much of a friend to me as sister Karen was.

☀ ☀ ☀ ☀ ☀

Wine cups in hand, we took the obligatory pictures of each other straddling the equator line, using my camera and the Polaroid of a soft-spoken Latino woman who sold the pictures for a dollar.

While nursing our second cup of wine, we spent a glorious hour in the museum that featured equator facts printed in eighteen languages. It was the opposite of American tourist spots, nothing cheesy or overpriced. And the park was full of national pride instead of t-shirts, clean and bursting with employees who pampered the guests because they genuinely wanted to do so.

Jilly and I wandered around, watching the children play and noting the diversity of visitors. The street food tasted fresh and awesome, served from sparkling-clean food trucks.

"Jilly, I'm in love with this country." We high-fived as she agreed.

Finding another bench, on the perimeter on the plaza this time, we sat and sipped our fourth cup of wine slowly. In a near whisper, Jilly said, "So... everything's cool?"

"Major cool," I said. But I knew it wasn't cool. Jilly knew it too. In fact, nothing was cool when it came to us and the alcohol circulating in our bodies.

True to form, knowing it wasn't cool to drink so much didn't stop me from drinking too much. The disease continued to blossom. But I think being Jilly's partner in alcoholism made it seem more manageable. There was less on the line, somehow, someone to share the blame. And if another person was also being stupid, then maybe it wasn't so stupid after all. Neither of us were in the gutter, right?

I thought about my supposed secret of not being able to do my "job," even a job I had designed to be non-taxing. Maybe I could excel in another job... maybe Jilly's daddy could buy me a job, too... a job where I didn't have to work.

No, Lela. You need a job so you can fuck it all up. Let the bottom fall out, let everything go to hell. You are defeated, anyway... it's just a matter of time before everybody else knows your secret.

☀ ☀ ☀ ☀ ☀

We drank through three more days in the city, hiding my "Surely I didn't do that!" memories behind a veil of tequila, beer, and sweet Ecuadorian wine. One night, we asked the concierge where we could go dancing; when we used the word "discotheque," he understood and hailed us a cab. We wore skimpy sundresses and the neon-pearl eyeshadow Jilly had brought for this very purpose.

The club was dark with sparsely placed black lights as you'd expect in an American club. Ear-splitting music, Latino-inspired and heavy with a dance beat, vibrated from speakers eight feet high and two feet wide.

I remember little; we danced with each other while surrounded by Ecuadorian sleazeballs licking their lips. No doubt, we made a spectacle of ourselves; we would have without the half-dozen shots of tequila.

Somehow, we didn't get raped in the disco and didn't fall down and break our legs. The next thing I knew, we were in a taxi. Jilly in the front seat rubbing her calves on the driver's neck. I remember yelling at her to keep her legs together so she would show her panties... and I remember her yelling back at me "Tricked you, Lela! I'm not wearing any!"

The next thing I remember is Jilly in the back seat of the taxi with me; who knows how that happened. She spoke to the driver, and only because I knew her so well, I understood her intention. She told him, "Mí amiga is leboñito," trying to say I was a lesbian. The problem was in the translation; she had said, "My friend is the beautiful."

I think now about how many times Jilly and I left ourselves vulnerable but somehow managed to survive. A patient angel watched over us, I suppose. (I know it now, for a fact, but at the time, I was simply grateful for a non-judgmental spirit.)

PANCHO & CHIQUITA
Chapter 34

"It's too dangerous, Ms. Jameson. All the tours have been canceled. I'm sorry."

"Exactly what do you mean by 'unrest on the border,' anyway? Isn't that always the case?"

"Yes, the war has gone on for years. But in the last few days, the Guatemalans have regained power and there is... what Americans call 'mayhem.' Tourists are being evacuated by your own government."

"So we can't go?"

"Not if you value your life, Ms. Jameson. Shall I whisk you a taxi to another destination?"

With just a slight pause to think, Jilly said, "Sí, Señor. To the bus station.

"The bus station, Jilly? Don't you think it would be–"

"If we can't see the rainforest, Plan B is to do something the natives do. So we're going on vacation. To Ecuador from Ecuador."

I looked at her with a question mark on my face. The mistrust lasted a full ten seconds though her confident air never waned. "Whatever you say, Ms. Tour Director, I'm all in."

"Just be prepared to carry your own bag. No bellmen there."

"Why am I not surprised?"

We taxied across town to the busy and noisy bus station. I guess I expected a Greyhound bus, and when I saw the refurbished school bus – the short size

– filled with a dozen chickens and two goats, I laughed. But we found seats among the natives and traveled two hours on pot-holed roads to the resort town of Baños, famous for its natural hot springs. The springs had earned a nationwide reputation, touted as a miracle cure.

We checked in to the nicest of the hotels, which was a dump. "Rooms" in cabin-like buildings spotted the property on a series of terraced levels that climbed the mountain. No amenities; it was like being in Girl Scout camp. The on-property restaurant was an Ecuadorian twist on a low-life concession stand.

We ambled to check the view of the hot springs. "Oh, shit!" I said, at the same time Jilly said the same. The view of the mountainside was breathtaking, but on the carved plateaus of the mountain, hundreds of naked Latino people bathed in greenish-gray water.

"No way I'm going in there, Lela." Jilly said.

"Me neither! Even the upper pool... see it way up there?" The tourist brochure had featured only this pool, right? With a glistening trickle of water flowing behind like a personal waterfall. It was beautiful though the climb to the entrance would be arduous. "There's a reason nobody is in that one, but–"

"But still, no way. Let's take a stroll through town and see the horse man."

"The horse man?"

"You'll see."

The town was about ten blocks long, with the shops just re-opening after the day's siesta. There were medical offices, an office supply store, and shops well-stocked with handicrafts – a variety of woven textiles in bright colors, carved wood icons and boxes, and plastic-wrapped candies. We both bought our souvenirs along the streets of Baños and enjoyed a nice day in a town not quite as clean as Quito, but just as friendly. The people were poorer, more "working class," but seemed just as happy as the Ecuadorians we had met since our arrival.

One woman, a shopkeeper, spoke to us in broken English. "Me in love American. I go soon." She gestured to ask Jilly if it was okay for her to touch her bright-blonde hair and she allowed it. The woman giggled, petting her head as if Jilly was a kitten.

A few paces later, Jilly announced. "Here it is. Our last stop." The sign over a canopied storefront said "Andes Tours."

The man behind the counter took my breath away. Latin men are noticeably sexy and shy, but this guy was an Adonis with a humble stance and sideways grin. Muy bueno... or caliente-hot, as Jilly would say.

Jilly spoke to the man quickly in Spanish, too fast for me to follow. I heard snippets of the nouns "horse" and "mountain," plus "gentle," and "turn around," and some numbers... ocho. Maybe ocho hours; eight. Connecting the dots, I assumed she had just booked a gentle horse ride in the mountains that lasted eight hours and we turned around halfway. Sounded kick-ass awesome to me... especially if the guide was the fine specimen behind the counter.

Jilly said adiós and turned to go. I stopped her in mid-turn. "No way I'm leaving without an introduction to the Ecuadorian God of Love. Do the honors, por favor."

A loud laugh from Jilly. "He's been checking you out since we walked in, anyway."

"Oh, you can bet I noticed! You blonde girls have it bad in South America. They think you're from Mars. Me? I'm just a bit... pale." I looked at the man but spoke to Jilly. "So tell him who his next lover will be." She spat a paragraph of Spanish. I heard "friend" and "pretty."

He flashed a smile that warmed my heart, half-boy and half-macho. Dark eyes, clear coffee-with-cream skin, and eyelashes longer than mine. I'd braced my arm for a handshake, but he touched my hand softly, cupping the palm, and brought it to his mouth. A kiss, soft but firm, as his eyes speared me like daggers. "Hello," he said in a throaty voice, "Hello, Lela, my love." My knees weakened and a buzz between my ears throbbed. A few other places throbbed, too.

"I...I..." Flabbergasted, overwhelmed, I couldn't speak.

"I es Jesus," he said, "Not American 'Jesus.' Poco, I am 'Zeus.'" My brow knotted. *What the hell does he mean?*

Jilly stepped in to explain. "'Poco' means 'short.' So his nickname is Zeus, short for Jesus, and not Jesus. Think about the spelling."

I got the joke and decided to give him some shit. "You no like Jesus?" His face instantly turned to panic, and he grasped my hand tighter.

"No! I *love* Jesús! Love, love, *love* Jesús. Adoro a Jesús!"

"Good... because I like *Zeus*. Your name." I wiggled my eyebrows and the look of relief on his face flashed, immediately followed by another adorable embarrassed smile. I was a sucker for a timid man who needed a brazen vixen like me to make the half-smile complete.

He added his left hand to the grip of my right and kissed it again. "Sí, sí! Lela love Zeus... Zeus love Lela!" His English was beautifully broken, so sexy.

Jilly told me later that we stared at each other for more than a minute, spilling love into each other's eyes. "You could see it dripping on the floor, Lela. Jeez! You're a little harlot – that's what you are."

"But tomorrow, I'll behave myself. I'm not jumping off a damn-good horse to jump onto the back of his... and I'm not letting him jump onto mine and slap the reins. No galloping for me. I'm scared of horses, kinda. But don't tell Zeus, okay. I don't want him to think I'm a candy-ass."

"Not an ounce of candy-ass in you, Lela."

We woke at dawn and walked to the Andes Tours office in the mist. Zeus' face lit up like a candle when we entered and I struggled to catch what he was saying but he spoke so fast! I tried a complete sentence: "Zeus, por favor, hablar moroso."

His reaction was instant, his eyes became saucers over a clown-wide grin. "Yes! I will speak slow! Lela! Slow!" It was like I'd told him he'd won the lottery. Again, his eyes penetrated mine; he looked into the folds of my soul. As my heartbeat raced, I tried to stop my feelings. *What, Lela? Are you in a romance movie or something? This is crazy shit. Stop acting like a schoolgirl!*

Jilly chimed in. "I think he likes your attempts at Spanish, Lela. He thinks it's cute."

"I think he thinks I'm cute all around," I said, not taking my eyes from Zeus. Jilly cleared her throat. Once. Twice. Then she waved her arms, trying to get our guide's attention.

Finally, she spoke. In Spanish, but I guess she asked when we would leave because Zeus moved fast, saying "Ahora, ahora!" That word meant now, I knew that much.

He rolled three mini-bikes from the back of the shop and gestured for us to choose one. Another gesture on how to start the tiny bike. He started his own, and we puttered to the street.

Ten minutes of cold, cold, cold wind in my face, though the bike couldn't go much faster than maybe 25 MPH. Ten minutes later, we arrived at a rickety barn on the mountainside. Jilly and I wandered around in the barn as Zeus saddled the horses, humming Spanish-sounding tunes. "Lela, remember you promised to behave."

"Hell, nothing to drink yet, and I don't imagine they'll be a beer stop. Sober for eight hours, I can behave myself. But Katy-bar-the-door when we get back to town."

"Maybe we can invite Zeus to our hotel..."

244

"Jilly! Don't say that! It'll be *your* fault if I get in trouble!" As we teased each other back and forth, Zeus walked between us and we fell into silence.

He spoke to Jilly in Spanish, still much faster than I could understand. We walked the horses to the mouth of the path and I attempted to mount the huge monster-animal. Thankfully, his description of "gentle" held; the horse didn't react to my multiple ineffective attempts to get in the saddle.

Finally, Zeus chuckled and pushed my butt as I rose and that was enough "oomph" to mount successfully. With a sly smile, I purred, "Gracias, querido," meaning, "Thank you, sweetheart," and his face ignited like a candelabra at full-light.

"Lela, don't show your fear. That horse knows," Jilly advised.

"Okay," I said, patting the horse's neck, "Good, horsey... sweet, gentle, well-trained horsey. Don't run off without me, okay?"

My attempt to ask Zeus the horse's name failed miserably because I tried to ask in Spanish. His face showed a complete lack of understanding. Jilly knew what I was asking and translated my question to Zeus, then translated his response: A female named Chiquita. I laughed. "Seriously? Like the banana! I love it!"

Another Spanish exchange between Jilly and Zeus, then Jilly said, "Mine is a male named Pancho, and he said 'let's get going.'"

"Pancho said that, or Zeus?"

"Ha, ha, smartass."

Zeus led the way on a white horse with a solemn walking pace. Around the first bend, he upped the pace a bit, and again fifty yards later. With each change, my fear increased; I braced myself, holding on tighter by gripping the horse's belly a little harder with my legs.

With the fourth change of pace, I gripped harder and pushed harder into the stirrups. In the flash of a second, Chiquita zoomed around our guide and galloped the uphill trail, white air bursting from her nostrils. I screamed words I can't remember; I'm sure the only one my mom would approve of was "Help!"

Zeus caught up with me a hundred yards later, speaking to the horse. "Shooooooooow, Chiquita, shoooooow." The command immediately calmed her, and though it took another fifty yards, she slowed and stopped. Zeus looked at me with concern, asking if I was okay... without words. I communicated that I was scared to death but unhurt.

"What is 'shooooooow?'" I asked.

He looked down with the adorable embarrassed-little-boy smile again, then struggled to find the words to explain. "Uh... quiet, happy... both."

Jilly stopped her horse easily as she joined us. "Jilly, tell him that 'shoooooow' sounds like an all-purpose command, for people, too," His response was a knowing nod with raised eyebrows, followed by a phrase I understood: "Vamoose!"

I realized my mistake after the fact. Duh. The horse had bolted because squeezing her belly was the command for "faster." It had been years since I'd ridden, but I felt stupid for not remembering that basic thing. Jilly laughed but assured me all was well now. I tried to show my fear of the animal in other ways, like screaming to Jilly. She carefully calmed me. "Shooooow, Lela, shoooooow."

Once I relaxed and could look around and enjoy the landscape, I was captivated. We had climbed to a high altitude by then, and everything was new. The flora and fauna of the Andes Mountains were diverse, and Jilly pointed out things I'd never heard of, like flowering wild-potato bushes and an unknown species of gnarly evergreen trees.

And instead of the Smoky Mountain Black Bear I feared in my "hometown mountains," llamas and alpacas roamed free. I gasped with delight as condors flew overhead.

We rode for hours before the rain came. Sprinkles became drops, then streams, then a waterfall pouring on our heads. Instantly soaked to the bone. Zeus dropped back to speak to Jilly, then veered off the trail to a lean-to garage connected to a house that had appeared randomly in the middle of nowhere. Under shelter, I lowered my coat hood to see Zeus staring at me with an award-winning smile.

"What?" I asked

"Hermosa," he said, "Hermosa mujer..." I asked Jilly for the translation; "Beautiful woman."

It was my turn to be embarrassed. I thanked him, keeping my head lowered. Unexpectedly, my stomach made a nervous flip-flop. It was a different feeling than yesterday's; I felt a romantic attraction to Zeus, not just a sexual one.

The rain continued to pound the earth; it seemed we'd be waiting a while. Zeus began a friendly conversation, asking surprisingly personal questions. When he asked if I had an "el spouso," I gestured "somewhat" with a slight back and forth movement of my hand. That cracked Jilly up and she asked if my okay-to-sleep-with-somebody permission slip from a previous trip still applied. I answered in Spanish: "Sí sí sí!" Zeus smiled as if he knew what we had said.

Hovering at the edge of the shelter, I could see the snow cap of Cayambe Mountain in the distance and let it become a Shangri-La in my mind. I found myself happily lost in a dream. Jilly asked about the mountain top and Zeus said it would be our turnaround point. I questioned that; it was too far away. We'd been riding for almost three hours already.

More Spanish to Jilly, which she translated: "This hot tour guide has misled us, it seems. He's trying to get us to camp in the mountains with him for the night." Somehow, I felt no fear or anger, not even surprise. Jilly's calm response to his "invitation" translated to say we couldn't camp but could sure use a beer.

"I know a village," he said in Spanish, "Beer all day." After having waited for almost an hour for the rain to slow, we trotted out of the lean-to and continued up the trail. The landscape now glowed with fluorescent green plants; the rain had brightened them like a black light brightens the color white.

Suddenly, the trail opened to become a double-wide road lined with storefronts. Ramshackle houses dotted the mountainside behind the stores. "What is the name of this village?" I asked Zeus.

Again, translated through Jilly, he had answered. "Sigchos." I attempted to repeat it but the word refused to roll off my tongue. In response to my stuttering Spanish, Jilly joked, "It translates to 'Fuck it, let's have a beer!'"

Front and center in the village of Sigchos sat a majestic cathedral. It was huge, with massive stained glass windows in arched shapes. We tied our horses to the post in front of the church and walked three doors down to what our guide called "el puesto de comida," a snack bar. Like dots, colorful outdoor umbrellas and wooden tables peppered the small patio in front of the food counter. "Cheerful," Jilly giggled.

No neon beer signs flashed in the windows, no wall coolers overflowed with beer. Quite the opposite, the owner of the snack bar scowled in disapproval when Zeus placed our order for three cervezas, eyeing him as if he was a child molester. His eyes widened in seeing the so-out-of-place blonde Jilly.

The owner's snippy reply translated to "Not cold and very expensive," to which Zeus replied, "No problem. Three of your best, please."

The national beer, Turtle Pale Ale, tasted awesome, even lukewarm. We spent the day in the village... laughing flirting, and making fun of incorrect Spanish-English translations. Halfway through my third beer, I began to suspect our guide Zeus knew a lot more English than he first let on. Halfway through my fourth beer, I didn't care. And after each of us had five, a low and slow series of bells rang out. Three dozen villagers paraded down the dirt road, on the way to the Catholic cathedral. Their black eyes stared us down for our "foreign, sinful ways."

I saw Zeus attempt to hide his face as he sat in silence. "Are you a Catholic, Zeus? A religious man?"

"Sí" was the beginning of a run-on sentence in a mix of English and Spanish. He crossed himself, still talking, confusing me even more. While he continued the rat-a-tat speech, Jilly threw her head back and laughed, slapping her knee.

"What's he saying, Jilly?"

"Oh, my God! He's hilariously in love with you!"

"What did he say?"

"Many things." When she stopped laughing again, she spoke through a mass of giggles. "Basically, he said he's a good Catholic boy, but already needs to go to confession for his thoughts about you. He's afraid his mother would... disown him for the sin he is hoping to commit tonight." With the third round of hysterical laughter, she raised her brown bottle for a toast. "Here's to Zeus!"

I laughed, too, snapping a look at Zeus, his face now filled with fear and guilt. He was wringing his hands and stress seemed to vibrate from his body like the gong of a tuning fork.

Trying to lighten the mood, I winked at him. His reaction was a moan and more wringing of the hands. He kept saying, "Dios, Dios," which Jilly said meant "God." Suddenly I felt bad, like I was leading a sheep astray, a sheep destined to be killed by the big, bad wolf. *Bad Lela, back off, girl! This is a good man and you're leading him where he doesn't want to go. Stop it! Right this second!*

I spoke softly. "Zeus..." His eyes filled with tears and he looked at me pleadingly. My expression was solemn when I said, "Shoooooow." The look of relief was obvious; his body visibly relaxed. With a smile, I raised my bottle. "To amigos, to friends." He reached to clang beer bottles as if he was desperate to do so, then he turned the beer upside down, draining it dry.

We agreed to leave before the church service was over. After six beers each, all three of us had a hard time staying on the horses on the ride down the mountain. I fell off twice and he hoisted me back on the horse. Jilly fell asleep in the saddle, or so it seemed. Zeus' eyes rolled back in his head a few times, I noticed. Our guide shouted a command of some sort, "Caminar!" Translation: "Walk!"

I took Chiquita by the reins and walked; we all did. In single file. As the path narrowed, Jilly and I sang Girl Scout songs, ridiculous children's songs like *The Wheels on the Bus Go Round and Round*, and all of them caused hearty laughs from a sobering Zeus.

He taught us Spanish slang and cuss words and giggled at our accents. His boyish grin on luscious mocha skin was a strong turn-on, but I had promised to back off. Promises to myself, however, were the ones most easily broken. I knew I could seduce him in the snap of a finger; we'd never meet again, right? But high on the mountain, my integrity held.

At last, Zeus stopped to gather his riders in a circle. "We eat now," he said.

"Thank God!" I breathed. Zeus snapped a look at me, I think reacting to my mention of "Dios." He smiled; something I'd done had made him happy and the innocent smile returned.

His saddlebag held a blanket for sitting and containers of cheese, plantains and other fruit, iced shrimp, and three bottles of water. All three of us ate like starving children, and it was like flipping a switch on my sobriety. The combination of exercise and food, and maybe the thin air, had sobered me up completely.

When we returned the horses to the barn, Zeus started the scooter motorbikes for us. It seemed this was where we'd say goodbye. A hundred thank you's passed between us, then I blurted the question I'd been holding inside. In half-and-half Spanish-English, I said, "Zeus, please come party with us. Wine? More beer? Dinner?" The smile on his face was endearing. *He wants to be with us! The story continues!*

Back in Zeus' office, Jilly twirled in a provocative dance and sang "Hot-hot-hot! Caliente!" We all laughed, then Jilly spoke quickly to Zeus and he answered in hundreds of words like he was spitting bullets from an automatic weapon. *How can she understand when he speaks so fast?* But she had understood and told me what he said. "I asked where to get Ecuadorian wine. We've got a stop to make."

Zeus followed us.

Suddenly – and I say suddenly because my memory fails me otherwise – the three of us were in the hot tub at our hotel, each drinking from our own bottle of wine. Like a pair of sloppy drunks, Jilly and I sang "A Hundred Bottles of Wine on the Wall," slurring our words. A laughing Zeus wore a pair of boxer shorts in blue and green plaid; Jilly and I were naked. It didn't seem to bother any of us that the water had a greenish tint.

I sang a current pop song in English, substituting Spanish cuss words here and there, as Jilly and Zeus sang backup. At some point, I choked on my wine, swallowing too much air, and coughed up a lungful of the pink-ish wine into the hot tub. We all jumped out, and my memory stopped with the first rash of goosebumps; it was cold as hell in the mountains at night.

In the next memory flash, I wore a skimpy dress, way too skimpy for the weather, with a cheering crowd behind me. I stood on the rungs of a bar stool, leaning forward to grip a shot of tequila in my lips, my hands behind my back. I stood up and threw my head back to shoot the tequila down my throat.

As I reeled from the effects of the shot, Zeus leaned me backward and kissed me deeply, greedily. The crowd continued to cheer, now clapping in time and chanting something in Spanish: I think "el amor," which means "love," but the "el" made it masculine. My guess, after the fact, was they were encouraging Zeus to make love to me. Notice the euphemism.

Then, oddly enough, I have flashes of an elbow-to-elbow crowd of ruffians at a cockfight and a memory of putting my face into Zeus' neck so he could "protect me" from whatever it was. He didn't soothe me, though; instead, he yelled with the crowd and shook his arm in time with the roomful of chants. It was 'ir' for "go." Said frantically and repeatedly, it sounded like the music in *Psycho* when Norman Bates opened the shower curtain, building to a crescendo that sent the smell of sweat in a cloud.

The final memory was being in bed with Zeus, but with Jilly beside us, passed out. On the verge of orgasm, I screamed, probably some version of "Yes-yes-yes... Fuck me, Zeus!" He didn't stop his work, but whispered back at me, "Shooooooooow, Lela, shoooooow."

I woke up naked and in Jilly's bed, wondering why. It was dawn; roosters were everywhere and their crows were constant. "What the hell kind of town *is* this, Jilly? Roosters? Please!"

"Ah! Live as the locals live! Let's get up and have coffee. Everybody's been up for hours already. We're late."

"Late my ass." But I found a sweatshirt and decent pants for the short walk to the hotel's concession stand. Jilly was right; people were everywhere. Watching them move so fast made my hangover worse, but two cups of the strong Ecuadorian coffee was a near-instant hangover cure.

As I watched a young woman scramble to clean the tables, I thought about Zeus. "Do you think he made it to confession before his momma disowned him?" I asked.

"I'm sure God will forgive him, Lela. It's not like you gave him much choice. Maybe you're the one who should go to confession."

"It's that damn Ecuadorian wine! That stuff is kick-ass."

"I'm sure the tequila helped, too."

"Yeah... it did. Should I feel bad? Shame on me?"

"You should feel bad only if he feels bad for taking you to a cockfight."

"I know! Isn't that bizarre? And the smell! Awful! Super-strong body odor. And... you know how blood leaves a taste in your mouth from just smelling it? Oh, it was gross-gross-gross. Jilly, I tried to look away, but... something happened. Then I don't remember much else.

"I still can't understand why you two came to *my* bed to start making love."

My brow knotted in trying to remember. "I think I was trying to convince him I was gay and the two of us were lovers."

"So you tried to *not* sleep with him after all that teasing? Damn, Lela."

"I don't know why I did it... any of it."

Jilly cocked her head and took a sip of her piping-hot coffee. "Why? That's an easy answer. B'cause you're a mixed-up kid, that's why."

"Mixed-up? What makes you say that so easily?"

She laughed. "Are you kidding? You don't think you're – quote – mixed up?"

"No more than *you* are."

"Touché, my friend."

"But I think I remember seeing his face over me when we were screwing..."

Jilly threw her head back and laughed. "Oh, hell! You don't remember that part?"

"No. And quit laughing at me."

"Oh, Zeus knew how to shut you up. Girl, you scream having an orgasm."

"Oh, God! Maybe I don't want to hear any more of your memories. I thought you were passed out cold!"

"I heard him, Lela. He shushed you with 'shooooooow,' then built up from there, screaming it during his own damn orgasm."

"Oh, no. I'm so embarrassed."

"You oughta be. Thankfully, it was just in front of me, not 'God and everybody,' as they say.

"My old friends return to haunt me: guilt, shame, and remorse. They're creeping up the base of my spine, Jilly. It's like... what would my mother say?"

"She would say you're a badass alcoholic that does stupid, dangerous things."

"And you know that because....?"

"Isn't that exactly what Jennifer told you?" Jilly knew how to put a lump in my throat.

On the flight home to Rockville, I had plenty of time to reflect on what I'd done. I shrunk into the window seat in shame, but not for the reason one would expect. The shame came from feeling no shame. I worried I had crossed some kind of invisible line on the way to becoming a sociopath.

The drinking wasn't an issue, I thought. I accepted my dependence on it and justified the things I did as normal consequences of drinking. For the most part, I could laugh about my behavior. Drunks are funny, right?

But having no shame in sleeping with Zeus... seducing him as a slut would seduce a John... while still pining for Jenna and sleeping with my husband. Hell, I focused on sex the instant vodka was introduced to the scene.

I said out loud, "Man, you *are* fucked up." My seat neighbor looked at me and nodded.

I'd lost count of how many people I'd slept with. In that instant, I knew something had to change... big time. I had no idea what to change or how to change it.

I'd never felt so lonely in my life.

DOWNSTAIRS
Chapter 35

About six months after we returned from Ecuador, a man showed up on Jilly's porch looking sheepish and, as she called it, "apologetically gorgeous." Though sober, he had accidentally crashed into her car that was parked too far from the curb in front of her house. Yep, parked like a drunk parks at three in the morning.

Jilly wore her long hot-pink furry robe and leopard-print slippers as they evaluated the damage. Her neighbors, all twelve of them, stared through their windows to gape at Jilly and the man named Dane. Maybe they could see the vibrations of love, passion, and adoration surrounding their bodies.

Jilly invited Dane inside to call his insurance agent. Twelve days later they were engaged and a month after that, they slipped by the courthouse to get married on the way to Atlanta. They arrived at Dane's Buckhead condo pulling a U-Haul trailer of Jilly's belongings.

She called me the day they met, the day they got engaged, and the day after they moved. Then no more calls from my BFF, the woman I had depended on for both sanity and insanity. My worst influence and my best friend disappeared in a heartbeat and I was despondent. I couldn't muster one iota of happiness for her; I only thought of how lonely I would be without her.

Another week in bed, waking only when Lola arrived. I decided Lola would become my best friend and caretaker.

Work-wise, she had a knack for Moonlight Jewelry handiwork, kept records like an OCD maniac, and took up my slack without a word. Thankfully, she didn't need supervision because I could rarely accomplish anything on my own, much less know what had to be done in the big picture of it.

About ten days after Jilly moved, I actually made it to my standing appointment with my therapist. My normal life resumed. As if "normal" had anything to do with it.

At work, my job was to buy the castings, tools, and hardware... spending money the business didn't have and wouldn't make any time soon. But going broke didn't bother me so bad. It took a long time for me to even realize it was happening.

Lola and I laughed a lot, smoked a lot of cigarettes, and traveled to dozens of craft shows. Many festivals where we sold jewelry were street fairs, with beer and wine flowing like a waterfall. I liked those fairs for many reasons. First, drunk customers buy more. Second, it kept me buzzed during the long hours of the sales day. Once I started drinking, usually to medicate myself through the disappointment of slow sales, I couldn't stop drinking. Day after day, night after night, sober Lola ran the booth, counted the money, closed down for the night, and drove us back to the hotel.

Back in Rockville, I depended on her for fun, too. She had a cowboy boyfriend: Mel Durren. The three of us met for happy hour at least once a week. Mel made me laugh and could drink me under the table. (I tried to match him but failed.) He ran a farm in east Rockville where he bred and trained quarter horses.

"I'm not going to brag about it, Lela, but my horses are the best in the Southeast." Mel drummed his fingers on the thick wooden table with his other arm around Lola's shoulders.

"Uh... Mel. Saying that *is* bragging. But Lola has told me all about your awards and stuff. Truthfully, I'm impressed." Mel beamed; even a confident man lies to hear shit like that. "In fact, Lola used the term 'celebrated breeder.' I like that. It sounds much more humble than 'best in the Southeast.'"

Lola spoke in her upbeat way. "But it's not just breeding that's earned him the reputation. It's Logan, his trainer. And Logan rides in the competitions... lots more awards there."

"I've heard you talk about Logan before, but he's never around. What's up with that?"

Mel chuckled. "Logan always wants to know when you come to our happy hours, Lela. He's... let's use the word 'intrigued.' Yeah, he's intrigued by you."

"But I've never met him! I should know somebody who is intrigued with me, don't ya think?"

"He can only get out on Tuesdays and Thursdays."

"Oh. He works a lot or something?"

"Uh... something like that."

Our introduction came the following week, a Tuesday. "Intrigued by me" was an understatement. It seemed he had already appointed himself a boyfriend, "hot for me" much more than intrigued. The flirting started with our introduction. He kissed my hand. Damn good-looking, about five years older than me but far more wrinkled, Logan sported a toothy cowboy grin that sent shivers down my spine. The one, glaring issue: his accent pegged him as a country boy from a rural county.

"Logan, not to piss you off or anything. I mean this to be nice. You're surprisingly intelligent for a redneck. McMann County's school of grammar gave you an advanced degree."

Logan threw his head back to laugh. "McMann County and my daddy educated me with a stick, not a damn carrot – that's fer sure. But that's all I know, Lela. I know how to run a farm and work like a dog. But I'm tough as nails."

"Able to leap tall buildings with a single bound?"

"Yep, call me Superman. Super Cowboy!" The exclamation, diluted with his lazy twang, made me laugh.

Logan was... odd. He called waitresses "Miss Ma'am," ordered his steaks well-done and over-tipped at restaurants and bars. He worked as the manager of a well-known body shop in Skylark and flashed hundred-dollar bills left and right. Tall and skinny, but every muscle was sculpted. Logan had the friendliest of faces, an aura of humility, and kind eyes behind wire-rim glasses. Perhaps the most odd, he never left a restaurant without stealing a coffee cup or a cream pitcher, sometimes a spoon. He didn't try to be sneaky about his thievery; he just walked out with his treasure and a broad smile.

The third time he showed at a Lola/Mel happy hour, he brought me a present. He'd been to Texas for a horse show and bought a cowboy hat for me: an expensive Stetson. When he plopped it on my head, he kissed me. I backed up, but his intentions were clear. More than once, he came *this close* to stepping over the line with his flirting. But to tell the truth, I liked it. No, I *loved* it!

I didn't know how much I liked him until we met at Mel's barn, got drunk on whiskey, and he carried me up the log staircase to make love in the barn helper's bed upstairs. Then I liked him a lot.

He was romantic and showered me with southern charm and roses, took me to expensive restaurants, and bought me sparkly presents. The four of us became a party-in-the-making, every Tuesday and Thursday, every week.

There was no doubt Logan was an alcoholic; Mel, too. Lola rarely drank at all but seemed to let our shenanigans roll off her back, never complaining about being the designated driver on our late nights.

Happy hours ended at three o'clock in the morning, sometimes later. We perused the bars, ate at all-night cowboy bars in East Rockville, and danced like idiots at Mel's "castle." Once we made a series of prank phone calls, including placing an order totaling $1,000 on Mel's credit card from a sex toy outlet.

Each time I asked why he could only party on Tuesdays and Thursdays, he dodged the question. If it was early in the night, I squirmed with suspicion; if it was after the three-drink line, I didn't care. Why should I care? I only wanted to party and act silly with a happy-go-lucky guy.

It wasn't until the third month that I found out he was married.

Lola said she'd been trying to tell me herself, but according to her, I was "a little too drunk to understand her warning."

She asked, "What are you going to do now?"

"Well, I've slept with married women before, but not married men. I don't quite know." I took a week off from the Logan/Mel/Lola party.

A lot happened in that week.

☼ ☼ ☼ ☼ ☼

"You're staying home tonight? But it's Tuesday…" Miller spoke behind the newspaper while lounging in the recliner, as usual.

"How do you know I have a pattern? Why are you checking up on me?"

"Well, Lela, dammit. You are my wife, ya know."

"Not really. Not anymore."

"We need to do something."

"You're right. But I don't want anything to change with Bo. This is not his fault."

"True…"

"And I'm afraid Andy will try for full custody if we divorce, so I'm not doing it."

"Who said divorce?"

"Ohhhhhh. You think we can fix this shit?"

"No." A long pause. "Not at all." He squashed the newspaper into his lap and popped the recliner to sit up straight.

"Then what?" My voice rose an octave; I felt some shit coming down.

"Could you... uh..."

"Could I what? Spit it out, Miller." I shot words like darts.

"Maybe, uh, could you... live somewhere else every-other-week? When Bo's not here?"

"What the fuck! No! You asshole! What the hell are you talking about? Why don't *YOU* move, then? Get your ass off that fucking recliner once in a while? Take all the time you want to read your fucking newspaper! Doesn't that sound good, you sonofabitch?"

"Quit screaming, Lela. That's not what I wanted this to be about."

"What the hell were you expecting, Miller?" I was gasping for air, shaking with anger.

"Hell... I don't know." His exasperated voice roared loud. "It's not like you've ever been calm if I've asked you to do something..."

"Just shut up... shut the hell up!"

I snapped my head away from his glare and stomped from the living room to the kitchen. Grabbing a bottle of wine and a big plastic glass, I continued stomping, for effect, in my walk down the steps.

In my studio, I gulped the wine, waiting for my heart rate to slow. Mad, scared, flabbergasted, distressed, and completely dejected. And mostly sad. Just fucking sad.

An hour later, I sneaked upstairs to get a fresh bottle of wine. I peeked into the living room... the bedroom... then tiptoed to the garage. No car. Miller was gone.

Sober enough to pull it off, I thought, I grabbed a few boxes from the garage and raced to the bathroom. Basic toiletries and my lighted makeup mirror; that's all I had room for downstairs. I found a small table and a stool to create a vanity. With three trips, I carried most of the current season's clothes down and loaded the closet in the bedroom beside my studio. It would now be my room.

This wasn't a one-time thing. I knew it would be my permanent residence. I reasoned it could stay this way without incident if I didn't rock the boat. Married, separated, but co-parents. I'd have to think of a good lie to explain it to Bo, but from now on, non-Bo days were mine alone, in the basement.

Afraid to keep going up and down the steps, afraid Miller would return before I finished moving, I worked fast. My heart beat like I was in a race... because I was. With the basics in place and somewhat organized, I sat down at my computer and lit up the keyboard with a letter. A fuck-you letter to Miller. The caps-lock button stayed on lock throughout the first page, followed by the second page of pleas and bargaining. The third page detailed a logical plan of how this arrangement would work for the three of us.

A lot had to happen fast. It was after midnight, making it the Friday I'd pick up Bo for our week. *No, it's MY week. There's nothing "our" anymore.*

All these years with that sonofabitch, that really nice guy who is a sonofabitch to me now... those years wasted. For nothing.

I gained a few trinkets, learned a few things, met a few people but otherwise, it was a bust. And it's all his fucking fault. The only thing I did was beg him to be lovable. But he can't do it. I should have listened to Vick Belford when he said Miller was a dud. It turned out to be the truth.

And I should have listened to Granny Liz when she saw Miller loved Bo more than he loved me. All true. I should have listened to everybody who warned me. I should have known and had the balls to leave years ago. Thank God we didn't have kids together, but why did I buy this expensive damn house?

Tears began in earnest. Only then did I realize I didn't have a bed downstairs; it hadn't even occurred to me. My thoughts went to a list of all the things I'd need to create a home for myself in the basement.

"Fuck him! I'm sleeping upstairs! He's probably not coming home, anyway. Maybe he's at his fucking girlfriend's place. I don't give a shit!" The volume of my words increased as I spoke, with the last few words a hysteric scream.

☀ ☀ ☀ ☀ ☀

I woke up at first light with a clear head and swollen eyes. Miller hadn't come home, but that was no surprise. Pushing the sadness out of my mind, I began a mental list of the day's must-do tasks, happy that Lola would be in to help me... and happy I wasn't due at a show that weekend.

Coffee. A notepad and my favorite purple pen. A box of Kleenex. The phone.

"Logan? This is Lela. Are you busy today? Can I borrow you and your truck to bring a mattress home?"

"Ashley Furniture Store? What's the most reasonably priced bed you carry, with a matching dresser? Free local delivery, right?"

"Comcast Cable, how soon can I get a connection set up in my basement?"

"Skylark Plumbing, can I schedule a man for this afternoon?" The lady offered bad news. "Rush charge of a hundred bucks!"

"Lola, can you come in early today? I need *lots* of help. And clean out your back seat. I need one of those dorm-sized refrigerators. The van can carry the bath cabinet and sink. The salvage store is a great place for one that small. Will you go with me?"

It was a busy day.

At four o'clock, I got Bo from after-school care and we headed to the baseball field for practice. I sat in the dugout as I always did. I acted the same, except I had zero words for Miller. He would find the truth soon enough. *Hell, he may not even notice! What an ass! Why did you ever marry him anyway, Lela? You knew this was coming!*

I caught my breath, willing myself to think slower, to concentrate on the baseball team. *Calm down, Lela, you're fine. This will work. Shoooooow.* I celebrated myself and doubted myself at the same time.

Bo and I got home first, and I led him downstairs to show off my new digs. I told him I'd grown tired of Miller's snoring. "It's keeping me awake," I said. Miller *did* snore and Bo thought it was hilarious, so the lie was believable. About an hour later, I heard the garage door open. Bo ran up to greet Miller, but I stayed where I was.

I heard Bo begging Miller to go downstairs with him, to see my new room "where you don't snore!' Miller refused, saying he had seen it already. Bo spent equal time upstairs and downstairs that night, never understanding the gravity of the change.

When I put him to bed on the third floor, he told me he liked my new bedroom and loved having a TV downstairs. With a sigh like a frustrated wife, he said, "So I can watch something else when Miller watches basketball all day." For some reason, that broke my heart the most.

There was a separate entrance downstairs though I had to walk in the sometimes-muddy side yard to get to and from the driveway. It was okay except in the rain. No rules, free to come and go as I pleased, I dated who I wanted and worked when I was sober.

Miller and I didn't speak unless Bo was the topic, which was just fine with me. I contributed zero money to household expenses... hadn't done so since paying off Miller's debts, but I continued to manage the household bills as I had since day one.

One Monday after the bank statement came in the mail, we had a massive fight when I asked Miller why he withdrew more than $600 from the ATM in one weekend. He exploded like a canon. "Don't you *EVER* question how I spend *MY* money," he screamed in a voice loud enough for the neighbors to hear. Though I should have backed down, knowing he was right, I flew off the handle myself.

Purposely dramatic, I stomped to the chest where I kept the financial records and slammed the files and piles on the table where Miller sat. "Fuck you! *You* do it then, motherfucker!" My voice was an equally loud scream. "*You* manage the damn bills! Track your own reckless spending!" I saw his face fall, which brought a big smile to mine.

Based on history, I knew he didn't want the job. Did I give a shit? Hell, no. His pride made him puff up when challenged... and my pride did the same. The difference was I had more power and knew how to use it.

Two failed marriages had taught me many things. One of them was how to be a Class-A Bitch.

☼ ☼ ☼ ☼ ☼

Slowly, the Meadow Ridge basement became cozy and homey for me. I continued the decorating... colorful towels and a paisley shower curtain for the bath, oversized artwork, designer bedding, and breezy window treatments to create a welcoming "upscale apartment." The living room was now full with a sectional sofa and dozens of throw pillows, contemporary side tables, and a coffee table made from an old cable spool.

Miller could have cared less about the downstairs décor, or if it existed at all. The exception was the ping-pong table, which was like a member of our family. On Bo weeks, we had day-long tournaments, and I always lost. Always. It was assumed beforehand and the source of many wisecracks... all in good fun.

On non-Bo weeks, the downstairs was off-limits for Miller. I'd sneak Logan in the basement entrance to spend the night, without worry of being caught. Because I didn't care what the Upstairs Asshole thought. Fuck him!

Over time, I got braver with my downstairs visitors, inviting visitors on Bo weeks, too. When I began seeing one of the J-girls, Jenna's friend, Bo caught us in bed when he woke up with diarrhea at two AM. Bad all around. So I reeled myself in, knowing something was soon to end my best-of-both-worlds life.

And something did happen. Too soon.

SAFE DEPOSIT BOX
Chapter 36

The one activity I did daily, without fail, was to check the mail. My fat dog Murphy and I had a ritual; he couldn't walk much further than the mailbox, but he'd do it for a treat (a piece of a rice cake, per the vet's obese-dog diet recommendation).

Every day, I opened the letters for Moonlight Jewelry and my personal mail then laid the bills and junk mail out for Miller. On this particular day, an unusual piece of correspondence came: the annual statement from the bank for our safe deposit box. It would be cheap, maybe $15, so I left it out along with the other bills and bullshit mail Miller now had to deal with.

I smiled to think about the last time I opened the safe deposit box. All those drawers! And the secrecy thrilled Bo; he played bank robber and told the security cop he was an international spy.

In all the years we'd been married, I had been the manager of household details and budgets, so I was the one to visit the box as needed. I doubted Miller had ever been there.

I was in the upstairs kitchen when he came home from work. Sipping his first scotch, he flipped through the stack of mail I had left for him, stopping to open the bank notice. Suddenly he was shouting, instantly angry and red-faced. "Safe deposit box? What the hell are you hiding from me?"

"I'm not hiding *anything*, Asswipe. No secrets in there. Just my dad's antique coins, the car titles, birth certificates, Granny's ring, a little cash... maybe something else; I don't know. We've had it for years." My explanation was as calm as a still pond; there was nothing to hide. But my calm demeanor seemed to anger him more.

Miller screamed, "I don't have a key! You bitch! You're stealing stuff behind my back!" His rage built to a point I'd yet to see. Suddenly scared of him, my heart rate zoomed and the circles of my armpits heated. Miller continued his tirade, accusing me of keeping secrets, stealing his mother's silver, hoarding cash, and more.

Finally, I interrupted the blubbering rant. "Calm down! Jeezus, Miller, if you want to see what's in the box, I'll give you the key."

"I don't want a fucking *key!*" He stood, balancing on the rungs of the bar stool and jabbing his finger at me with every syllable. He shouted, "*FUCK YOU!* What I want is … I want you *OUT!*" I had never heard him go that far; even when he asked me to live elsewhere, he never said it so strongly.

I had a sneaky feeling of fear the out-of-the-ordinary bill might give him pause, but I never expected such an extreme reaction. Watching Miller ready to blow a fuse, I willed myself to remain calm. *Deep breath, Lela. Shoooooow!*

With a sigh, I looked him square in the eye; the only outward sign of my anxiety was the swinging of my foot under the breakfast table. "*Out?* Where the hell could I go, dear? I have no money."

He screamed, shaking with anger. An alarming shade of red, his face morphed into one of pure evil and I gasped. *Who's crazy now, motherfucker?*

With an emphasis on every pronoun, he screamed, "That's *your* problem, Lela-Bitch. *You* have screwed me long enough. This is a sham, a joke! You're a fucking lunatic and I'm tired of trying to pretend you're normal and that we have a normal life. This is *IT!* You're *out!* Starting *today!*" He glared at me, breathing through his mouth in a ragged rhythm. "This is *insane!* So far from normal!"

"Normal? If you could see reality, you'd realize *I* am the normal one, Miller, but this relationship has been a joke for a long ti–

"*You?* You're normal?" He threw his head back to laugh, a coughing huff of a laugh that bordered on wicked. "What an *idiot* you are!" I waited for the string of insults, sure to come.

"You're *far, far* from normal. You drink too much, your fucking Bi-Polar moods go off the chart, you nag the hell out of me, and say inappropriate things in public that embarrass *everybody!* Can't you *see* this? Are you *blind?*"

"These are not facts. You're making this shit up... I guess to justify your own agenda. I don't think you really want me to leave, anyway."

"Oh yes! That's *exactly* what I want! You're so out of it, Lela! My friends make fun of *me* because *you* are a nitwit. So I pay the price for your stupidity, your twisted view on life, your fucking falling-down-drunk bullshit."

When he stopped to take a breath, I let my heartbeat continue its rise but refused to react to his obviously wrong remarks. "Anything else, my dear?"

"Fucking-A there's more! Your so-called business is a joke, just a way for you to justify more vodka. More vodka, more vodka, and *more* vodka. Lela, you're an alcoholic from hell! And I just can't handle it anymore. He sunk his head into his hands as if exhausted from all the false statements. After a beat, he lifted his head and screamed. "So just get the fuck out of my house!"

I lost it, now screaming as loud as Miller had. "If anybody's leaving this house, it's *you* because all this..." My gesture was meant to show the entire house. "This house is for *Bo!* So Bo and I will stay here, trying to keep things as stable as possible." My voice had risen an octave or two.

Miller laughed like a witch. "*Stable?* Are you fucking *kidding* me? There's *nothing* stable here! And how are you going to afford a house payment, you idiot? You think this house is free?"

"You and your million-dollar salary will pay the house payment, Miller. The judge will demand you support me, anyway."

"Lela, you're fucking crazy. Out! OUT! *OUT!* I can't stand it one more minute!"

"I can't afford it!" By then, I was red-faced and screaming just as he was.

"Jeezus, Lela! Quit buying so much vodka and you'll have plenty of money. Just get *OUT!* And I mean for*ever.* It's over. We're done. *I want a divorce!*" His face was crimson and he struggled for breath with double-sized oval nostrils.

I sat in silence, staring at him, studying his face and the chest hair that peeked out of his shirt collar.

Maybe he thought my change in expression had changed my understanding because he re-upped the screaming. "Don't you hear me, dammit? Start packing! And don't take a damn thing that's mine, you bitch. Thieving bitch!"

Being called a bitch infuriated me; he knew it did. The reason for my sensitivity was easy to pinpoint. The rape by my brother-in-law came flooding back, with him calling me Lela-bitch over and over, again and again.

I glared at Miller, then closed my eyes, feeling the vibration of anger in my ears. *No! That feels awful. Open your eyes!* But all I could do was stare straight ahead, too upset to cry. *Keep your shit together, Lela. Stay in control! Breathe in through your nose... out through your mouth. Breathe... breathe.*

As I gained control, I smiled. The stakes were high now. For my own protection, and his, I had to remove my feelings... wipe them from the slate and begin the conversation anew. A truly honest reaction to his name-calling could cause me to attack him in a blind rage. It had happened before and I'd brought blood.

Miller noticed my smile and exploded with anger. Oh yes, he was growling mad. For a flash, I thought about our wedding, the first official time I doubted his love for me. My doubts were real, and the truth had come out long ago. *Lela, you've been hanging on way too long. And for what? You're miserable... move on.* I choked out six words. "You really want me to leave?"

He looked surprised... as if hearing the phrase out loud was a shock. He paused and looked away but nodded a definite yes. I responded without hesitation, rambling. "Then you get your wish, Shithead. I'll move and you won't see Bo Winston again. Never! Remember, asshole, you're not even *related* to him! Don't worry, you Fuckwad-Sonofabitch, I'll leave as soon as I can. And you'll pay for everything. Every penny. I'm leaving you, Miller."

"Good fucking riddance!" His nostrils flared again and his arm jerked as he raised a hand to wipe the sweat from his upper lip.

With a deep sigh and in a smartass voice, I continued, "Okey-dokey-then... I'll see a lawyer tomorrow. *I'll* do the legal shit, though you know more about it than I do. How many divorces for you now, Miller? Three? I'm sure you know the process. Call your ridiculous lawyer-friend, the one who plays golf barefoot and drinks too much."

I laughed, knowing the stupidity of his lawyer. *You can screw Miller to the wall, Lela. You're going to hire a smart lawyer to go against his buffoon. Yep, you'll get alimony, temporary support, the whole bit. Just keep a level head. Don't fuck it up.*

Still breathing like a dragon, Miller barked, "I don't think my 'lawyer-friend,' as you say, drinks any more than *YOU*, Lela. Because *you're* the one with the problem!" I could see he was determined to continually push my buttons.

I shot back. "But I never snorted my business up my nose and let my wife bail me out! Look what I've done for you, you inconsiderate asshole! I've carried you for *years*. Now it's *your* turn."

Miller said nothing, tearing the bank notice into pieces and throwing them in the air. I acted as if nothing was wrong, confident I'd one-upped him forevermore.

Though my nerves were pulsating, I willed myself to play it cool. I nonchalantly grabbed a bag of chips from the appointed kitchen basket and popped one in my mouth. The crunch was ear-splitting and within seconds, my throat became desert-dry, the chip scratching tender tissue.

A slight cough, then I could swallow, thank God. Determined, I continued my pretense and sauntered out of the kitchen, crashing into his shoulder as he stepped sideways to stop me. "Get the fuck out of my way, Asswipe."

Passing into the living room, I purposely plopped onto the sofa, grabbed the remote, and flipped through a dozen channels. Short blasts of sound from the TV, each lasting only one second, pounded the walls like the beat of a drum. As if all my senses were heightened, I could hear Miller's ragged breathing yards away at the kitchen bar.

I settled on one channel and stared at the TV, seeing nothing. As I pretended to be perfectly fine, tears flowed down my cheeks. First just a few tears, then more, then I broke down. No way to eat the chips now; my throat had shrunk to the size of a decimal point.

Thirty seconds later, I slammed the bag of chips on the coffee table, scattering crumbs on the hardwood in a four-foot circle. "I should've listened to Granny Liz," I said with a snarky calm, "And I should've refused that stupid ink pen." Then I carefully walked downstairs to mix a drink. A double, no doubt. Or maybe a triple.

In a daze, I sat on my sofa, reliving the fight. *Is he right? Do other people think I'm an alcoholic and an idiot?* I thought of a few examples, from that night at the Addys to the time I got drunk and fell on the curb while we all walked to the stadium. Each time I thought I'd covered all the embarrassing moments, I'd think of another.

It's true, Lela. You get shit-faced and do stupid things. And about buying more and more vodka... he may be right on that, too. Checks written to the liquor store equal what I pay to the daycare, almost every week.

I leaned forward, having finished my drink. I spoke to myself. "How long have you known you were an alcoholic, Lela?" *Since you were... maybe sixteen?* *Yeah, but nobody else can say it to me... that's just rude! Fuck you, Miller McKeown. Bo and I will be just fine. F-I-N-E. Fabulous, Incredible, Noteworthy, and Extra-Excellent.* "Take THAT, motherfucker!"

A new beginning can be an opportunity to grow or another opportunity to fail. Flip a coin.

☼ ☼ ☼ ☼ ☼ ☼ ☼ ☼ ☼

SNEAK PEEK AT BOOK FOUR
Up Next: "Unmanageable"

Chapter 1: THE GREEN HOUSE

The day after I moved in, the toilet overflowed, spilling shitty water all over the bathroom. I called the landlord, and she sent a plumber to the house immediately.

After he fixed the toilet, I walked the plumber to his truck. He stopped in the driveway and looked up. "What in the world were they thinking?" he said, referring to the color of the house. It was a basic split-foyer but with green wood siding. Not just "green" but G-R-E-E-N, a color somewhere between lime and chartreuse. "Who would choose that color *on purpose?*" he asked, perplexed.

I could only shrug. "Maybe that's why the rent is so low."

"Well, the neighborhood is nice... your landlord is nice. Surely this is a mistake." He stepped to the left for another angle, now looking into the eaves. "But the paint job is fresh, brand new. Go figure."

Yep, the color turned heads, maybe a few stomachs, but the screaming-green house was a rare find. Ninety percent of the rental houses in West Rockville exceeded my budget, but this was one of the nicer ones. I was lucky.

Three bedrooms, a fenced backyard for Murphy the fat Sheltie, a two-car garage, new carpet, and neat as a pin. All for $500 per month. The landlords even mowed the yard as part of the deal.

☼ ☼ ☼ ☼ ☼

"I love this room, Mom! So big! But please tell me we'll get rid of this bunk bed soon. Don't you think I've outgrown it by now?"

"Fourteen is not too old for a bunk bed, Bo. And good news, kiddo: the small sofa fits on the far side of your room, under the window. Your sleepover friends can crash there."

Continuing my tour guide narration, I stepped to the door of the next upstairs room. "This is what's *supposed* to be the Master bedroom but it will be my studio. Your G-Daddy will help me put it together with long countertops like the old one."

Bo blew a huff of a sigh, rolling his eyes. "Yeah, your dad is used to helping you move, right? One more time..." his voice trailed off.

"Bo, stop it! Don't be a smart-mouth to your mother."

"Just stating the truth, Mom."

I ignored his snarky teenage attitude and took a few more steps down the hall. "And this is my bedroom."

"The smallest room, Mom? Why?"

"There are more important things than my little place to sleep."

I saw Bo's face twist as he realized I had sacrificed my space so he could have more. "But... my room is *part-time* for me. Mom, *you* should have the biggest one."

"No, buddy. You're the biggest and the best around here!" Bo eyed me sideways, doubting my sincerity, I suppose. But when I could do something nice, I did it... maybe trying to make up for being a drunk and crappy mother. I didn't exactly display the Mother of the Year trophy on a foyer shelf.

Two days after I moved into the green house, my parents came to Rockville for a long weekend, spending two nights with my oldest sister Jennifer and her kids. In those days, I tiptoed around Jennifer, sipping wine instead of gulping. Underneath, I seethed, resenting her for forcing me to pretend.

Though my oldest sister and I used to be good buddies, partying together with our common friends, she'd confronted me four times over the last few years, accusing me of having "an alcohol problem." Fuck her. "I'm fine," I had said, but she just rolled her eyes.

On Saturday, Daddy and I went back to "Miller's house" in Skylark. My soon-to-be-ex greeted us with the warmth of an ice cube. Fuck him. Daddy and I worked in the basement, removing the same countertop he'd installed in the studio three years ago. Then I helped load everything in his truck, the *old* truck. "How did you talk Mom into riding in 'Old Joe,' Daddy?"

Scratching the shiny part of his mostly bald head, he chuckled. "She fussed the whole time, Lela... said she'd never-ever do it again." Daddy imitated Mom's high-pitched voice. "Eeew, Rick! The door panel is diiiiirty! Oh, Rick! My aching baaack!" I laughed at his impersonation of her. Back to himself, he shared his true feelings. "She's a love, but she sure can raise a ruckus."

"Did she throw a Benningham fit?" It was a family joke referring to Mom's side of the family, a parody of their calm and steady nerves, their notoriously even tempers. Daddy laughed by slapping his knee and honking through his ample nose. The melody of Daddy's horselaugh had been the same since I was a child. Heartfelt, it happened often.

The next morning, he came to attach the countertop around the perimeter of the huge upstairs bedroom at the screaming-green house.

Daddy also cut three pieces of plywood to cover the floor so three rolling chairs could move easily. He ended the day in one of his silly moods and we had a rolling-chair race across the floor. I would've won if he hadn't cheated... which made the loss even more hilarious.

As we always did, Daddy and I focused on having fun no matter the importance of the task at hand. My father was childlike and easy to laugh, never short of jokes and pranks. Simply put, I adored him. Always had.

As the last part of his mission, Daddy added shelves above two workstations. The corner area, the largest by far, was for Lola, my long-time assistant. I imagined her sitting there, Cherokee-Indian DNA coursing through her veins, throwing chunks of long, black hair over her shoulder... yes, she would work well in the space. "If she doesn't like it, Daddy, I'll fix it. My goal is to make Lola happy, no matter what. Without her, I'm lost."

Though I wouldn't admit it, Lola was the one who ran the business while I drank and made bad decisions. She worked part-time during the week but the schedule was flexible.

Lola knew what to do, no supervision required. She'd said things like, "The bracelet display needs attention. Can I work extra hours to do it?" I didn't ask what she wanted to do or how much it would cost, I simply agreed.

Or she'd say, "We need to restock the consignment booth at Skylark Crafts. I'll do inventory tomorrow." Again, I'd just nod and thank her for taking charge. Without Lola, there would have been no Moonlight Jewelry.

And now with more room but less sense, I would add another assistant.

The yet-to-be-hired second helper would work at the smaller workstation Daddy had defined with a counter and shelves above. "Lola, we just need hands... a factory worker, a mindless servant." She agreed. I ended with the stark reality. "But you tell her what to do because you keep tabs on the inventory, right?"

"Right. I'll take care of it, Lela. Just run an ad... maybe in the same newspaper where you advertised for me."

"I'll do it as soon as I'm settled."

"Uh... maybe do it before that."

"Why?"

"Because 'being settled' never really happens around here." Lola's sheepish smile didn't *seem* like an accusation, but it was. In my addled state of mind, I was oblivious to Lola's hints. Well, oblivious to most everything by that time. She never told me she knew I was incapable, never shamed me about it, just took control of more and more business tasks as my abilities ebbed.

When her boyfriend suggested the problem might be my excessive drinking, she insisted it wasn't. "It's her Bi-Polar medicine," she insisted. And she was more than half right.

When my former psychiatrist questioned my lies about "moderate" alcohol consumption, I fired him and started seeing another doctor. The new doc was an overweight gray-haired Dr. Cook who must have been in cahoots with every drug rep in the Southeast.

He prescribed seven different anti-depressants and mood stabilizers, plus Adderall for focus, and a massive dose of something to help me sleep. I usually woke up drunk and disoriented... and sorting out all those pills was one helluva feat. It seems I was always out of one prescription, so I'd skip it then double up when I got the refill. I could never get it straight.

Lola offered to take charge of my medication but I adamantly refused. Pissed, I shouted at her, "What do you think I am, Lola? An idiot? Incapable of taking care of myself?" I was livid... so livid I didn't realize her lack of response was a big, fat "yes" in disguise.

Raised to be a Southern sweetheart of a woman, Lola was a giver, and she considered it her job to be my caretaker. She took care of the business as if it was her own.

As she witnessed me shrinking deeper into the Land of Lost Alcoholics, she doubled her efforts in trying to protect me. A loyal employee, a good friend, and my greatest enabler. Thanks to Lola, I reached my bottom slowly... painfully... like a suicide bomb with a mile-long fuse.

Chapter 2: INAUGRAL FIRE

The night after Daddy and I put the studio together, I realized that ugly green house represented my freedom, my "new start." I could change direction, renew a dedication to quality. The word "quality" repeated in my mind over and over though I didn't quite know what it meant.

I repeated the word as I lit the first fire in my stone fireplace. A stack of split logs came with the house, a leftover from the previous tenant, I assumed. The wood was a little wet, but it lit and made the house smell like a wondrous forest. I sat on my new sofa and watched the logs crackle and pop. Alone, my thoughts turned to the serious side. *Have I done the right thing by moving out? Am I really up for starting all over again? Do I really drink too much, like he said? Do I even understand what ruined the marriage?*

Maybe I didn't *want* to understand why the marriage was over because I thought all fingers of blame pointed at Miller. He'd screwed me over. Lying to me about wanting a family, lying about his addiction and money problems, stealing the woman I thought I loved, lying about his hopes and dreams, the essence of his entire being! *You didn't see those things coming, Lela. But after you found the truth, you continued the marriage. You forgave him and blamed yourself. But it's not your fault! You got screwed!*

Even at the start, I knew Miller loved Bo more than he loved me. I had told Karen, even, but I ignored it and the pain it caused. No, I *chose* to ignore it. *Another bad decision, Lela. Drunken wisdom.*

Wanting only to be a father to Bo, Miller McKeown stomped all over my heart, seemingly on purpose. I couldn't help but blame myself. After all, I drank a lot. And I ignored the red flags, staying the course and staying hopeful that he would grow to love *me*, too. I just kept drinking and fucking up and forgiving shit; I didn't leave him until he forced me to go.

Yep, Miller was a hard-boiled heartless ass, born and raised that way.

The divorce wasn't yet final and wouldn't be for a while. My lawyer, a female up-and-comer nicknamed "Rabid Dog Annie," had drafted a separation agreement and a list of things Miller would pay on my behalf. For "temporary support," we asked him to pay my rent, car payment, auto insurance, phone bill, and $500 in cash per month for "household support." That arrangement would change with the final divorce settlement to become permanent alimony if I played my cards right.

The legal demand for temporary support was a pie-in-the-sky opening offer by Rabid Dog Annie, the point used to begin negotiations. Yet Miller accepted it without bargaining. His attorney, nothing more than an unreliable and lazy friend, had advised him to sign it. *What a dumbass! Goes to show how stupid Miller McKeown is... I'll ride this one out for as long as I can.* My attorney agreed.

For the final decree, I would ask for alimony in the same amount, but Annie said the judge would limit the length of payments to two years or so, she said. But for now, it was open-ended, as if he was "giving" me the money. Even a legal newbie like me understood he should move forward as fast as possible.

The profit I made from Moonlight Jewelry barely covered utilities and groceries. I used the cash I received at craft shows to pay for incidentals like prescriptions, shampoo, vodka, and makeup, and a piece of clothing here and there. I wasn't rich by any means, but I lived well and with no worries... and no thoughts of the future.

My "financial management rule" stood: I paid myself first each month, whittling it down to set aside a whopping $20 for my savings account. Twenty bucks. By the time I got to the bank, that's all that was left. Still, I thought I'd planned everything beautifully, and patted myself on the back for my financial responsibility. *Smart Lela, you're gonna go far, kid, doing the right thing. Just remember... "Quality." That's your mantra, your promise to the world.* I still didn't understand what the word "quality" meant in relation to my life at the time, but it sounded good.

"Quality," I said, and threw another log on the fire. I fixed a drink, placed it on my newly polished coffee table, and dashed out the backdoor for another seasoned log. Just as I added to the *"quality"* fire, I saw the beetles. They ran full-speed-ahead, darting from the heat as each log began to char. Hundreds of beetles... racing across and down the stone hearth and onto my beige carpet like a flock of birds in a two-foot-wide parade. Their steps in unison, it was a crowded and creepy beetle stampede.

I freaked, gasping so deep that I choked. Like a rocket, I drove to the Mini-Mart and bought every bottle of bug killer they had, eight cans if I remember right. When I returned, there were no beetles in sight so I tiptoed to the fireplace with the first can of bug spray in-hand.

No. Aerosol cans and fire. No. I remembered the camping weekend with the church Youth Group. "Ka-boom would make it worse, Lela," I spoke out loud. "You need water. Quality water."

My heart pounded, threatening to make me sober as I worked. The third bucketful was the one that flooded the firebox, sending black gritty water onto the new beige carpet. Now crying, I found a few old towels and tried to blot up the stain. That's when I felt two beetles crawling up the back of my leg – *under* my jeans.

Yep, scared sober. Dammit.

I mixed a drink and double-timed it upstairs to my bedroom, closing the door behind me. The first week in the new house... I hope this catastrophe isn't an omen, a sign of more bad things to come. And I hope beetles can't climb the steps.

I fell asleep wondering if the soon-to-come bug man would comment on the oh-so G-R-E-E-N of the house.

CHAPTER 3: INHERENTLY STUPID

Tuesdays and Thursdays were still reserved for Cowboy Logan, and our dating had expanded to include a few Wednesdays and weekends, too. I hated that he was married and nagged him about it, but my whining was drowned in vodka, forgotten with cocaine, and covered with Stetson hats.

We ate at expensive restaurants, then high-tailed it to Mel's gigantic house on the horse farm for a few chugs of his moonshine and a soak in the hot tub. Always partying, always crossing the border to impropriety – except for Lola; she made sure we didn't hurt ourselves.

That September, the four of us drove to Texas to pick up Mel's newly pregnant horse, spending the weekend as tourists, remembering the Alamo and sniffing the Fort Worth Stockyards. Somewhere along the way, we went to a rodeo where I fell down in the stands and was trampled by the crazy mob. "Here, drink this!" Logan directed, passing me a pint of vodka. "Like the Germans used to do."

"The Germans?" I asked.

"Whatever! The Vikings? Somebody. Like the cowboys use whiskey."

I took a swig, rubbing my left ankle, the one somebody had stomped flat. Straight vodka was never my shtick, but I took four generous gulps that afternoon, my appointment with Dr. Smirnoff.

Logan pulled me into his lap and poured vodka over the cuts on my legs and elbows. "Antiseptic. But this one might need stitches."

"Did the Vikings get stitches?"

He didn't reply; his eye-roll said all. I continued, "Then pour more vodka. Just don't waste too much."

"This one's gonna leave a scar."

"Texas souvenir. Give me that bottle!"

Lola and I were inseparable friends by this time and she had moved to the perfect party house, what we called "The Cliff Hanger." It was a cabin-like, three-room house balanced on the side of a mountain, yet it sat in the center of west Rockville. Heart-shaped leaves of ivy surrounded the house and wrapped the trunks of the oak trees that guarded the front entrance.

"More Madonna!" I screamed. Lola wouldn't let me operate the stereo anymore... not since I fell into the cabinet and crashed the shelves. As she changed the CD, I begged her, "Dance with me!" She refused; I considered that an emergency. "Anybody! Help! I need a dance partner!"

I had ten choices: eight drunk women about my age and two drunk guys a few years older. We made up the Saddlebag Gang, and Lola's Cliff Hanger was our headquarters.

The Saddlebag Gang rules matched the ones from our three years of girl's beach trips: no boyfriends allowed. Baron and Blitz didn't count; they were just friends, part of the gang. Besides, they were the ones who hauled in the kegs and tapped them so proficiently. The kegs were permanent fixtures, as was the puzzle box full of weed, kept under the sofa.

Friday nights, Girl's Night Out, brought the same name tags we had worn on beach trips in years prior: *"Hello My Name Is"*... we had a never-ending supply. We each had our favorite; I was usually Tess Tosterone. Others were Jenny Tailya, Connie Lingus, Sandy Slits, Dixie Normus, Lola's favorite, Lisa Greement. The guys remained "Knot Here" and "Visitor" and served as our security team until they, too, got drunk and unable to pay attention.

Then, on Saturdays after our Girl's Night Out, we took turns telling each other what dumb stuff happened and what stupid thing each of us had done. Usually, memories from the night before came in three varieties: vague, embarrassing, and ridiculous.

☼ ☼ ☼ ☼ ☼

I made sure to plan entertainment for most of my nights because I was afraid to be alone... afraid of myself and any remaining beetles. I dodged the fear and feelings of self-hate by relying on a lot of vodka and a bit of creativity.

"This is a flirty little dress!" I said to myself, "And some kick-ass high heels. Oh-la-la! Anybody would believe this is a date outfit." Lipstick on, I drove the five miles to my favorite neighborhood bar, the Titanic Bar and Grille. It was a respectable place, popular with folks in their 30s and they'd done a great job with the theme. Huge graphic murals of black-and-white glaciers wrapped the walls, the bar was "the captain's bridge," complete with an oversize ship's wheel, and accents of riveted steel peppered the place.

The bartender, Jamie, knew me well and had my vodka-tonic on the bar before I sat down on a stool. He said in a loud voice, "Are you meeting another one who stood you up?"

"Hush, Jamie! Are you trying to give it away already?"

I sat alone, looking at my watch every few minutes and eyeing the groups of men who had stopped by for happy hour. I flashed them innocent, shy-girl smiles... then I'd look at my watch again. As planned, one of the guys would ask to buy me a drink. "No, I'm waiting for my date... but I think I've been stood up."

In the bellowing voice of a man determined to rescue a damsel in distress, the man would invariably puff out his chest and say, "Stood up? Now, who would stand up a pretty woman like you?"

Success!

Free drinks for the rest of the night and an opportunity to play the vixen. Using sex as power, playing men like toys. Sometimes I would take them home with me, but rarely. Instead, I would have them take me to play pool, to a club, or go on an all-night shopping spree. I was the consummate bad girl, and I was damn-good at it.

☼ ☼ ☼ ☼ ☼

Logan and I went to the Titanic with Lola and Mel one night after having too many drinks at a two-for-one happy hour down the street. Mel urged Logan to do his trademark thievery. "Get the spider plant this time, Logan,"

Mel said. Cowboy Logan dug up the live plant from the flower box beside our booth. Holding it by the roots, he walked out of the Titanic as if nothing was amiss.

Logan was a kleptomaniac; I never figured out why because he had a shitload of money. That cold Thursday night, I said, "Great houseplant! You've outdone yourself! And it sure beats a coffee cup or another sugar bowl."

Instead of upsetting me, Logan's kleptomania made me laugh... especially that night because he gave me the plant. "I'll need a pot and a way to hang it, too, Logan. Can you steal that for me?"

"From where?" Then he stopped himself. "Hell no! I just do restaurants. I don't want to get in trouble, ding-dong."

If alone and bored on winter nights in my screaming-green house, I drank myself to oblivion and spent hours crying and feeling sorry for myself. Then I'd pick up the phone, searching for "help" that couldn't help me at all. I was just bored and lonely.

"Have her call me ASAP. I'm in crisis!" I left a message with my therapist's answering service around ten PM. When she called back, I was no longer upset... too drunk to hold a thought for more than sixty seconds. Through peals of laughter, I told her I had a column of snot that reached the floor, but otherwise, I was fine. She sent me a bill for $50 for that "appointment" and I never called her again outside of office hours.

With my therapist off the list of possibilities, I perused the yellow pages to find a friend. Never thinking I was taking time from somebody who honestly needed help, I entertained myself by calling crisis lines: The Suicide Crisis Line, Sexual Assault Crisis Line, Narcotics Anonymous, any "Help!" phone number listed. With a drink in hand and a well-thought-out story, I'm sure my act frustrated those who answered because I refused to be helped by their scripted words. I simply repeated my supposed pain and problems over and over.

Only one guy hung up on me.

I whined to the older man who answered the AA Hotline, "But drinking makes me feel better... helps me hate myself less."

He answered calmly. "As I said, there's a program to take away those bad feelings without having to drink... a program that will give you a new freedom and a new happiness."

"But I'm a private person! I can't talk about my problems in front of people!"

"You don't have to talk. Just listening will help."

"Listen to a degenerate alcoholic? Ha! Who in their right mind would take advice from a drunk?"

"A drunk who no longer drinks isn't a degenerate. In fact, you'll find them to be quite wise."

"That's such bullshit! I wouldn't give the motherfuckers the time of day."

"So do you want to get sober?"

"Sometimes."

"Is right now one of those times?"

"No."

"Are you drunk right now?"

"Yes."

"Then I don't have time for your bullshit." And he hung up.

Alcoholics didn't play, it seemed. He had seen through my verbal tapestry of bullshit, knowing I was toying with him.

After the crisis lines lost their appeal, I made other types of cries for help. While men are usually the ones who make booty calls, I was the caller. I worked my way down a list posted on my fridge. The only requests: show up in a hurry, armed with joints and beer.

My life had become unmanageable, and I knew I had to do something about it, sooner rather than later. But underneath my bravado, I also knew I was too far gone to do it on my own.

Maybe there's a way out that doesn't require so much effort on your part, Lela. POOF! You're sober! Yeah... that's the way to do it.

About two months after moving to the screaming-green house, I found myself drunk in the early evening, crying my eyes out and fed up with being lonely and stupid. I called the AA Hotline again, sharing my honest truth. The girl said, "The 5:30 meeting, 2317 West Park Boulevard. I'll meet you there."

I slipped into the meeting room late, cried every minute I was there, and slipped out before the closing prayer. The girl I was supposed to meet... I didn't even look for her.

My mind was busy on the way home. I don't know who I was talking to or who I was arguing with, but the steam of my anger billowed from the silver van.

I'm supposed to get sober based on THAT bullshit? Hell, no! Those fucking people are weird, talking about how magic happens from not drinking... butterflies coming out of their butt and crap. For me, going a few HOURS without a drink is like dying a slow death. So HAPPINESS without it? No way! It could never happen for me.

Tears began as I felt myself sink further into hopelessness, quickly followed by the bravado that said I was perfectly fucking-fine and didn't need help, especially from the weirdos in that room.

The guy saying he'd been sober for fifteen years – I call bullshit. It's impossible! And the dude lied in front of all those people! He's cheated somewhere along the way and he's lying about it, so why would I trust anything he says?

A REAL alcoholic can't get sober, no matter what AA says. LISTEN TO ME!!! That stupid meeting was a farce! AA just isn't for me. In fact, the whole concept is inherently stupid.

☼ ☼ ☼ ☼ ☼

– END OF SAMPLE –

MORE ABOUT ME

First, always first, I'm a proud and grateful recovering alcoholic with 21 years' sobriety. That's who I am.

My life and career have always been about writing, and it started when I was a kid. I gathered a collection of compound words, color-coded and OCD-organized. I still have that tattered paisley notebook on my bookshelf. No shit.

Thirty years a copywriter, then twelve as a certified picture framer, and many jobs in between. Then something happened (it's a huge something), and I began writing for fun in my 50s.

My tidbits landed in AA's *Grapevine* magazine and a few online journals, then a story about my dog was featured in *Chicken Soup for the Soul.*

Hmmmm... maybe this is going somewhere.

As if meant to be, about a week later, an author-friend challenged me to write and publish a full book. "Just one rule," he said, "Write what you know."

I didn't know writer's terminology, so I took his advice literally. I thought it meant writing your life story. Only later did I find that the phrase means *based on* what you know. Huge difference.

The words came easily, and I spent the next three years writing my life story, which became seven top-selling books.

Who'da thunk it?

Mostly, I hope to help others; that was the whole point.

With the series complete, I'm now writing weird books under the pen name Patty Ayers. Updates to come.

I live in East Tennessee with a panoramic view of the Great Smoky Mountains, surrounded with cozy and calm here in my little condo. If I'm not writing, you'll find me tinkering or playing tug-of-war with my distinguished editor, Stormin' Norman the Schnauzer.

Combining creativity with my OCD, I also have a side biz called *Kid's Art in Stitches* – I embroider children's stick-drawings in crazy-bright colors. Stitch by stitch, the result is happy.

By the grace of Dude, I've been sober all day long.

I wish you the same.

FIND OUT WHAT HAPPENS!

UP NEXT: Unmanageable

See all books on my Author Page:
amazon.com/author/lelafox

Join me on *The Front Porch* for a weekly dose of inspiration,
funny stuff, and my take on life and recovery.

Sign up at lelafox.com

A review is anonymous, helps others, and takes just a minute.
Go to the Amazon listing, scroll to the bottom,
and click the gray "Write a Review" button

Did you like the book? Tell the world!

Made in United States
Orlando, FL
15 April 2023

32130691R00161